William Miller, PhD, MLS
Rita M. Pellen, MLS
Editors

Libraries
Beyond Their Institutions:
Partnerships That Work

Libraries Beyond Their Institutions: Partnerships That Work
has been co-published simultaneously as *Resource Sharing &
Information Networks*, Volume 18, Numbers 1/2 2005/2006.

*Pre-publication
REVIEWS,
COMMENTARIES,
EVALUATIONS . . .*

" **A** collection that WILL INTEREST NOT
ONLY LIBRARY MANAGERS AND
ADMINISTRATORS, BUT ALSO LEADERS
OF SOCIAL SERVICE ORGANIZATIONS,
GOVERNMENT AGENCIES, AND INFOR-
MATION VENDORS. The contributions
highlight a variety of initiatives, including
K-20 information literacy projects, staff
and customer training, international li-
brary-to-library collaborations, and models
for group purchasing by private academic
institutions."

Barbara J. Stites, MLS
*Executive Director
Southwest Florida Library Network*

Libraries
Beyond Their Institutions:
Partnerships That Work

Libraries Beyond Their Institutions: Partnerships That Work has been co-published simultaneously as *Resource Sharing & Information Networks*, Volume 18, Numbers 1/2 2005/2006.

Libraries Beyond Their Institutions: Partnerships That Work, edited by William Miller and Rita M. Pellen (Vol. 18, No. 1/2, 2005/2006). *A guide to the wide variety of partnerships between libraries and institutions within their own universities, municipalities, or government units.*

Libraries Within Their Institutions: Creative Collaborations, edited by William Miller and Rita M. Pellen (Vol. 17, No. 1/2, 2004). *A guide to the wide variety of partnerships between academic libraries and other areas within their own institutions.*

Cooperative Efforts of Libraries, edited by William Miller and Rita M. Pellen (Vol. 16, No. 1/2, 2002). *Explores a wide variety of cooperative initiatives at regional, statewide, and international levels.*

Joint-Use Libraries, edited by William Miller and Rita M. Pellen (Vol. 15, No. 1/2, 2001). *Presents nine examples of situations in which libraries of different types share a building.*

Networks and Resource Sharing in the 21st Century: Re-Engineering the Information Landscape, edited by Mary Huston-Somerville and Catherine C. Wilt (Vol. 10, No. 1/2, 1995). *"Enlightening and portends things to come for those who do not step up and embrace the new electronic information technology as an important business tool." (Bimonthly Review of Law Books)*

Impact of Technology on Resource Sharing: Experimentation and Maturity, edited by Thomas C. Wilson (Vol. 8, No. 1, 1993). *"A refreshing expansive view of library resource sharing." (Special Libraries)*

Periodicals Circulation Statistics at a Mid-Sized Academic Library: Implications for Collection Management, edited by John A. Whisler (Vol. 5, No. 1/2, 1990). *Providing an indication of the relative use of journals in an average academic library, this book will help serials and collection development librarians who must decide to which titles their library will subscribe and how those titles will be maintained in their collections.*

The Public Library in the Bibliographic Network, edited by Betty J. Turock (Vol. 3, No. 2, 1987). *Learn the facts about joining a bibliographic network and the effects that participation can have on your public library's operation.*

Coordinating Cooperative Collection Development: A National Perspective, edited by Wilson Luquire (Vol. 2, No. 3/4, 1986). *"A wealth of interesting and useful information, as well as a smattering of knowledge and even wisdom." (Newsletter of Reference and Adult Services Division, American Library Association)*

Experiences of Library Network Administrators: Papers Based on the Symposium "From Our Past: Toward 2000," edited by Wilson Luquire (Vol. 2, No. 1/2, 1985). *Network administrators describe the origin, history, and process of their organizations.*

Library Networking: Current Problems and Future Prospects, edited by Wilson Luquire (Vol. 1, No. 1/2, 1983). *"Compulsive reading. Highly recommended." (Library Review)*

Libraries Beyond Their Institutions: Partnerships That Work

William Miller
Rita M. Pellen
Editors

Libraries Beyond Their Institutions: Partnerships That Work has been co-published simultaneously as *Resource Sharing & Information Networks*, Volume 18, Numbers 1/2 2005/2006.

The Haworth Information Press®
An Imprint of The Haworth Press, Inc.

New York • London • Victoria (AU)
www.HaworthPress.com

Published by

The Haworth Information Press®, 10 Alice Street, Binghamton, NY 13904-1580 USA

The Haworth Information Press® is an imprint of The Haworth Press, Inc., 10 Alice Street, Binghamtom, NY 13904-1580 USA.

Libraries Beyond Their Institutions: Partnerships That Work has been co-published simultaneously as *Resource Sharing & Information Networks*™, Volume 18, Numbers 1/2 2005/2006.

Cover design by Lora Wiggins.

Library of Congress Cataloging-in-Publication Data

Libraries beyond their institutions : partnerships that work / William Miller, Rita M. Pellen, editors.
    p. cm.
    "Libraries beyond their institutions : partnerships that work has been co-published simultaneously as Resource Sharing & Information Networks, Volume 18, Numbers 1/2 2005/2006."
    Includes bibliographical references and index.
    ISBN-13: 978-0-7890-2908-9 (hc. : alk. paper)
    ISBN-10: 0-7890-2908-1 (hc. : alk. paper)
    ISBN-13: 978-0-7890-2909-6 (pbk. : alk. paper)
    ISBN-10: 0-7890-2909-X (pbk. : alk. paper)
    1. Library cooperation. 2. Libraries and community. I. Miller, William, 1947- II. Pellen, Rita M.
III. Resource sharing & information networks.

Z672 .L47 2005
021.2–dc22
                                                                                    2005001513

Indexing, Abstracting & Website/Internet Coverage

This section provides you with a list of major indexing & abstracting services and other tools for bibliographic access. That is to say, each service began covering this periodical during the year noted in the right column. Most Websites which are listed below have indicated that they will either post, disseminate, compile, archive, cite or alert their own Website users with research-based content from this work. (This list is as current as the copyright date of this publication.)

Abstracting, Website/Indexing Coverage . . . . Year When Coverage Began

- *AATA Online: Abstracts of International Conservation Literature (formerly Art & Archeology Technical Abstracts)*
  <http://aata.getty.edu> 2004

- *Academic Abstracts/CD-ROM* 1995

- *Academic Search: database of 2,000 selected academic serials, updated monthly: EBSCO Publishing* 1996

- *Academic Search Elite (EBSCO)* 1996

- *Academic Search Premier (EBSCO)*
  <http://www.epnet.com/academic/acasearchprem.asp> 1995

- *ACM Guide to Computer Literature <http://www.acm.org>* 1985

- *Business Source Corporate: coverage of nearly 3,350 quality magazines and journals; designed to meet the diverse information needs of corporations; EBSCO Publishing*
  <http://www.epnet.com/corporate/bsourcecorp.asp> 1995

- *Cambridge Scientific Abstracts is a leading publisher of scientific information in print journals, online databases, CD-ROM and via the Internet <http://www.csa.com>* 1989

(continued)

(continued)

- *Internationale Bibliographie der geistes- und sozialwissenschaftlichen Zeitschriftenliteratur . . . See IBZ* <http://www.saur.de>. 1995

- *Journal of Academic Librarianship: Guide to Professional Literature, The* 1997

- *Konyvtari Figyelo (Library Review)* 1996

- *Library & Information Science Abstracts (LISA)* <http://www.csa.com> 1989

- *Library and Information Science Annual (LISCA)* <http://www.lu.com> 1998

- *Library Literature & Information Science* <http://www.hwwilson.com> 1995

- *MasterFILE: updated database from EBSCO Publishing*. 1996

- *MasterFILE Elite: coverage of nearly 1,200 periodicals covering general reference, business, health, education, general science, multi-cultural issues and much more; EBSCO Publishing* <http://www.epnet.com/government/mfelite.asp> 1995

- *MasterFILE Premier: coverage of more than 1,950 periodicals covering general reference, business, health, education, general science, multi-cultural issues and much more; EBSCO Publishing* <http://www.epnet.com/government/mfpremier.asp> 1995

- *MasterFILE Select: coverage of more than 770 periodicals covering general reference, business, health, education, general science, multi-cultural issues and much more; EBSCO Publishing* <http://www.epnet.com/government/mfselect.asp> 1995

- *National Clearinghouse for Primary Care Information (NCPCI)*. 1995

- *OCLC ArticleFirst* <http://www.oclc.org/services/databases/>. 1990

- *OCLC ContentsFirst* <http://www.oclc.org/services/databases/> 1990

- *OCLC Public Affairs Information Service* <http://www.pais.org> 1984

- *PASCAL, c/o Institut de l'Information Scientifique et Technique. Cross-disciplinary electronic database covering the fields of science, technology & medicine. Also available on CD-ROM, and can generate customized retrospective searches* <http://www.inist.fr> 1984

- *Referativnyi Zhurnal (Abstracts Journal of the All-Russian Institute of Scientific and Technical Information–in Russian)* <http://www.viniti.ru> 1987

- *SwetsWise* <http://www.swets.com> 2002

(continued)

Special Bibliographic Notes related to special journal issues
(separates) and indexing/abstracting:

- indexing/abstracting services in this list will also cover material in any "separate" that is co-published simultaneously with Haworth's special thematic journal issue or DocuSerial. Indexing/abstracting usually covers material at the article/chapter level.
- monographic co-editions are intended for either non-subscribers or libraries which intend to purchase a second copy for their circulating collections.
- monographic co-editions are reported to all jobbers/wholesalers/approval plans. The source journal is listed as the "series" to assist the prevention of duplicate purchasing in the same manner utilized for books-in-series.
- to facilitate user/access services all indexing/abstracting services are encouraged to utilize the co-indexing entry note indicated at the bottom of the first page of each article/chapter/contribution.
- this is intended to assist a library user of any reference tool (whether print, electronic, online, or CD-ROM) to locate the monographic version if the library has purchased this version but not a subscription to the source journal.
- individual articles/chapters in any Haworth publication are also available through the Haworth Document Delivery Service (HDDS).

Libraries Beyond
Their Institutions:
Partnerships That Work

CONTENTS

ABOUT THE EDITORS

William Miller, PhD, MLS, is Director of Libraries at Florida Atlantic University in Boca Raton. He formerly served as Head of Reference at Michigan State University in East Lansing, and as Associate Dean of Libraries at Bowling Green State University in Ohio. Dr. Miller is past President of the Association of College and Research Libraries, has served as Chair of the *Choice* magazine editorial board, and is a contributing editor of *Library Issues*. He was named Instruction Librarian of the Year in 2004 by the Association of College and Research Libraries Instruction Section.

Rita M. Pellen, MLS, is Associate Director of Libraries at Florida Atlantic University in Boca Raton. She was formerly Assistant Director of Public Services and Head of the Reference Department at Florida Atlantic. In 1993, Ms. Pellen received the Gabor Exemplary Employee Award in recognition for outstanding service to FAU, and in 1997, the "Literati Club Award for Excellence" for the outstanding paper presented in *The Bottom Line*. She has served on committees in LAMA, ACRL, and ALCTS, as well as the Southeast Florida Library Information Network, SEFLIN, a multi-type library cooperative in South Florida. Honor society memberships include Beta Phi Mu and Phi Kappa Phi.

Introduction:
Cooperation Outside of Institutions

For this volume, we were interested in exploring external cooperation beyond participation in OCLC or other bibliographic utilities. We wanted to discover the variety of ways in which libraries cooperate with non-library entities outside of their own institutions, such as community organizations, governmental agencies, vendors, or city governments. It is the rare library that exists in a vacuum; most are part of a system, such as a university or a municipality, and all libraries exist in a broader societal context which requires interaction and cooperative activity. In order to best serve those who need them, libraries must cooperate widely with entities other than themselves.

These articles on cooperative activities between libraries and entities beyond the institutions of which they are a part span a very wide spectrum indeed. Janet Nichols, Lothar Spang, and Kristy Padron discuss collaborative activities between their library and K-12 educators to promote information literacy. Carolyn Snyder, Howard Carter, and Mickey Soltys discuss a variety of partnerships between their academic library, regional education consortia, and OCLC, as well as within their own institution. For instance, they have developed 14 courses for the Online Lyceum, a project of the Association of Research Libraries which creates online learning opportunities and helps institutions save money on travel costs for professional education. Elizabeth Curry, a professional consultant, discusses her work on a state-wide project to train librarians to lead collaborative community projects.

David Wright discusses problems and successes in creating a consortium of private institutions in Mississippi, for the purpose of acquiring licensed elec-

[Haworth co-indexing entry note]: "Introduction: Cooperation Outside of Institutions." Miller, William. Co-published simultaneously in *Resource Sharing & Information Networks* (The Haworth Information Press, an imprint of The Haworth Press, Inc.) Vol. 18, No. 1/2, 2005/2006, pp. 1-3; and: *Libraries Beyond Their Institutions: Partnerships That Work* (ed: William Miller, and Rita M. Pellen) The Haworth Information Press, an imprint of The Haworth Press, Inc., 2005/2006, pp. 1-3. Single or multiple copies of this article are available for a fee from The Haworth Document Delivery Service [1-800-HAWORTH, 9:00 a.m. - 5:00 p.m. (EST). E-mail address: docdelivery@haworthpress.com].

http://www.haworthpress.com/web/RSIN
Digital Object Identifier: 10.1300/J121v18n01_01

tronic information at favorable prices. Also focusing on consortia, Maris Hayashi considers the relationship of individual librarians to library cooperatives, and how a mutually beneficial relationship can exist to enhance service at member libraries, especially as consortia provide opportunities for training.

Just as Flynn, Gilchrist, and Olson discussed assessment as an internal institutional process in our earlier volume on cooperation within institutions, *Libraries Within Their Institutions: Creative Collaborations*, Martha Kyrillidou discusses it as an external collaboration as she describes ARL's Statistics and Measurement Program, which is an "active collaboration at the national and international level," involving partnerships with the National Center for Education Statistics, NISO, ALA/ACRL, ASERL, IFLA, SCONUL, and other entities.

Nancy Kranich considers the role of libraries in promoting civic engagement, educating citizens, and bringing them together to strengthen participation in democratic processes. Kenning Arlitsch, Nancy Lombardo, and Joan Gregory discuss sharing their institution's resources with overseas partners, with a particular focus on interlibrary loan and health science resources. Romelia Salinas and Richard Chabrán describe their very innovative efforts, as librarians with university support, to work with Hispanic community groups and prepare them for the integration of digital information into their work. Julie Todaro provides a "who, what, when, where, and why" of community collaborations for libraries.

Julia Kelly and Louise Letnes describe the development of AgEcon Search, an "alternative method of delivering research results to many potential users." This web resource, the result of cooperation between academic institutions, academic libraries, professional associations, and government agencies, disseminates the grey literature of agricultural and resource economics. Charles Humphrey describes a collaboration between Canadian academic libraries and Statistics Canada on a data literacy program designed to foster more informed use of available data.

Claudine Jenda describes the extensive network of U.S. Patent and Trademark Depository Libraries, and the collaborative partnership between the Patent and Trademark Office and these libraries. Finally, Ken Marks details a process of collaboration between his library and a commercial vendor, to test and implement a new inventory control product.

Taken together, the articles in this volume illustrate the remarkable range of cooperative activities in which libraries are engaged, locally, nationally, and even internationally. Increasingly, we see librarians realizing that their institutions are part of the total fabric of society, and need to be linked in a variety of ways to the world around them, and not only by participation in bibliographic utilities. There is a growing understanding of the key role libraries have in the development of civil society, and a realization that we have an obligation to enhance the integration of digital information, not only for students in academic settings, but also much more broadly throughout all levels of society. We applaud this activist stance as librarians reach out to cooperate, both within their local context and beyond.

William Miller
Director of Libraries
Florida Atlantic University

Building a Foundation for Collaboration:
K-20 Partnerships in Information Literacy

Janet W. Nichols

Lothar Spang

Kristy Padron

SUMMARY. The authors have developed collaborative partnerships with K-12 educators and school library/media specialist students to promote information literacy. This article traces the history beginning with on-site workshops collaboratively developed by K-12 and university library staff; a continuing education course in information literacy for teachers and school librarians; an in-service workshop prepared collaboratively by a high school staff and university librarians; and a graduate-level library science course in information literacy for school library/media specialist students. Suggestions are provided for promoting information literacy partnerships between K-12 schools and universities, known as K-20 information literacy. *[Article copies available for a fee from The Haworth Document Delivery Service: 1-800-HAWORTH. E-mail address: <docdelivery@haworthpress.com> Website: <http://www.HaworthPress.com> © 2005/2006 by The Haworth Press, Inc. All rights reserved.]*

Janet W. Nichols, MSLS, is Coordinator of Instruction and Information Services (E-mail: janet.nichols@wayne.edu); Lothar Spang, AMLS, is Public Services Librarian (E-mail: lothar.spang@wayne.edu); and Kristy Padron, MLIS, is Instruction Services Librarian (E-mail: kmpadron@wayne.edu), all at the David Adamany Undergraduate Library, Wayne State University, Detroit, MI 48202.

[Haworth co-indexing entry note]: "Building a Foundation for Collaboration: K-20 Partnerships in Information Literacy." Nichols, Janet W., Lothar Spang, and Kristy Padron. Co-published simultaneously in *Resource Sharing & Information Networks* (The Haworth Information Press, an imprint of The Haworth Press, Inc.) Vol. 18, No. 1/2, 2005/2006, pp. 5-12; and: *Libraries Beyond Their Institutions: Partnerships That Work* (ed: William Miller, and Rita M. Pellen) The Haworth Information Press, an imprint of The Haworth Press, Inc., 2005/2006, pp. 5-12. Single or multiple copies of this article are available for a fee from The Haworth Document Delivery Service [1-800-HAWORTH, 9:00 a.m. - 5:00 p.m. (EST). E-mail address: docdelivery@haworthpress.com].

Digital Object Identifier: 10.1300/J121v18n01_02

KEYWORDS. Information literacy, collaboration, college and university libraries/services to schools, K-12 outreach

With the opening of the David Adamany Undergraduate Library in September 1997, the Wayne State University Library System strengthened its commitment to building collaborative relationships with K-12 partners. Historically, the libraries had provided circulation privileges and on-site instruction for advanced placement and honors students from area schools. During the planning and staffing of the Undergraduate Library, we envisioned a broader goal of working in tandem with area schools to promote information literacy. The authors have been involved in these efforts and have shared this vision since the opening of the Undergraduate Library. Their experiences serve as a foundation for continued efforts in establishing educational partnerships with their K-12 colleagues. The following questions helped to shape and direct their efforts.

SHOULD ACADEMIC LIBRARIANS BE INVOLVED IN ESTABLISHING PARTNERSHIPS WITH K-12 SCHOOLS?

The answer is an enthusiastic "yes!" Both the American Association of School Librarians (AASL) and the Association of College and Research Libraries (ACRL) have defined information literacy as the foundation for their instructional efforts. The teaching and reinforcement of information literacy skills is recognized as critical to lifelong learning and the foundation for each organization's instructional efforts. In 1998, AASL and ACRL formed a joint task force to look at ways to encourage closer collaboration between K-12 and post-secondary librarians. The AASL publication of *Information Power* (1998) and the subsequent ACRL publication of *Information Literacy Competency Standards for Higher Education* (2000) made clear the commonalities the organizations and their members share in preparing students to meet the information challenges of the 21st century. The *AASL/ACRL Blueprint for Collaboration* (2000) identified existing collaborative partnerships and made recommendations for future collaborative efforts between the American Library Association (ALA) divisions and their members.

One K-12/university library partnership focused on educational technology in K-12 classrooms. A collaborative program between Duke University and the Durham (NC) Public Schools paired technology mentors from the university library staff with public school teachers. Teacher participants received both formal classes and one-on-one mentor sessions. This program was developed as a pilot program that could be duplicated in other school systems (AASL/ACRL Task Force 2000).

Another K-12/university partnership involved teaching lifelong learning skills to high school students. The University of California at Irvine libraries created a two-year pilot program called School Partnership for Instruction, Research, and Information Technology (SPIRIT). SPIRIT was funded by a grant from the University of California School-University Partnership Program. A goal of SPIRIT was to help increase the number of students that meet and exceed University of California at Irvine's admissions requirements (AASL/ACRL Task Force).

Based upon the work of the Task Force, the AASL/ACRL Standing Committee on Information Literacy was established. The committee has planned and delivered joint presentations at the 2003 AASL National Conference and at the 2004 ALA Annual Conference to further the professional associations' commitment to K-20 collaboration for information literacy. There is strong professional support for developing collaborative partnerships in K-20.

- *What Possibilities Exist for Collaboration between Academic Librarians and Their K-12 Colleagues?*
- *How Do University Librarians Establish Collaborative, Ongoing Partnerships for Information Literacy?*
- *What Do These Partnerships Look Like?*

Prior to the opening of the Undergraduate Library, focus groups including school library media specialists, administrators, and classroom teachers met and, based upon their discussions, developed a plan for a university library-K-12 partnership. While they expected that traditional instruction of K-12 students would continue as a part of the focus of the Undergraduate Library's instructional goals, they suggested establishing a more collaborative partnership with K-12 educators. By working with those educators as colleagues to advance information literacy through faculty workshops, the efforts of the partnership would be greatly increased. Allowing teachers time and assistance in integrating information literacy into their curriculum would impact those teachers' classes for years to come.

With this goal in mind, grant funding was obtained through the Herrick Foundation for the development of two pilot projects with area schools: Ferndale High School and Northwestern High School. The Herrick Project was developed over a three-year period of planning, on-site workshops, and evaluation. Professional staff in the Undergraduate Library collaboratively planned in-service workshops with teachers, school librarians/media specialists, and administrators from the two area high schools. Participants were introduced to the Big6™ model of information literacy (see p. 9) and planned research assignments that integrated this model into their existing curriculum. Workshops were presented over a 2-year period at the high schools. Details of the project are available in articles published by Nichols (1999, 2001), and Krugler and Nichols (2000).

During this time, the commonalities of instructional goals between the K-12 educators and the instructional librarians from the University were evident. They saw information literacy as a foundation for lifelong learning to be taught and reinforced throughout a student's education. Educators involved in the Herrick Project clearly valued the opportunity to work collaboratively with their university colleagues (Krugler and Nichols).

Based upon the success of the Herrick Project, the authors sought additional opportunities for partnering with K-12 colleagues. During the summer of 2000, the College of Education at Wayne State University invited faculty to develop and teach in-service classes for Detroit Public School teachers. The authors developed and conducted a week long, hands-on information literacy workshop for teachers called *Information Literacy*. Participants earned graduate credit through the College of Education. *Information Literacy* provided participants the opportunity to create lessons that integrated an information literacy model into their existing curriculum. It also gave participants practical experience with collaboration, instructional design, and information literacy models. The course's main objective was for participants to put theory into practice by developing a research lesson that followed the Big6™ model of information literacy, which will later be discussed in this article. The content and evaluation of the course are discussed in an article in written by the authors (Nichols and Spang 2001).

The authors had anticipated teaching their information literacy course the following summer, only to learn that funding was no longer available through the College of Education. At this point it appeared that opportunities for further information literacy partnerships had stalled. However, this was not the case. A suburban school library media specialist contacted the authors in fall 2001 after reading their article in the *The Big6™ eNewsletter* (2001) in which they outline the information literacy course they had taught. She was on the North Central Association accreditation committee for her high school and had convinced her colleagues to include information literacy as one of their school goals for the upcoming accreditation visit. She inquired if developing a workshop such as that described in the article might be possible.

After lengthy e-mail correspondence, the authors met with the accreditation team at the high school and outlined the possibilities for a workshop. Subsequently, the high school team and academic librarians met with the high school principal to plan for delivery of a half-day information literacy workshop to the entire high school staff during a scheduled teacher in-service day. Planning included a follow-up intensive workshop for interested teachers. We conducted the introduction to information literacy with hands-on activities in the high school library media center using the school's wireless laptop computers and recruited interested faculty for the summer workshop. However, remodeling of the school library media center, along with the library media specialist leaving for another job, sidelined the plans for that workshop. Here the authors learned how crucial human relationships are to developing partnerships of this kind. Although the administration and faculty were supportive, without the leadership of the school library media specialist the project and partnership did not continue.

Still firmly committed to the value of working with K-12 educators to further information literacy instruction, the authors looked for other partnering opportunities. Both authors have taught as adjunct faculty in the Library and Information Science Program (LISP) at Wayne State University since the summer of 2002. After that summer, we approached the director of LISP regarding the development and teaching of an information literacy course for pre-service library media specialists. With strong encouragement, we prepared a course proposal that was accepted by the program. The course, *Issues in Librarianship: Information Literacy*, was taught in summer 2003 and summer 2004.

While the content of *Issues in Librarianship* is directed to school library media specialists, one LISP student with a concentration in public libraries participated in the summer 2003 course. There were inquiries regarding the summer 2004 course from LISP students with concentrations in academic libraries. In these cases, the students have indicated a strong interest in information literacy in order to better work with K-12 teachers and students who use the public library. In the case of LISP students with academic library concentrations, they are aware of the emphasis on information literacy in the academic setting as well.

The Big6™ model for information literacy is used as the structure for the course. This model was developed by Robert Berkowitz and Michael Eisenberg, and is commonly used to teach information and technology skills in the K-12 setting. Big6™ delineates research and problem-solving strategies into 6 steps and provides an essential framework for approaching information-based questions (Big6™ 2004). The first step is Task Definition, or defining the problem and needs for information. The second step is Information Seeking, where possible sources of information are brainstormed and then evaluated. The third step is Location and Access, where information sources are located and information is found from them. The fourth step is Use of Information; the information seeker reads, hears, or physically processes the information from its source and extracts the necessary information. The fifth step is Synthesis: the information seeker gathers, organizes, or presents the information he has found. The final step is Evaluation, where the seeker judges the information obtained as well as the quality of the problem-solving or research process (Big6™ 2003). Educators find valuable curricular and staff development materials through the Big6™ website at http://www. big6.com (2004).

The course *Issues in Librarianship* is conducted as a practical, hands-on workshop for students. The instructors work as colleagues in assisting in the planning and development of a unit integrating information literacy into the curriculum or staff development program tailored to each participant's particular situation. Participants have the opportunity to collaborate with an academic librarian and to gain practical experience in developing information literacy lessons. Just recently, one of last year's participants posted to the listserv for Michigan Association for Media in Education (MAME), the statewide association of school librarians/media specialists, her comments on the usefulness of the course in preparing for introducing the Big6™ to her middle school faculty.

The possibilities for K-20 collaboration are as varied as the individuals and organizations involved, but do share some commonalities:

1. Programs should be developed collaboratively. The authors were very sensitive to the possible perception on the part of the K-12 partners that in some way the university members of the team might feel they needed to "show the K-12 people how things should be done." In all of the projects just cited, we saw all members as equal stakeholders in the planning and instruction. This is key to a collaborative relationship.
2. K-12 members of the planning teams indicated that having university partners did lend what they called "credibility" to their efforts.
3. A K-12 team of a building-level administrator, respected classroom teacher, and library media specialist further lent both credibility and support to the efforts. Having an administrator involved in both the planning and delivery of the on-site workshops is integral to the success of the partnerships.
4. When appropriate, planned in-service should be delivered on-site so that participants are using familiar and available technology.
5. Teachers need time to plan, to work with their colleagues, to experiment with resources, and to develop meaningful activities integrated into the curriculum. Just introducing resources and/or technology without time for planning carries no long-term benefits.

6. Networking with K-12 colleagues "opens the door" to collaborative possibilities. We have presented the results of our information literacy partnerships at K-12 conferences and have published the results of these partnerships in K-12 professional literature. As a direct result of this networking, an on-site K-12 workshop was presented and a school library media specialist from western Michigan commuted to attend a five-week information literacy class. Based upon her work during the class, she returned to her school to present the workshop she developed to her teachers and has become an information literacy leader within her school district. Results of successful partnerships need to be presented to "potential partners" at K-12 conferences and in K-12 publications.

7. "Think big, plan small." Having a vision provides the focus and direction for collaborative efforts. Expect that initial projects may seem small, but in our experience there is a ripple effect at work. Looking back over the past seven years of collaborative efforts, long-term professional partnerships have developed. We now have contacts in area schools and work closely with these teachers, library media specialists, and their students on a variety of continuing outreach projects.

8. Look for partners on the university campus. The College of Education is a natural partner for K-20 collaboration. Partnering with colleagues to provide information literacy instruction to students receiving teacher education training and those returning for continuing education courses may provide networking opportunities that can lead to developing partnerships.

FUTURE POSSIBILITIES

Two recent publications reinforce both the importance of information literacy as a basis for lifelong learning and the importance of developing K-20 collaboration to prepare students for success in the 21st century. *Understanding University Success* (Conley 2003) documents the results of a three-year study to determine what college freshmen need to know to succeed academically. This report identifies "Knowledge Skills & Foundations" as *information gathering: notes and research* and a*nalysis, critique, and connections*. The publication of this report links high school and college standards, and clearly identifies information literacy as a foundation for success, enabling K-20 educators to have documentation to support and encourage articulation.

Learning for the 21st Century (Partnership for 21st Century Skills) identifies K-12 and higher education partnering as MILE, or a "Milestone for Improving Learning and Education." The report identifies the essential skills that people will need to be successful in the 21st century. Again, both information literacy and the need for K-20 partnerships are clearly identified as critical to the effort to meet the educational needs of today's students.

We see these reports as a foundation for future grant efforts on their part to further develop information literacy partnerships within the K-20 educational community. Because of the identification of information literacy and K-20 articulation in reports generated by the higher education and business communities, there is now a strong foundation outside of the library profession to encourage and support continuing efforts to develop K-20 information literacy partnerships.

REFERENCES

AASL/ACRL Task Force on the Educational Role of Libraries. 2000. *Blueprint for Collaboration.* ACRL White Papers and Reports. <http://www.ala.org/ala/acrl/acrlpubs/whitepapers/acrlaaslblueprint.htm> [accessed March 26, 2004].

American Association of School Librarians. 1998. *Information power.* Chicago: American Library Association.

Association of College & Research Libraries. 2000. *Information literacy competency standards for higher education.* Chicago: American Library Association.

Big6™. 2004. *Big6™: Information literacy for the information age.* <http://www.big6.com> [accessed April 28, 2004].

_____. 2003. *What is the Big6™?* <http://www.big6.com/showarticle.php?id=415> [accessed June 4, 2004].

Conley, David T. 2003. *Understanding university success: A report from Standards for Success: A project of the Association of American Universities and The Pew Charitable Trust.* Eugene, OR: Center for Educational Policy Research.

Krugler, Becky A., and Janet Nichols. 2000. Building partnerships for staff development. *Media Spectrum* 27: 24-25.

Nichols, Janet. 1999. Building bridges: High school and university partnerships for information literacy. *NASSP Bulletin* 83: 75-81.

Nichols, Janet W. 2001. Sharing a vision: Information literacy partnerships (K-16). *College & Research Libraries News* 63: 275-77+.

Nichols, Janet W., and Lothar Spang. 2001. A summer information literacy workshop for teachers. *The Big6 Newsletter.* Summer. <http://www.big6.com/showarticle.php?id=287> [accessed March 26, 2004].

"Learning for the 21st Century." Partnership for 21st Century Skills. <http://www.21stcenturyskills.org/downloads/p21_Report.pdf> [accessed March 26, 2004].

Building Bridges:
A Research Library Model
for Technology-Based Partnerships

Carolyn A. Snyder
Howard Carter
Mickey Soltys

SUMMARY. The nature of technology-based collaboration is affected by the changing goals and priorities, budgetary considerations, staff expertise, and leadership of each of the organizations involved in the partnership. In the context of a national research library, this article will describe Southern Illinois University Carbondale Library Affairs' partnerships with campus organizations such as Information Technology, with Illinois regional education consortia, and with national organizations including the Association of Research Libraries and OCLC, Inc. *[Article copies available for a fee from The Haworth Document Delivery Service: 1-800-HAWORTH. E-mail address: <docdelivery@haworthpress.com> Website: <http://www.HaworthPress.com> © 2005/2006 by The Haworth Press, Inc. All rights reserved.]*

Carolyn A. Snyder is Director of Foundation Relations and Professor of Library Affairs (E-mail: csnyder@lib.siu.edu), Howard Carter (E-mail: hcarter@lib.siu.edu) and Mickey Soltys (E-mail: msoltys@lib.siu.edu) are both affiliated with Library Affairs, all at the Southern Illinois University Library, 605 Agriculture Drive, Carbondale, IL 62901.

[Haworth co-indexing entry note]: "Building Bridges: A Research Library Model for Technology-Based Partnerships." Snyder, Carolyn A., Howard Carter, and Mickey Soltys. Co-published simultaneously in *Resource Sharing & Information Networks* (The Haworth Information Press, an imprint of The Haworth Press, Inc.) Vol. 18, No. 1/2, 2005/2006, pp. 13-23; and: *Libraries Beyond Their Institutions: Partnerships That Work* (ed: William Miller, and Rita M. Pellen) The Haworth Information Press, an imprint of The Haworth Press, Inc., 2005/2006, pp. 13-23. Single or multiple copies of this article are available for a fee from The Haworth Document Delivery Service [1-800-HAWORTH, 9:00 a.m. - 5:00 p.m. (EST). E-mail address: docdelivery@haworthpress.com].

KEYWORDS. Collaboration, distance education, information technology, instructional support, partnerships, research libraries, technology

INTRODUCTION

Library Affairs (the Library College) at Southern Illinois University Carbondale has extensive experience with technology-based partnerships on campus and outside the University and is illustrative of the service opportunities and challenges of such collaborative efforts. These partnerships have been impacted by important factors in each participating organization including changing goals and priorities, budgetary considerations, staff expertise, and leadership. Within the mission of the university, the Library Affairs' focus has been on service to library users and significant contributions to regional and national cooperation. The Library has embarked on several major partnerships and on a number of more focused collaborative activities. Some continue today with minor modifications, while others have changed significantly, and others no longer exist.

CAMPUS PARTNERSHIPS

Library Affairs began engaging in technology-based partnerships in the early 1990s. The partnerships and collaborative endeavors have been possible because of a series of strategic decisions by the Library to update the staff and equipment of the outdated Learning Resources Center. The unit was renamed the Instructional Support Services (ISS) Department and was refocused to include the expertise and resources to lead in the development of technology-based services to support teaching faculty, teaching assistants, and other instructional staff. At the same time, expertise and equipment within the Library Systems Services Department were significantly upgraded and expanded to enable Systems to develop state-of-the-art technology-based services. These changes required the support of the Vice President for Academic Affairs and other campus administrators. Library resources were reallocated, and new funding was secured from the campus and from outside the university. While this has been an evolving process, these significant organizational and staffing changes were made by the end of 1992.

The restructuring of its instructional support services positioned the SIUC Library for technology leadership on campus and for the first of a number of creative partnerships in the technology area. The initial focus was on collaboration with organizations and individuals on campus with the goal of enhancing technology-based services for Library users. In 1992, Library Affairs entered into a significant partnership with Computing Affairs (now Information Technology). Although these two units report to two different campus vice-chancellors, they have developed successful collaborations while maintaining their separate organizations. Since these two organizations each have their own culture, priorities, and budget conditions, this creates challenges that have affected the overall continuity of the partnership.

A recent literature search yielded little information about collaboration between separate library and IT units. The Coalition for Networked Information (CNI) has taken a leadership role in supporting and publicizing collaboration between libraries and information technology units with various campus organizational structures. Some examples were described at the CNI Fall 2000 Task Force Meeting project briefings where presenters included representatives from Dartmouth College and Mount Holyoke College. At Dartmouth, a joint library/IT planning process resulted in the development of the concept and design for a new library wing, housing both library and computing services, such as the reference desk and academic computing consulting services. Mount Holyoke participated as part of CNI's initiatives to provide a structured environment for institutional teams to develop collaborative projects related to networking and networked information resources (CNI, 2000).

Other successful collaborative projects include the Information Arcade at the University of Iowa, the development of campus information policies at the University of North Carolina, Chapel Hill, and new courses in the CNI's New Learning Communities program (Lippincott, 1998). Northwestern University renovated an entire floor of its main library in 2001 and located the primary departments for direct support of faculty in one cooperative space. This joint effort brought together the library's collection management function with academic technologies and digital media services (Snyder, Carter, and Soltys, 2002). The University of Washington Libraries were recognized as the 2004 university winner of the Association of College & Research Libraries Excellence in Academic Libraries Award for their *Uwired* effort that "highlights the effectiveness of the libraries in working collaboratively with other campus offices to promote and support effective uses of technology in teaching and learning" (*College & Research Libraries News*, March 2004).

At SIUC, the first collaborative Library and Computing Affairs technology project was the joint development of the campus-wide information system (CWIS) and the subsequent development of the Library's own information network, LINKS. "CWIS and LINKS gave SIUC students, staff, and faculty the improved ability to retrieve information about campus activities, and provided unprecedented access to library materials at this institution and at other research libraries" (Snyder, Carter, and Soltys, 2002).

Library Affairs and Computing Affairs formed a team named CIRCA/2001 for the development of CWIS and other collaborative endeavors. Six Computing Affairs staff led by an assistant director moved to the Library where they shared space with library members of the team led by an assistant director/associate dean. Team members from both organizations shared space in the newly renovated area that had previously housed the card catalog. The renovation was funded by the campus administration, and the partnership had support from the highest administrative levels. CIRCA/2001 continued at full strength into the mid-1990s with a focus on network access to information resources. Because of changing Information Technology (IT) priorities, the team operated at a reduced level in the late 1990s. During this period, most joint services were eliminated, reduced in scope, or provided solely by the Library.

In January 2001, IT and Library Affairs again agreed to strengthen their collaborative activities to enhance services for campus faculty, students, and staff. Members of the IT staff moved to the Library in 2001 with the goal of forming a cohesive team with Library staff. The newly named Academic Technology Center (ATC), located in the Library, brought together the services of the IT Customer Service Center (CSC), Library Affairs Instructional Support Services (ISS), and Library Affairs Systems Services. CSC is the IT central point of contact for campus computer users. The CSC staff troubleshoots computer and connectivity problems for faculty, students, and staff. The ISS mission is to assist instructors in employing technology to meet their teaching objectives. ISS provides such services as custom web programming, web course development, digital imaging and graphics, distance learning, instructional development, instructional evaluation, instructional technology support, technology tools and resources, video production, and interactive video support (Carter and Rundblad, 2003). Library Systems Services is responsible for the Library's computer workstations, networks, and servers. It also provides technical support and training to Library staff and others.

The ATC focus reflected the changes in campus technology that had occurred during the previous decade and the changing needs of the campus community. The first project the ATC team addressed was the urgent need for training in the routine use of popular desktop software, such as word processing, spreadsheet, and database programs. Training in these widely used products was not available anywhere on campus. Using the Library Affairs seminar series (for bibliographic and computer instruction) as a model, two-hour workshops were offered with no charge to faculty, students, staff, or other patrons. Teams comprised of one IT person and one library staff member designed and taught each ATC seminar. The effectiveness of ATC during its first year was documented in the evaluations of the seminars (Snyder, Carter, and Soltys, 2002), changing priorities, reduced staff budgets, and personnel turnover resulted in the withdrawal by June 2003 of most IT participation in the seminar series.

However, the ATC found other partnership opportunities to exploit. In one case, an instructional designer assigned to the CSC was relocated to work full time in ISS to use her instructional development expertise. She assisted instructors in designing and developing web-based components for their courses. This arrangement continued for about a year until the person left the University. Another example is the cooperation between the WebCT administrator in ISS and the Help Desk in CSC to assist students and instructors with WebCT-related problems, such as resetting passwords and providing access to course materials. Members of the IT staff also worked with members of ISS to write a document to provide campus guidelines for the development of accessible web pages. It explained the applicable standards and provided tips to web developers for achieving those standards. The document was made available on the ATC web site.

In 2003, IT and the Library expanded their cooperation across the campus in support of a Chancellor's initiative allocating $1 million a year to improve the University's teaching and learning environment and to enhance the quality and increase the quantity of instructional technology equipment in auditoriums and classrooms. Some of the money was designated to improve the physical characteristics of the classrooms including seats, flooring, lighting, and ADA compliance issues. IT and Library staff members worked with representatives of Plant and Service Operations, faculty members, consultants, and vendors to design the instructional technology system configuration and implement the installation of the new equipment.

Library Affairs has had considerable responsibility for classroom support for half a century. Its ISS Department manages the operations in Lawson Hall, a facility with 4 large auditoriums each seating approximately 280 persons and 6 smaller auditoriums each seating about 75. ISS also delivers audiovisual equipment to classrooms and auditoriums across campus. The Chancellor's initiative included placing new podiums, computers, projectors, video equipment, and smart technology in 21 large auditoriums including Lawson Hall and in 22 smaller classrooms. Academic departments were given the responsibility for managing and maintaining 11 of the classrooms used primarily by their students. ISS supports and maintains equipment in the large auditoriums and remaining general use classrooms.

While collaboration between library and technology organizations has been important for the last decade, it is essential in the current economic environment of public institutions of higher education such as SIUC. Duplication of services and expertise is not fiscally responsible and often not possible financially. The foundation for successful collaboration has been built between

Library Affairs and IT. Other opportunities exist for partnerships with other facilities on campus that provide technology support to students and faculty. One promising area for further cooperation involves ISS and the New Media Centers (NMC) in the Colleges of Liberal Arts and of Mass Communications and Media Arts. In the early 1990s, Library Affairs collaborated with the two New Media Centers to support and assist faculty in the incorporation of technology into courses. The NMCs have continued to work closely with IT, but the early collaboration with the Library did not continue.

The NMCs are physically located in each college's building. They provide students and faculty of the two colleges the functionality that is focused on needs related to the curriculum and specialties of the particular college and its departments. Since the New Media Centers are primarily self-help facilities, the Centers' staff members primarily insure that the equipment functions properly and that the facilities are secure. Although substantial initial funding for the NMCs came from the New Media Consortium, a not-for-profit organization established in 1993, funding is now the responsibility of each college. As part of a campus planning and budget task force study, leaders from ISS and the NMCs have discussed ways to realize efficiencies and eliminate duplication of services. Preliminary findings are that the services not driven by functionality should be directed to ISS, since ISS has the resources and provides services to all of the campus. NMCs have the functionality but are too under-funded and under-staffed to provide many services, such as web page creation and web hosting. At some future time it may be possible and desirable to combine the IT labs, NMCs, and ISS as a campus-wide resource center providing services and functionality to students, faculty, and staff.

Library technology collaboration with faculty and students was extended in 1993 by the implementation of the Geographic Information Systems service unit. The Library had convened a group of SIUC GIS users who, at their first meeting, expressed the need for a coordinator of GIS activities on campus. They noted that the Library seemed a likely choice because of its centrality and status as a repository of data available to all. The Library then hired an expert in geography with responsibilities that included the convening of regular GIS user meetings to keep members abreast of developments on current projects and thereby assist them in avoiding unwanted duplication of effort and expense (*Zetetikos*, 1994). The GIS services continue to be effective because they meet the users' current research and curricular needs. The Library's GIS expert provides training to a number of departments ranging from Administration of Justice to Zoology and assists faculty and students with data displays for their research and presentations. He also works with area high school teachers to conduct GIS orientation sessions for their classes.

REGIONAL COOPERATION

On the regional level, collaboration with community colleges in the southern third of Illinois and the SIU Edwardsville campus has been a significant activity for the last decade. Starratt and Hostetler (1997) wrote

> The Library has taken an often unique, integrative role in affording distance learning opportunities within SICCM (Southern Illinois Collegiate Common Market) and SIHEC (Southwest Illinois Higher Education Consortium) as it provides much more than traditional library services to the university and to the distance learning program. Library Affairs is solely responsible for the technical, instructional development, and administrative aspects of delivering SIUC's distance learning efforts within the two consortia, as well as for working with its partners to deliver library services to its remote users. Many of the Library's services which directly support the distance learning program have been centered in the SIUC Library since the late 1940's; others, however, have a more recent origin and reflect the Library's efforts to reallocate resources to new technology in recognition of shifts in the teaching, learning, and research environments. (pp. 21-22)

Library Affairs at SIUC was designated as the "hub" for an interactive video network for SICCM, one of the ten Illinois higher education consortia. Library Affairs faculty and staff led in providing distance learning training through the Regional Center for Distance Learning and Multimedia Development established in the SIUC Library in 1994 and active through 2003 when funds from the Illinois Board of Higher Education were no longer available. Faculty and staff from 12 southern Illinois community colleges and nearly 40 high schools received training through the Regional Center. The SIUC Library faculty and staff continue to supply the expertise for development of the interactive video network and for technical support for SICCM-member institutions. More recently, the distance learning technical staff in Library Affairs provided the expertise for development of an Internet-based (H.323) configuration for the SICCM distance learning initiative. The interactive video network continues to provide the technology for a significant amount of the distance learning activity in the SICCM service region; the Internet-based network provides a viable and inexpensive gateway to other Illinois instructional and state agencies. This regional cooperation is also an illustration of changing priorities and funding patterns. While the technology support from SIUC continues, the instructional development support is now the responsibility of the individual community college campuses (Snyder, Carter, and Hostetler, 2004).

Another way to build partnerships is to find new ways to use existing capabilities. The currently under-used interactive video network is a case in point. A cooperative effort has recently begun that involves the University's Disability Support Services (DSS), Division of Continuing Education, IT, and the interactive video staff in ISS, to provide remote sign language interpreting using its video network capability. DSS identified the need to provide American Sign Language interpreting services around the region but is fiscally restrained from sending interpreters to remote locations. The video network allows for the transmission of synchronous interpretation to remote sites by SIUC-based interpreters. Using ISDN-based (telephone) and IP-based (Internet) technologies, qualified sign language interpreters can support deaf and hard-of-hearing people in classrooms, meetings, and events across the state or virtually anywhere in the country without leaving the SIUC campus. The receiving location can view the interpretation on a video or computer monitor or video projection system. Demonstration tests conducted with an Illinois community college and another with a Missouri university received unanimous praise for the service.

NATIONAL COLLABORATION

Partnerships have been established with institutions beyond the campus or the region. In 1999, Library Affairs began an innovative project to create web-based professional development opportunities for the national and international library community. The Online Lyceum is a collaborative partnership between Library Affairs and the Association of Research Libraries' Office of Leadership and Management Services (ARL OLMS). This initiative provides a learning environment that integrates the innovative use of technology at SIUC with time-tested content from ARL and OLMS. This collaboration is the outcome of ARL's exploration of distance education options and a strong commitment by the Library Affairs Dean and the ARL Executive Director to support the new initiative. The Online Lyceum was designed to help institutions save money on travel costs for professional education, provide opportunities for librarians to enhance technology skills, and provide an anywhere, anytime learning environment (*Zetetikos*, 2000).

To date, fourteen courses have been developed for the Online Lyceum. The first course, Training Skills Online, was developed over a period of three months during the spring of 1999 and successfully delivered in May. Content developers from ARL worked closely with web developers, instructional designers, and librarians in ISS. Discussions centered around the methods that had been used to deliver the in-person course, web-based instructional tools currently available, and methods for continued communication and collaboration among the team members. A significant amount of time was devoted to working with content developers on the effective use of technology, including bulletin boards, chat rooms, e-mail, and electronic journal entries. Since 1999, OLMS has delivered a continuous schedule of Online Lyceum courses. As content has changed or technology has advanced, the ARL-ISS team has updated the courses and their functionality for completeness and currency. Revenue received for development of the ARL courses has allowed Library Affairs to fund personnel positions, upgrades to equipment and software, and other priority needs that could not be funded from the Library's regular budget. The outcome of this joint effort was not only the delivery of a successful series of online courses for ARL but also the development of a new model for collaboration in the online environment.

Other SIUC national collaborations have included the development of a copyright course with the American Library Association (ALA) and the development of a cataloging course for the Online Computer Library Center, Inc. (OCLC). The ALA project followed the model of the ARL Online Lyceum process with the ALA Copyright Office providing the content and ISS providing the instructional design and technical development. The completed course was delivered in 2001.

The collaboration with OCLC followed a different process. The director of the OCLC Institute wanted to provide an introductory course in the basics of the MARC bibliographic format by online delivery or in a stand-alone CD-ROM mode. Discussions were begun with ISS to create such a course in 2002 with the support of the Library Dean. Following a company re-organization, OCLC's vice president for member services was assigned responsibility for the OCLC Institute. The Institute has responsibility for seminars, workshops and other professional development learning events. A partnership was established in 2003 between OCLC, Library Affairs, and the Missouri Library Network Corporation (MLNC), an OCLC-affiliated network in St. Louis. OCLC designated Toolbook as the development software to be used. ISS created the content and the instructional design, and did the technical programming. MLNC provided content expertise. A prototype lesson module was developed by ISS and critiqued by representatives of OCLC, the MLNC, and ISS for content, tone, graphic style, and functionality in a meeting in St. Louis. Incorporating the feedback, ISS developed a six-lesson course with a course introduction, overview, and a glossary. At significant points of development, telephone conference calls were held for all partners to review, critique, and amend the course materials. The completed course was delivered in January

2004. OCLC then began conducting usability studies on the course. The revenue received from developing this course helped Library Affairs fund one programmer and one instructional design position in ISS for the duration of the project. OCLC hopes to market the course to its member institutions worldwide, and the contract specifies that Library Affairs will receive royalties for each sale of the course.

PARTNERSHIP CHALLENGES

The factors affecting the success and duration of local, regional, and national collaborations and partnerships include the changing goals and priorities, budgetary considerations, staff expertise, and leadership of each of the organizations. The CNI Working Together professional development program participants in a review of collaboration identified factors motivating collaboration and mitigating against successful partnerships in institutions. The group described the following motivating factors:

> executive mandate in both merged units and in separate units, scarcity of financial resources, the desire to consolidate overlapping functions and activities, the need to incorporate the other professional group's perspectives into project design, the interdependence of librarians and information technologists, the need to develop new services in the networked environment, and overall institutional survival. (Lippincott, 1998, p. 84)

The CNI group also listed factors that mitigate against successful partnerships in their institutions. These factors include:

> the significant amount of time needed to invest in successful partnerships, lack of financial resources for projects, "territory," campus geography (making face-to-face meetings or development of joint facilities difficult), personality conflicts, differences in organizational culture, lack of respect for the other profession, and failing to see the benefits of partnerships. (Lippincott, 1998, p. 84)

Whether collaboration is on the same campus or with regional or national partners, it requires considerable effort. Successful collaborations are the result of sustained commitment from all parties. While SIUC's technology-related collaborations have been extensive and multi-faceted in the pursuit of service excellence, they no doubt illustrate the factors affecting such collaborations and partnerships in academic libraries. The changing goals and priorities of the Library and the other organizations involved have influenced the nature and continuation of each partnership and collaborative activity. The IT and Library partnership has ranged from strong and intense to reduced activity to a renewed sharing of expertise and physical proximity and is a good example. Changing leadership and staff, changing institutional environments, and changing organizational priorities have all had an impact on each Library partnership and collaborative activity.

REFERENCES

"ACRL Honors the 2004 Award Winners," *College & Research Libraries News* 65 (March 2004): 140. Available online at: <http://www.ala.org/ala/acrl/acrlpubs/ crlnews/backissues2004/march04/04winners.htm>. Last accessed April 29, 2004.

Carter, Howard, and Kevin Rundblad. "The Village of ISS," *Information Technology and Libraries* 22 (June 2003): 54-60.

Coalition for Networked Information. "CNI Fall 2000 Task Force Meeting: Project Briefings" (December 7-8, 2000). Available online at: <http://www.cni.org/tfms/ 2000b.fall/PBrief_2000Ftf.html>. Last accessed May 26, 2004.

Lippincott, Joan K. "Working Together: Building Collaboration Between Libraries and Information Technologists," *Information Technology and Libraries* 17 (June 1998): 83-86.

Snyder, Carolyn A., Howard Carter, and Jerry Hostetler. "Distance Education Support in University Libraries," *Journal of Library & Information Services in Distance Learning* 1:2 (2004).

Snyder, Carolyn A., Howard Carter, and Mickey Soltys. "ATC: All That Collaboration," *Library Administration & Management* 16 (Fall 2002): 194-7.

Starratt, Jay and Jerry C. Hostetler. "Distance Learning and Library Affairs: Technology Development and Management at Southern Illinois University at Carbondale," in Snyder, Carolyn A. and James W. Fox (Ed.). *Libraries and Other Academic Support Services for Distance Learning*, (Greenwich, CT: JAI Press, 1997): 17-30.

Zetetikos: Morris Library Annual Report: 1993 (Southern Illinois University Carbondale, 1994).

Zetetikos: Morris Library Annual Report: 1999 (Southern Illinois University Carbondale, 2000).

Play with the Slinky®:
Learning to Lead Collaboration
Through a Statewide Training Project
Aimed at Grants for Community Partnerships

Elizabeth A. Curry

SUMMARY. How can training develop the philosophical commitment that library staff members need to successfully lead collaborative projects? How do conversation as a training model and play as an activity shape the collaborative learning process? How do we stimulate libraries and library staff to assume leadership roles in community building? This article is a study of a statewide training process designed to create opportunities for librarians to learn to lead collaborative community projects. It highlights the content, exercises, and methods used to stimulate learning. The workshops were facilitated as models of collaboration, and play, as well as sites of conversation about collaborative philosophy and techniques. *[Article copies available for a fee from The Haworth Document Delivery Service: 1-800-HAWORTH. E-mail address: <docdelivery@ haworthpress.com> Website: <http://www.HaworthPress.com> © 2005/2006 by The Haworth Press, Inc. All rights reserved.]*

Elizabeth A. Curry is currently in the Doctoral program at the University of South Florida Communication Department, PO Box 1735, Lutz, FL 33548 (E-mail: elizabethcurry@tampabay.rr.com). She is a trainer and consultant who specializes in leadership, collaboration, team development, and strategic thinking.

[Haworth co-indexing entry note]: "Play with the Slinky®: Learning to Lead Collaboration Through a Statewide Training Project Aimed at Grants for Community Partnerships." Curry, Elizabeth A. Co-published simultaneously in *Resource Sharing & Information Networks* (The Haworth Information Press, an imprint of The Haworth Press, Inc.) Vol. 18, No. 1/2, 2005/2006, pp. 25-48; and: *Libraries Beyond Their Institutions: Partnerships That Work* (ed: William Miller, and Rita M. Pellen) The Haworth Information Press, an imprint of The Haworth Press, Inc., 2005/2006, pp. 25-48. Single or multiple copies of this article are available for a fee from The Haworth Document Delivery Service [1-800-HAWORTH, 9:00 a.m. - 5:00 p.m. (EST). E-mail address: docdelivery@haworthpress.com].

Digital Object Identifier: 10.1300/J121v18n01_04

KEYWORDS. Collaboration, leadership, training, interpersonal communication, discourse, organizational play, storytelling

SETTING THE SCENE WITH SLINKY® PLAY

Laughter and chatter ripple throughout the group. Excitement and a bit of confusion permeate the room when I invite workshop participants to open the boxes labeled "magic springs," a generic brand of the retro toy Slinky®. They don't need instructions on what to do, they just begin playing. Suddenly, plastic Slinkys® in bright rainbow colors are sliding back and forth from hand to hand, back and forth, back and forth as twenty librarians engage in play. The sliding plastic rings make zinging noises that become a humming sound. Different rhythms and different speeds combine to create a busy sound that fills the room. People are smiling, some with glee, some with embarrassment, a few with confusion. I walk around the u-shaped configuration of tables, chatting and also playing with my Slinky®. Back and forth it slides, zing, zing, humming.

Then I begin to refocus the group. I use the Slinky® like a clapper with quick smacks together. People look up as the rhythm changes. I smile broadly, "OK, Are we ready? I can feel your creativity surging so let me explain why you each have a Slinky®." I pause and ask again, "Are we ready?" I pause. The voices quiet and people begin to turn their attention to me. Some still play with the Slinky® but more quietly. "I have a fun exercise to start our day. It will prepare us to look at different ideas on leadership and collaboration. We are going to *think outside the box* and try to look at things from many different perspectives. There are no right or wrong answers when you are searching for innovative ideas or when you seek to understand others' ideas, not just correct or contradict them."

I pause again and look around the tables. "The activity is to make a list of the different ways a Slinky® can be used, other than as a toy. The ideas do not need to be practical or workable. They can be wacky and crazy. We are brainstorming not evaluating," I emphasize. "No right or wrong answers. Our goal is to see how many ideas we can generate and find as many creative ideas as possible. There are only two rules. One, please number your list as you write the ideas. Two, you have fifteen minutes to complete the activity. I hope that each person can try for a minimum of twenty ideas. Any questions? Are you ready?" No one speaks but heads nod, so I give the signal to begin. People are writing, playing with the Slinky®, staring, and thinking as I walk around. I notice that two young women in blue jeans, Joanne and Becky listed on their nametags, are whispering and only Becky is writing. A woman in a peach colored pantsuit, Sylvia, holds the Slinky® up to her ear to dangle. John, a man in a blue golf shirt, stands up and drops the Slinky® to the floor. Annie, a woman with short curly brown hair, throws the Slinky® out in front of her across the table. When the writing seems to slow down and participants are searching for ideas, I coach them, "Think about different rooms in your house or your daily routine."

People are sharing ideas under their breath and laughing. Someone says, "Oh, I got a good one . . . a toothbrush holder!" Voices around the tables are rising: "a coffee cup holder, a steering wheel cover, a telephone message organizer." Finally, Craig asks me, "Can we share ideas, can we work together on a list, combine our lists?"

I repeat the question in a loud voice for the whole group. I reply, "I never said you couldn't work in teams and this is a session on collaboration." They laugh and form a group of three here, a group of two in another corner, sharing ideas and laughing. "Time is almost up. You have two more minutes," I warn. Then I ring a bell and announce, "Time's up." As the participants look up and sigh I pause and say, "We are going to look at the task and then reflect on the process." Amid much laughter, we determine the number of ideas and share our most creative ideas. We talk about ways of assessing quantity and quality. Then I ask, "So what did you see happening during this exercise?" They eagerly share their observations. We discuss how the first five or ten ideas come fairly quickly, but it gets harder after that–for some people. One person mentions that it is difficult not to evaluate ideas. James says that my coaching helped, and the ideas people muttered under their breath served to inspire others. The group agrees. One idea spawned another. Working together and sharing ideas, combining lists demonstrated the power of teamwork and many relevant observations about collaboration.

I wrap up this exercise suggesting that there are times when we need creative brainstorming and times we need decision-making. Rather than look for obstacles and reasons we can't work together, I suggest they remember one phrase when they try to develop twenty possibilities for collaborative projects or activities: What will it take to make this work? I call their attention to a resource in their packet from *Collaborative Creativity: Unleashing the Power of Shared Thinking* (Ricchiuto, 1997). We've experienced diversity, shared thinking, teamwork, and creativity.

As a training model this was an icebreaker, but it was much more of an experiential exercise to involve people in discovering key concepts. It was also designed to reinforce the notion that during the workshop we will be open to new and even "wacky" ideas as we pool our resources to gain new knowledge. The fun and laughter created positive emotions that stimulated innovative thoughts (Fredrickson, 2003). In this article, I will explore notions of how play and positive emotions are useful to learning, leading, and collaboration. Play can stimulate creative ideas, free people from fear of criticism, establish a safe environment to take risks, and foster a sense of community (Csikszentmihalyi, 1990; Linder, Roos, & Victor, 2001; Rieber, Smith, & Noah, 1998). I also will try to demonstrate Kenneth Gergen's theory that the critical stance of knowing (1) contains the conversation, (2) silences marginal voices and fragments relationships, (3) erodes community, (4) creates social hierarchy, and (5) contributes to broad cultural organizational enfeeblement (Ludema, Cooperrider, & Barrett, 2001, pp. 190-191; McNamee & Gergen, 1999). I demonstrate a more collaborative way of knowing and learning (Clinchy, 1996). I propose that collaborative communication training strategies and collaborative project development encourage conversations from multiple voices, enhance relationships, build a sense of community, promote equality, and begin to change our world one project at a time.

INTRODUCTION AND PROJECT OVERVIEW

"Collaboration is a social imperative. Without it we can't get extraordinary things done in organizations" (Kouzes & Posner, 2002, p. 242). Collaboration involves a complex array of knowledge, skills, and abilities, yet librarians without the training or background to support successful projects may be faced with organizational goals encouraging outreach to community agencies. Frequently, the collaboration is initiated by a funding source, a special project, or overture from another group. Many of these projects are very successful and grow into long-term continuing services. Some projects are fraught with difficulties or even fail because the collaborative foundation or philosophy is not sufficiently developed. I propose that we consider collaboration as a process, not just a project or an event. The project is the result of the process of building a relationship, which requires interpersonal communication. Collaborative endeavors require a high level of leadership, a way of thinking that embraces diversity, openness to possibilities, acceptance of different perspectives, and the goal of seeking commonalities.

This article is a study of a statewide training process designed to create opportunities for librarians to build on a foundational collaborative philosophy, learn collaboration communication skills, and become leaders in community collaboration. The workshops were facilitated as models of collaboration as well as sites for discussing collaborative techniques, brainstorming ideas for projects, and questioning assumptions. The article addresses the following questions:

- How can training develop the philosophical commitment that library staff members need to successfully lead collaborative projects?
- How does conversation as a training model shape the collaborative learning process?
- How do we stimulate libraries and library staff to assume leadership roles in community building?
- How do we foster collaborative approaches to the needs of those in the community that transcend organizational boundaries?

I explore strategies related to these questions in the context of the North Carolina Powerful Partners workshops. I highlight aspects of the content, exercises, and methods, which I used to stimulate learning about leading collaboration. The staff of the State Library of North Carolina had the vision for enhancing collaborative skills and fostering community building. It was my privilege to work with them as they shared their vision with me. In a collegial environment we planned, implemented, and evaluated the project. I would particularly like to acknowledge Sandy Cooper, State Librarian; Penny Hornsby, Federal Programs Consultant; and Ron Jones, Youth Consultant at the time of this project. Ron's flexibility, sense of humor, and tireless efforts made our travel throughout North Carolina together a rewarding adventure. I also benefited greatly from Ron's keen observational skills and perceptive feedback on the workshops. Our conversations and collaboration resulted in a special professional friendship, which helped me grow and develop.

COMMUNICATION LINKS LEADERSHIP AND COLLABORATION

I concur with a host of scholars who believe that both collaboration and leadership are based on communication and developing relationships. "At the heart of collaboration is trust. It's the central issue in human relationships within and outside organizations" (Kouzes & Posner, 2002, p. 244). The literature on collaboration refers frequently to trust as well as respect, equity, shared power, facilitative leadership, communication, and dialogue (Angelis, 1999; April, 1999; Bennis, Spreitzer, & Cummings, 2001; Johnson, Zorn, Tam, Lamontagne, & Johnson, 2003; P. Mattessich, Monsey, and with assistance from Roy, 1997; P. W. Mattessich & Monsey, 1992; Muronaga & Harada, 1999; Spreitzer & Cummings, 2001; Winer & Ray, 1994). Major examples would be the leadership work of James M. Kozues with Barry Z. Poser and Peter Senge.

Through their extensive research Kouzes and Posner have developed their five practices of leadership presented in *The Leadership Challenge*: (1) Model the Way by clarifying values, (2) Inspire Shared Vision by enlisting others, (3) Challenge the Process by experimenting and taking risks, (4) Enable Others to Act by promoting cooperative goals and sharing power, and (5) Encourage the Heart by recognizing contributions of others and creating a sense of community (Kouzes & Posner, 2002). In each of these practices, collaborative relationships and communication are stressed. Another example is Peter Senge's learning organization and the five disciplines which have been described as leadership disciplines (April, 1999; Senge, 1990). Senge's disciplines stress our interrelatedness, focus on thinking of collective systems, and emphasize the importance of communication and dialogue.

From a communication perspective, Kenneth Gergen also proposes that we look at the context of how we are related and interdependent in his work on relational and generative theory (Gergen, 1994, 2000, 2001). Generative theory focuses on the power of language to create alternatives, open possibilities, and offer different ways of perceiving and understanding the world. With relational responsibility, the process is valued more than the product as we strive for continuous engagement and reflection. In generative theory, action and discourse are integrally linked. "Talk is how we can most effectively create change" (McNamee & Gergen, 1999, p. 169). We use discourse as a way of relating and creating meanings that guides our actions. Communication is transactive not representational because "people understand through communication not prior to it" (Soukup, 1992, p. 5). Communication is not simply a technique we use within the change process. Another interpretation I espouse is that conversation is the context for change. Kurt April describes the process of leading change through conversation.

> Producing intentional change, then, is a matter of deliberately creating through communication and conversation, a new reality or set of social structures. If this is the case, then the change process actually occurs within, and is driven by, conversation and communication, rather than the reverse. It is my assertion that intentional change is produced through the development of these conversations. (April, 1999, p. 231)

So, in this article, I pair collaboration and leadership, positioning both as communication based. Based on that premise, I consider the training model, which is also based on teaching collaboration and leadership through conversation and interpersonal experiences.

LEADERSHIP

Scholars from numerous disciplines have studied leadership for hundreds of years with the main conclusion that it is a very complex and sometimes ambiguous concept. James McGregor Burns, a major figure in the field, concluded that leadership is "one of the most observed and least understood phenomena on earth" (Witherspoon, 1997, p. ix). One library author found over 100 definitions of leadership, such as situational leadership, servant leadership, Emotional Intelligence, or team leadership (Riggs, 2001).

At a recent conference, Dr. Mark D. Winston from Rutgers University pointed out that there has been very limited scholarly research on library leadership although there have been many news or opinion articles in the library press. Librarians have often focused on management skills more than leadership concepts in our professional events, publications, and library education curriculums (Winston, 2004). Leadership as a topic of concern has surfaced in the face of constant changes, which have caused more and more librarians to emphasize broader political, social, and environmental trends as the starting place for planning. Effectiveness became more important than efficiency. Only 10% of ALA accredited programs offer leadership training; however, there is growing interest in the face of potential crisis of leadership in the field (Winston, 2004). Dr. Winston acknowledges that the leadership literature is interdisciplinary and that the prolific business literature is particularly relevant to library and information management. He still encourages more leadership research specific to libraries and librarians.

Much of the literature agrees that leadership is important because it enhances the success of the organization in meeting its goals. However, the leadership literature incorporates a wide variety of approaches to the basis of leadership: (1) traits, (2) skills, (3) styles, (4) contingency, and (5) team or group. Often the five approaches are combined. The Center for Creative Leadership reports that the most significant success factor for a leader is building relationships. Many leadership experts, such as Warren Bennis, Kouzes and Posner, Daniel Goleman (Goleman, Boyatzis, & McKee, 2002), and others, propose that self awareness is central for leaders to understand self and others. Patricia Witherspoon elaborates on the concept of leadership as self awareness and adds that leadership is a relationship building process based on communication (Witherspoon, 1997). *The Next Library Leadership: Attributes of Academic and Public Library Directors* contains a comprehensive overview of leadership traits and professional qualities which include a wide range of skills necessary for collaboration (Hernon, Powell, & Young, 2003). Leaders must be able to communicate effectively in order to achieve goals in areas, such as change, community building, visioning, political skills, strategic planning, and teamwork.

Some people talk about the changing leadership paradigm from hierarchical roles to a more collaborative interdependent approach. I enjoy Betsy Wilson's characterization that the "Lone Ranger" approach to leadership is dead. "We are beginning to recognize that collaborative leadership combines the power that is inherent in the act of leading with the greater power that comes from shared visions and actions" (Wilson, 2000, p. 698). Her vision for the next century demands that libraries collaborate in community building. More and more colleges and universities are calling for "engaged scholarship" (Boyer, 1996), PLA's planning process focuses on community needs, multi-type cooperatives see partnerships in community building as a major trend for the millennium (Bolt, 2000), and the topic has received increasing attention throughout the profession. Kathleen de la Peña McCook has exhorted all types of libraries to look beyond our institutional walls, become more active in community initiatives, and find a place at the table (McCook, 2000).

TRAINING POWERFUL PARTNERS TO COLLABORATE

Collaborative learning has been researched and reported on regarding various levels of education from elementary grades to college classes. John Agada from the University of Wisconsin has presented a model for incorporating collaborative skills into library and information science education. His approach is anchored in interpersonal skills with cognitive and affective modeling (Agada, 1998). I found virtually no other research literature on teaching collaboration skills to librarians. Much of what we have learned about collaboration is based on the experience with specific projects, conference presentations, and articles about those projects; however, in this article I want to begin a process of looking at collaboration and training.

Any training in leadership or collaboration skills must balance the conceptual and philosophical foundations with the practical skills, while providing opportunities for dialogue, self-reflection, and assessment. With adult learners, a variety of techniques and learning styles must be incorporated into any program. Learning to lead, communicate, and build collaborative relationships is a "life long" endeavor. A holistic approach to personal development of leadership is a process, not a quick fix (Doh, 2003). Training includes modeling, coaching, feedback, experiential activities, personal assessments, and a safe place to experiment, explore, and take risks. Participants need to have motivation, the capacity for strategic thinking, basic communication skills, emotional intelligence, an orientation toward on-going learning, and the desire to lead (Doh, 2003).

POWERFUL PARTNERS PROJECT

The Powerful Partners project sponsored by the State Library of North Carolina consisted of several phases starting with a series workshops offered in multiple locations throughout the state for librarians and media specialists, broadly defined as the Leadership and Partnership Basics for Collaboration. Applicants submitted brief proposals for mini-grants to fund attendance at these training sessions. Attendance was required for participants to qualify for phase two, Advanced Collaboration Workshops covering grant project development with a team of librarians and community members working together. Attendance at these training sessions was required before submitting a grant proposal for funds allocated specifically for collaborative projects. Grant funding was linked to the learning objectives of the training sessions, and the criteria included collaboration success factors covered during the training. From 1999 to 2001, almost $400,000 was allocated to this project, and from 2001 to 2004, almost $500,000 was budgeted.

The Powerful Partnerships project supported the LSTA (Library Services and Technology Act) Plan of the State Library of North Carolina. The State Library's strategic plan for services called for leadership from libraries and librarians in every North Carolina Community in order to accomplish the following goals: (1) Children and teens benefit from the combined resources and efforts of a community focused on education and the healthy development of youth; (2) Children and teens in North Carolina access a full range of ideas and information; (3) Children and teens in North Carolina receive programs and services that stimulate their imagination, curiosity, and growth; and (4) Children and teens in North Carolina interact with adults who foster and guide their development as readers and learners. The major outcome we anticipated was that children and teens receive services strengthened by collaboration of agencies in their community.

The first workshop focused on leadership and collaboration by addressing topics, such as the difference between leading, controlling, and facilitating; types of authority and power; styles of influence and persuasion; levels of commitment in building collaboration; and the steps in building partnership relationships. The second stage of training was a two-day work session where librarians could not attend unless accompanied by one or two community partners. This was a work session where collaborative teams drafted a plan and outlined a grant proposal for a collaborative project. The sessions were models of collaboration as the group addressed needs statements for clientele not institutions, barriers to collaboration, success factors, group development, communication, recognition, and grant guidelines. This article is an overview of the process and the workshops. The North Carolina project focused on collaborative projects for youth and the leadership of public and school librarians; however, the process and training have applications for all types of libraries. In the following sections, I discuss the Leadership and Partnership Basic workshop and then the Advanced Collaboration Workshop. The final part of this article is a conclusion reflecting and summarizing the project lessons.

LEADERSHIP AND PARTNERING WORKSHOP

Before participants attended the workshops, they received a Homework and Sneak Peek packet with a self assessment inventory, several articles about collaboration, and material on persuasion and influence (Conger, 1998; Covey, 1992; Kriegel & Brandt, 1996; Ricchiuto, 1997). When participants read materials in advance, the time during the training sessions can be spent on interactive activities and discussion more than lecturing for content. These advance packets also tend to help reluctant participants feel more comfortable. The Homework and Sneak Peek materials maximize the impact of the training, encourage reflexivity, and reinforce application of the concepts.

I could summarize my approach to training with one of my handouts, a mini-poster of the Chinese proverb says: "Tell me and I'll forget. Show me and I might remember. Involve me and I'll understand." The Slinky® exercise I described in the beginning of this article set the tone for the day. Next, I outlined the purpose, process, and anticipated payoffs of the workshop, including my expectations for a highly interactive, creative, fun day. (Note that the following description does not correlate to exact times in the workshop and the break times are not addressed. I frequently engaged participants in activities that called for them to move around the room. We had a casual atmosphere with formal and informal breaks.)

The guiding vision was posted on flip chart paper in colorful lettering in several places, "With leadership from libraries and librarians in every North Carolina community children and teens learn to read, love to learn and have access to the world." These three phases *learn to read, love to learn*, and *access the world* were our touchstones throughout the first training phase and the later advanced session. In my overview I acknowledged that we had a great deal to cover–enough for four or five days. The major topics were: Leadership Styles, Change Readiness, Power and Authority, Styles of Influence and Levels of Cooperation, and Resources Available on Team Building. I stressed that the agenda, time, and topics would be adapted to their needs. In a sense, I offered the participants shared control of the day. I invited their collaboration and acknowledged the greater sense of purpose.

Interviews following the completion of the project noted that I frequently used the word "share," and I framed the day as a partnership among the participants and myself. Modeling collaborative learning as well as discussing it is critical to this type of training. I asked participants to contribute ideas and then rank a list of group behaviors called recipe for successful groups. Then we created a chart with everyone's top four priorities. Our discussion was a model of how people have different expectations when groups form and there is a need to clarify what group members think is important overall. I presented participants with a tool to help them remember that different people saw things differently, a kaleidoscope (often called a prism or *dragon's eyes*). This was the first of our Memory Anchors, something I use to reinforce concepts and act as reminders after the participant return back home. As a follow-up, I invited participants to individually complete a worksheet on their expectations for the day, what they wanted to get out of the session, and what they might contribute. Sharing comments was optional. The worksheet was to remind people to assume personal responsibility for their individual goals and needs. However, the discussion was useful to me as a facilitator and underscored the collaborative possibilities for shaping the session.

Changing leadership paradigms was the next module. I introduced the differences in more hierarchical leadership styles and the move to more collaborative leadership styles. We looked at levels of controlling and facilitating, moving from telling to asking or inviting solutions (Rees, 1991). Controlling might be more library focused and facilitating can become more client centered. In small groups we tried a few examples of ways to change a controlling statement to a facilitating statement. Instead of proposing the library solution, the exercise starts at identifying community needs. Instead of defining a partner as a funder or supporter, the exercise asks partners for ideas and commitment to working together for the community. The strategy of asking and inviting more than telling was also a skill I tried to model in my training.

Change is another major topic related to collaboration. We used a self-assessment exercise so participants could look at their change readiness skills. Using colored dots, we charted individual scores to represent the overall group in a graph. People worried a bit about if their scores were good or bad which was an opportunity to reinforce self awareness and awareness of others. Each person looked at the chart and wrote three sentences about the group. Our discussion was based on these descriptions and observations on process. The group discussed things such as whether being highly resourceful could sometimes be a drawback, the generally low tolerance for ambiguity, along with the perception of ourselves as adaptable. There were no "right" answers, so we could engage more readily in a rich, thought provoking discussion.

The exercise also was another demonstration of diversity in groups. We moved to exploring how we are influenced and can influence others. Our approach was based on persuasion or influence as mutual learning processes and collaborative communication, not win lose negotiations. Persuasion can galvanize change and forge solutions through conversation and dialogue (Conger, 1998). Each person wrote his or her own description or definition of power, authority, and influence on three postnotes. Then in small groups they rearranged ideas into similarities and differences. Discussion of small group reports touched on both positional power and expert power as authority, relational power, and charisma used to influence others, and issues of whether power was good or bad (Covey, 1992). This exercise led into exploring styles of influence, ways we are influenced, and thinking of what might influence others. Another self-assessment led to using examples for each style of influence: assertion, expertise, political skills, preparation, presentation, and client centered. As we tried different approaches and discussed the results, we concluded that it was difficult to stay open to options and not try to advocate for your own ideas. We talked about the shades of difference in manipulation, negotiation, persuasion, and collaboration. We also realized how often people use a combination of influence styles with community collaboration because groups are diverse. An important note was that the assessments, styles, and categories were used as springboards for discussion and reflection not as labels.

After lunch and door prizes, we used the story of *Stone Soup* (Brown, 1975) as a framework for discussing collaboration. Participants shared comments, such as: "The villagers were afraid to share because they had limited resources." "The soldiers didn't force farmers to share, they invited them to learn how to make soup from just water and a stone." "The soldiers inspired the farmers with a vision of soup fit for a king." "Alone villagers had little but together they made something great." "People followed the early risk takers." "At the end they had a relationship so they celebrated together." The question "Was it ethical for the soldiers to trick people into collaboration?" spurred a lively discussion of whether it was indeed trickery. At that point, I saw the workshop group willing to question each other's assumptions and pursue a lively discussion geared toward understanding. It was a moment of meaning for me as I experienced the power of using a story to spur discussion and the sense that the workshop participants were becoming a collaborative learning group. Our Memory Anchors were polished stones that served as reminders that collaborative projects are like stone soup. The story was our springboard to definitions and levels of collaboration, *Building Blocks of Interdependence* as we moved from categories of interaction: Networking and Communication to Cooperation, then Coordination and finally Collaboration. Based on the following definitions we played, "Is it Collaboration Yet?" by looking at projects and comparing structure, authority, communication, funding, and resources involved.

Cooperation is characterized by informal relationships that exist without any commonly defined mission, structure, or planning effort. Information is shared as needed, and authority is retained by each organization so there is virtually no risk. Resources are as separate as are rewards.

Coordination is characterized by more formal relationships and understanding compatible missions. Some planning and division of roles are required, and communication channels are established. Authority still rests with individual organizations, but there is some increased risk to all participants. Resources are available to participants and rewards are mutually acknowledged.

Collaboration is a mutually and well-defined relationship entered into by two or more organizations to achieve common goals. . . . Collaboration connotes a more durable and pervasive relationship. Collaborations bring previously separated organizations into a new structure with full commitment to a common mission. Such relationships require comprehensive planning and well defined communication channels operating on many levels. Authority is determined by the collaborative structure. Risks are much greater because each member of the collaboration contributes its own resources and reputation. Resources are pooled or jointly secured and products are shared. (P. W. Mattessich & Monsey, 1992, p. 39)

As we concluded our session, I briefly introduced steps to partnership relationships, success factors, omit teambuilding resource material, and a planning worksheet, all of which would be the basis for the next steps in the project. Phase Two involved mini-grant proposals to fund a team of librarians and community partners to travel to the Advanced Collaboration Workshop, a grant and project development session.

To end the day, I touched on the importance of evaluation and feedback, modeling a plus-delta exercise and explaining it to participants. The full agenda with fast paced exercises, a fun and relaxed environment, Memory Anchors, prizes, and lunch were all mentioned as pluses. Suggestions for enhancements and minor changes focused on logistics and preliminary information. We acknowledged that the Powerful Partners project/process was in the process of being developed so there was some ambiguity, which caused some discomfort. We also added another closing ritual where everyone gets the last word. Sometimes I called the exercise sharing our *Light Bulb Moments*. During this time, we went around the room and each person had the opportunity to make a comment. This was a time when people often shared the thoughts that have been especially meaningful for their personal/professional development.

ADVANCED COLLABORATIVE PROJECT PLANNING WORKSHOP: CREATING A ROAD MAP

Only people who had completed the first workshop were eligible to apply for funding to bring partners to the second workshop. In order to qualify for funding of a community project, librarians had to bring one or two partners to the workshop to work as a team. Public librarians, school media specialists, directors, and youth specialists brought partners, such as representatives from the Boys and Girls Club, County Health Department, Migrant Education Program, Museum of Life and Science, County Hispanic Services Department, Community College, churches of various faiths, Chamber of Commerce, Resource and Referral Center, Education Foundation, County Volunteer Services, and Children's Theater. The room set-up for this day-and-a-half session was different than the u-shape of the introductory workshop. We put tables in a chevron shape, to facilitate teamwork and group discussions. Based on preliminary project statements, two teams with similar projects were grouped at each table. Major learning goals for this day and a half workshop were: (1) to understand collaboration stages and success factors and (2) design a collaborative project that would be the basis for submitting a grant proposal that met the criteria for LSTA and the North Carolina Powerful Partners project. So this was a grant writing and project planning workshop as well as a collaboration training. The half-day was designed to allow participants to share ideas on collaboration and community needs. The second full day was structured as a work session to write the grant proposal.

We started the half-day with some humor by giving each person some money–play money in the form of a tablet. This reinforced that announcement that everyone could receive funding if they followed the guidelines carefully and specifically addressed the collaboration factors in those guidelines. The grants were not competitive except in terms of meeting guidelines. My introductory remarks stressed that we were all working together and teams would help each other with feedback at the same time as they drafted their individual proposals. Participants' knowledge ranged from no grant writing experience to many years of successful grant writing, so I acknowledged the expertise of the group by asking people to tell us a bit about their experience. I sincerely invited those with experience to add their ideas to any information I provided. I also encouraged people to meet each other during breaks. I positioned networking as a critical leadership and collaboration skill, the act of finding resources and possibilities. Throughout the day people reported on their contacts, their new social capital. So we modeled and practiced the skill.

Each person received a Memory Anchor, a stress ball in the shape of a globe, to remind us that in the process of focusing on grant guidelines our work was to change the world one project at a time. After reviewing the state vision and goals posted on the walls again, I asked members of each group to discuss their community needs and develop a statement according to the guidelines from the grant:

- Identifies the specific inadequacies of the service/program in terms of the target audience's needs/problems, not the partner's
- Relates to a community need identified by the collaboration team and is a solution designed by the team
- Demonstrates that needs to be addressed by the project are not currently being met or are being met inadequately
- Is supported by statistical evidence that demonstrates and documents the gap between the current situation and the desired change
- Explains why and how the target group was chosen is of reasonable dimension
- Makes a compelling case
- Is jargon-free, interesting to read and as brief as possible (State Library of North Carolina, 2000-2001)

The challenge was not to feature the name of the organization or the solution in the needs statement designed to focus on the community. Posting each group's statement around the room gave us a sense of purpose and commitment. However, we also agreed as a group that the original needs statements would be reviewed and revised at the end of the second day. This demonstrated project development as a non-linear process based on collaborative conversations.

As a group, we reviewed definitions of cooperation, coordination, and collaboration (P. Mattessich et al., 1997). Next, the teams developed lists and shared stories about what were obstacles to collaboration and what promoted successful collaboration. The general discussion showed how the obstacles and success factors mirrored each other and the stories helped the group get acquainted. We used a worksheet, based on the 19 success factors identified by Mattessich and Monsey and the Amherst H. Wilder Foundation, for each person to rank the five factors they thought that were most important. We charted the results with colored dots and discussed how this model could be used in the planning process (Appendix).

The 19 factors in six categories were included in the grant guidelines stating that in order to be funded the application must demonstrate a plan to address the factors. It is interesting to note that there was a distinct difference in rankings at different workshop locations around the state. In one area, the factor with the most votes (almost unanimous) was "political and social climate." In another area political climate ranked low but "open and frequent communication" was selected by most of the participants. "Concrete attainable goals" was also highly ranked. The category of "skilled convener" or facilitator was rarely ranked as a top priority. One reply to that was that they rarely had funds for outside facilitators. Other participants offered suggestions for ways to get skilled facilitators, which resulted in a brief exercise to demonstrate the concept of "What would it take?" To conclude the half-day portion of the workshop, participants were given a grant writing handbook and a copy of *Collaboration handbook: Creating, sustaining and enjoying the journey* (Winer & Ray, 1994). We used blue cards and yellow cards as evaluation for the session: yellow for anything that worked well for people and blue for any changes they wanted to suggest. Later, we met for dinner and informal entertainment by the fire as a way to continue our conversations and community building.

We began the second day by discussing the results of the yellow and blue cards and worked out a few minor changes to the room arrangement based on feedback. The collaboration factors exercise from the previous day served as a guide for various topics within the workshop outline. These were also reflected in the grant proposal guidelines. The teams challenged themselves to identify other partners, clarify decision-making, list the resources that partners could provide and outline joint agreements, and develop a communication plan. We very specifically covered each section of the grant guidelines including goals, objectives, and action plans. The interaction came as groups shared and consulted with each other. One more experienced group perhaps contributed more than others, and not all participants were deeply interested in all the projects. However, my job as facilitator was to draw connections to key points that would impact everyone. I used humorous stories to illustrate some points and lists to clarify some information.

As a way to experientially illustrate the complexities of collaboration partners, the positives and potential difficulties, we played Nerf ball. We stood and formed two large circles or teams. After we practiced throwing one ball around the circle for partners to catch, six additional balls were introduced. This exercise and processing by participants brought out a variety of issues in team building and collaboration. For example: "Was there one leader or did we all have responsibility to coach each other, communicate with each other? Did we pay attention to the success of other participants or only watch our own ball? Did we have fun and accomplish the task? What do you do when someone drops the ball?" In addition, the exercise provided the change of pace we needed to continue drafting the grant proposals.

Evaluation is a key section of the grant proposal and the collaborative process. In addition to an evaluation plan tied to project objectives, we discussed adding components that evaluated team development. We reviewed several examples of tools that could be used to solicit feedback from team members on criteria such as meeting facilitation, focus, and communication. Another example led team members to evaluate aspects of development such as group cohesiveness, level of interpersonal support, acceptance of diversity, and satisfaction with participation (Kormanski & Mozenter, 1987, p. 233). A third aspect of evaluation was celebration, which involved recognition of the group's accomplishments and individual contributions. We concluded our workshop by practicing creative ways to acknowledge and thank others. I placed a variety of objects on a table such as: a flashlight, an ABC book, a glass star, hammer, candle, toy yo-yo, brass plated Number 1, smile mug, silk flowers, and toy microphones. Each person or group selected an item that they would use as a recognition symbol, Memory Anchor, or award.

At the end of the day, the groups gave sample presentations. One group sang a humorous song. One group gave a more formal presentation with the candle and an award about lighting the way to the future. Another group used the parable of the boy who saved starfish on the beach. We shared silly presentations, clever recognitions, and touching moments. At that point, an evaluation seemed almost anticlimactic, but I invited the group to give feedback in a plus delta exercise and pointed to it as a model. Initially, there were many positives and almost no improvements suggested. When I told a story of how my family always looks for what would make a gourmet meal "just a little bit better," the group proceeded to discuss their ideas for enhancing the workshop. Several people mentioned that they understood the constraints or why something was done, but they thought it could have been done differently. I think my sincere openness and request for feedback, even if the ideas were minor suggestions, made a difference. One comment was that we acted on suggestions from the first day. I saw the changes in the room arrangement as minor, but to the participants it signified the collaborative environment. The last form of evaluation was to ask people to think about how they would rate their participation and were if they satisfied.

CONCLUSION

The goal of the Powerful Partners project and the training was to stimulate libraries and library staff to assume leadership roles in community building and to foster collaborative approaches to the needs of those in the community that transcend organizational boundaries. This article was my attempt to reflect on ways that training could be used to develop the philosophical commitment library staff members need to lead collaborative projects successfully. I explored how conversation can be used in training to shape a collaborative learning process. The modeling of collaborative behaviors during the workshops was also a critical aspect of the learning process.

Did the youth and teens in North Carolina learn to read, love to learn, and gain access the world? Did libraries and librarians in North Carolina provide leadership so that the combined resources and efforts of a community focused on education and the healthy development of youth? The major outcome we anticipated was that children and teens would receive services strengthened by collaboration of agencies in their community. One measure of success could be that, in the first year, twelve of seventeen proposals for community projects were funded because they addressed the nineteen collaboration success factors. Libraries invested the time to develop projects with their partners so that almost $300,000 was distributed to community projects. Twelve community teams received funding through the leadership of the library to be part of changing our world one project at a time. This article is about the training, but I recognize that further study of the actual projects would provide more data on the benefits to the participants, libraries, and communities.

I propose that collaborative communication training strategies and collaborative project development encouraged conversations from multiple voices, built a sense of community, and promoted equality. I want to emphasize that the exercises and techniques are not enough to create the collaborative learning environment. I tried in this article to show how a facilitator trusts the process and shares control as well as responsibility. The boundaries between facilitator and participants blur at times. Suspending judgment and promoting acceptance of diverse points of view are critical. You can take a risk if you are not focused on being right or wrong.

Positive emotions and play were important to the communication and the collaborative relationships during the workshops. How do we develop creative, flexible problem solvers? Research shows that when people experience positive emotions they expand their thinking and become more creative and flexible (Fredrickson, 2003). People are also more likely to be open to new information. Positive emotions lead to the discovery of novel ideas, pursuit of innovative actions, and development of stronger social bonds. People with positive experiences are less likely to become stuck on their own point of view or come to premature closure on issues being considered. This contributes to working within a collaborative philosophy. Research on the value of *serious play* has proposed that play can lead to intense personal commitment and involvement, particularly in creative environments (Csikszentmihalyi, 1990; Linder et al., 2001; Rieber et al., 1998). Play can act to free people from self-criticism and a critical stance toward others. I hope that my descriptions of the serious play in the Powerful Partnership workshops communicated the sense of commitment, involvement, and empowerment that participants experienced when we found serious play in our activities.

Throughout the workshops, I shared stories of my experiences in a humorous way. I used personal stories and traditional tales as a type of collaborative literacy, engagement in the literature that reinforces both the concepts and the ability to discuss these concepts in a collaborative environment (Wood, Roser, & Martinez, 2001). I often described times when I did something "wrong"–but I stressed that it was a learning experience. I have told people my personal stories such as Questioning the Authority of the Library Sign Police, The Day a Rule Closed the Auditorium, Asking a Partner to Marry You on the First Date, and Being Invited to Collaborate But Our Name Isn't on the Program. My stories encourage others to share their stories and we can inductively learn from those stories. We remember those stories and share those stories in a way we don't share lists, rules, and policies (Bochner, 1994; Browning, 1992; Ellis, 2000; Ellis & Bochner, 1996, 2000; Finlay & Hogan, 1995; Simmons, 2001). In this article, I began with the Slinky® story. I'll close with a vignette from the time after the last workshop concluded, the time when people often come to chat informally with the facilitator.

PORTRAIT OF FACILITATOR

The sounds of animated conversations, shuffling papers, packing of notebooks, and farewells have died down. I hear flip chart paper being pulled from the walls and wadded up, refreshments being cleaned up, and AV equipment being packed. As I chat with several of the last participants, I see Tim out of the corner of my eye. He is waiting to talk to me individually and he doesn't move into the group around me. Tim, a dark haired young man in his late twenties wearing jeans and a plaid button down shirt, had not spoken much during the beginning of the day. He frequently had his eyes down writing, taking notes. He would laugh readily at times and he listened to his partners, two full-figured women who were perhaps old enough to be his mother. Tim surprised me at the end of the workshop by organizing his team to sing a song to demonstrate a recognition plan for their project. The team was so funny that the other participants gave them a wild round of applause. Finally, I edged over to him as the other participants left. I smiled broadly and leaned on the edge of the table to relieve the deep ache in my feet. He said, "This day was much better than I thought." I laughed. He continued, "This morning when you said there was no right or wrong, I thought you were a little whacked, but now I get it."

I replied, "I am a bit zany at times, but I think it helps make the day fun. And as I explained, fun helps people to see things differently. I'm glad it worked out OK for you. It seemed like your team has a solid project proposal, to say nothing of your fabulous song!"

"Thanks. You know the Nerf ball game really got me thinking about how groups work together–or don't work so well. It was my favorite." Tim could see Ron packing up the equipment; everyone else was gone. "I just wanted to tell you that I don't usually talk much at workshops. I doodle and draw–but I listen. Today, you made it really comfortable, and I feel good about my team–and our project. I wanted to give you something for a thank you." Tim handed me a small sketch on one of the blue index cards, an abstract line drawing of a woman's face with intricate designs framing her face like hair. "It's a portrait of you," he said shyly and then smiled. "You said we should thank people, acknowledge them, so I am." His brown eyes were wide and his eyebrows were arched with anticipation.

"Oh, I love it!" I exclaimed immediately with sincerity. "You won't believe this but I collect drawings and portraits of me that my artist friends and family have done over the years. This one will be really special." I smiled broadly with real surprise and appreciation. I think to myself how he has internalized our discussion and how hard the recognition process can be for some people. I feel a sense of satisfaction that the day was a safe place to experiment and learn.

I framed that sketch and it still hangs in my hallway. Each time I glance at it, I remember the Powerful Partners project, the collaborative spirit of effective workshops, the impact of conversations, the power of play, and the relationships that develop as we form our learning communities.

REFERENCES

Agada, J. (1998). *Teaching collaborative skills in library and information science education (LISE).* Paper presented at the American Society for Information Science (ASIS) Midyear Conference, Orlando, FL.

Angelis, J. (1999). Building dynamic coalitions: A communication model. *Illinois Libraries, 81*(1), 29-32.

April, K. A. (1999). Leading through communication, conversation and dialogue. *Leadership & Organization Development Journal, 20*(5), 231-241.

Bennis, W., Spreitzer, G. M., & Cummings, T. G. (Eds.). (2001). *The future of leadership: Today's top leadership thinkers speak to tomorrow's leaders.* San Francisco: Jossey-Bass.

Bochner, A. P. (1994). Perspectives on inquiry II: Theories and stories. In M. Knapp & G. R. E. Miller (Eds.), *Handbook of interpersonal communication* (pp. 21-41). Newbury Park, CA: Sage Publications.

Bolt, N. (2000). Collaboration, partnering, and community building: Their impact on multitype cooperatives. In S. Laughlin (Ed.), *Library networks in the new millennium: Top ten trends* (Vol. 3). Chicago, IL: Association of Specialized and Cooperative Library Agencies, American Library Association.

Boyer, E. L. (1996). The scholarship of engagement. *Journal of Public Service & Outreach, 1*(1), 11-20.

Brown, M. (1975). *Stone Soup: An Old Tale.* New York, NY: Charles Scribner's Sons.

Browning, L. (1992). Lists and stories as organizational communication. *Communication Theory, 2*, 281-302.

Clinchy, B. M. (1996). Connected and separate knowing: Toward a marriage of two minds. In N. R. Goldberger, J. M. Tarule, B. M. Clinchy, & M. F. Belenky (Eds.), *Knowledge, difference and power: Essays inspired by women's ways of knowing* (pp. 205-247). New York: BasicBooks.

Conger, J. A. (1998). The necessary art of persuasion. *Harvard Business Review, 76*(3), 84-96.

Covey, S. R. (1992). *Principle-centered leadership.* New York, NY: Fireside Book by Simon & Schuster.

Csikszentmihalyi, M. (1990). *Flow: The psychology of optimal experience.* New York, NY: HarperCollins Publishers.

Doh, J. P. (2003). Can leadership be taught. *Academy of management, learning & education, 2*(1), 54-67.

Ellis, C. (2000). Creating criteria: An ethnographic short story. *Qualitative Inquiry, 6*(2), 273-277.

Ellis, C., & Bochner, A. P. (1996). *Composing ethnography: Alternative forms of qualitative writing* (Vol. 1). Walnut Creek, CA: AltaMira Press.

Ellis, C., & Bochner, A. P. (2000). Autoethnography, personal narrative, reflexivity: Researcher as subject. In N. J. Denzin & Y. S. Lincoln (Eds.), *Handbook of qualitative research* (pp. 733-768). Thousand Oaks, CA: Sage Publications.

Finlay, M., & Hogan, C. (1995). Who will bell the cat? Storytelling techniques for people who work with people in organizations. *Training & Management Development Methods, 9*(2), start page 6 (electronic source: ProQuest).

Fredrickson, B. L. (2003). The value of positive emotions. *American Scientist, 91* (July/August), 330-335.

Gergen, K. J. (1994). *Realities and relationships: Soundings in social construction.* Cambridge, MA: Harvard University Press.

Gergen, K. J. (2000). *An invitation to social construction.* Thousand Oaks, CA: Sage Publications.

Gergen, K. J. (2001). *Social construction in context.* Thousand Oaks, CA: Sage Publications.

Goleman, D., Boyatzis, R., & McKee, A. (2002). *Primal leadership: Realizing the power of emotional leadership.* Boston: Harvard Business School Press.

Hernon, P., Powell, R. R., & Young, A. (2003). *The next library leadership: Attributes of academic and public library directors*. Westport, CT: Libraries Unlimited.

Johnson, L. J., Zorn, D., Tam, B. K. Y., Lamontagne, M., & Johnson, S. A. (2003). Stakeholders' views of factors that impact successful interagency collaboration. *Exceptional Children, 69*(2), 195-209.

Kormanski, C. L., & Mozenter, A. (1987). A new model of team building: A technology for today and tomorrow. In J. W. Pfeiffer (Ed.), *The 1987 annual: Developing human resources* (pp. 227-237). San Diego, CA: Pfeiffer & Company.

Kouzes, J. M., & Posner, B. Z. (2002). *The leadership challenge* (Third ed.). San Francisco: Jossey-Bass.

Kriegel, R., & Brandt, D. (1996). *Sacred cows make the best burgers: Developing change-ready people and organizations*. New York, NY: Warner Books.

Linder, M.-O., Roos, J., & Victor, B. (2001, July 5-7, 2001). *Play in organizations*. Paper presented at the EGOS Conference, Lyon, France.

Ludema, J. D., Cooperrider, D. L., & Barrett, F. J. (2001). Appreciative inquiry: The power of the unconditional positive question. In P. Reason & E. Hilary Bradbury (Eds.), *Handbook of action research participatory inquiry and practice* (pp. 189-199). Thousand Oaks: Sage Publications.

Mattessich, P., Monsey, B., & with assistance from Roy, C. (1997). *Community Building: What makes it work: A review of factors influencing successful community building*. Saint Paul, MN: Amherst H. Wilder Foundation.

Mattessich, P. W., & Monsey, B. R. (1992). *Collaboration: What makes it work: A review of research literature on factors influencing successful collaboration*. St. Paul, MN: Amherst H. Wilder Foundation.

McCook, K. d. l. P. (2000). *A place at the table: Participating in community building*. Chicago: American Library Association.

McNamee, S., & Gergen, K. J. (Eds.). (1999). *Relational responsibility: Resources for sustainable dialogue*. Thousand Oaks, CA: Sage Publications.

Muronaga, K., & Harada, V. (1999). The art of collaboration. *Teacher Librarian, 27*(1), 9-14.

Rees, F. (1991). *How to lead work teams: Facilitation skills*. San Diego, CA: Pfeiffer & Company.

Ricchiuto, J. (1997). *Collaborative creativity: Unleashing the power of shared thinking*. Akron, OH: Oakhill Press.

Rieber, L., Smith, L., & Noah, D. (1998). The value of serious play. *Educational Technology, 38*(6), 28-37.

Riggs, D. E. (2001). The crisis and opportunities in library leadership. *Journal of Library Administration, 32*(3 & 4), 5-17.

Senge, P. (1990). *The fifth discipline: The art and practice of the learning organization*. New York, NY: Doubleday.

Simmons, A. (2001). *The story factor: Secrets of influence from the art of storytelling*. Cambridge, MA: Perseus Publishing.

Soukup, P. (1992). Interpersonal communication. *Communication Research Trends, 12*(3), 1-36.

Spreitzer, G. M., & Cummings, T. G. (2001). The leadership challenges of the next generation. In L. W. Bennett, G. M. Spreitzer, & T. G. Cummings (Eds.), *The fu-*

ture of leadership: Todays top leadership thinkers speak to tomorrow's leaders (pp. 241-253). San Francisco: Jossey-Bass.

State Library of North Carolina. (2000-2001). *EZ-LSTA Powerful Partners collaboration grants: Information & Guidelines.* Raleigh, NC.

Wilson, B. (2000). The Lone Ranger is dead: Success today demands collaboration. *College & Research Libraries News, 61*(8), 698-701.

Winer, M., & Ray, K. (1994). *Collaboration handbook: Creating, sustaining and enjoying the journey.* Saint Paul, MN: Amherst H. Wilder Foundation.

Winston, M. D. (2004). Realizing the leader within us. Daytona Beach, FL: Florida Library Association Conference.

Witherspoon, P. D. (1997). *Communicating leadership: An organizational perspective.* Boston: Allyn and Bacon.

Wood, K. D., Roser, N. L., & Martinez, M. (2001). Collaborative literacy: Lessons learned from literature. *The Reading Teacher, 55*(2), 102-111.

APPENDIX

Collaboration Success Factors

RANKING	YOU	GROUP

ENVIRONMENT

	YOU	GROUP
1. History of collaboration or cooperation in community		
2. Collaborative group seen as leader in community		
3. Favorable political, social climate		

MEMBERSHIP CHARACTERISTICS

	YOU	GROUP
4. Mutual respect, understanding and trust		
5. Appropriate cross section of members		
6. Members see collaboration in their self interest		
7. Ability to compromise		

PROCESS-STRUCTURE

	YOU	GROUP
8. Members share a stake in the process and outcome		
9. Multiple layers of decision making		
10. Flexibility		
11. Development of clear roles		
12. Adaptability		

COMMUNICATION

	YOU	GROUP
13. Open and frequent communication		
14. Established formal and informal links		

PURPOSE

	YOU	GROUP
15. Concrete, attainable goals and objectives		
16. Shared vision		
17. Unique purpose		

RESOURCES

	YOU	GROUP
18. Sufficient funds		
19. Skilled convener		

Adapted from: *Collaboration: What Makes It Work*, by Mattessich & Monsey, Amherst H. Wilder Foundation, 1992.

Library Consortia:
Do the Models Always Work?

David A. Wright

SUMMARY. Successful models of statewide library consortia are evident in many locations. Academic libraries in independent institutions of higher education in Mississippi must seek alternate affiliations since they do not participate in the MAGNOLIA consortium for public institutions. What does the future hold, especially for database licensing for libraries that are not able to participate in a statewide project? Profiles of some existing and emerging consortia in other states are provided as potential models for the state of Mississippi. *[Article copies available for a fee from The Haworth Document Delivery Service: 1-800-HAWORTH. E-mail address: <docdelivery@haworthpress.com> Website: <http://www.HaworthPress.com> © 2005/2006 by The Haworth Press, Inc. All rights reserved.]*

KEYWORDS. Cooperation, Mississippi, consortia, college and university libraries, MAGNOLIA (Mississippi Alliance for Gaining New Opportunities through Library Information Access), PALMS (Private Academic Libraries of Mississippi)

David A. Wright, BSEd, MSLS, is Library Director, Leland Speed Library, Mississippi College, Clinton, MS 39058 (E-mail: wright@mc.edu).

[Haworth co-indexing entry note]: "Library Consortia: Do the Models Always Work?" Wright, David A. Co-published simultaneously in *Resource Sharing & Information Networks* (The Haworth Information Press, an imprint of The Haworth Press, Inc.) Vol. 18, No. 1/2, 2005/2006, pp. 49-60; and: *Libraries Beyond Their Institutions: Partnerships That Work* (ed: William Miller, and Rita M. Pellen) The Haworth Information Press, an imprint of The Haworth Press, Inc., 2005/2006, pp. 49-60. Single or multiple copies of this article are available for a fee from The Haworth Document Delivery Service [1-800-HAWORTH, 9:00 a.m. - 5:00 p.m. (EST). E-mail address: docdelivery@haworthpress.com].

There are many successful models of statewide library consortia, some of which have been in existence for nearly three decades. But what happens when a state does not have a history of cooperation between institutions? What alternative strategies should libraries employ to gain the benefits of consortia when there is not a strong commitment to resource-sharing among various types of libraries? Libraries in independent institutions of higher education in the state of Mississippi face the future with these questions and the accompanying uncertainties in an attempt to provide quality information and resources to students and faculty.

In library consortia, there is strength in numbers. Numbers of libraries working together increase negotiating abilities with vendors. When the MAGNOLIA (Mississippi Alliance for Gaining New Opportunities through Library Information Access) project was formed in 1997 and funded by the state legislature, it was billed as linking more than 1,100 public, school, and academic libraries to EBSCOhost databases.[1] The Mississippi legislature funded MAGNOLIA under the Council for Educational Technology (CET), an entity established by the legislature in 1994 to advise on matters of technology related to several state educational partner agencies. All types of publicly supported libraries are represented by the agencies within the jurisdiction of CET. However, when the plans for MAGNOLIA were being formed, libraries in independent institutions of higher education and private elementary and secondary schools were not invited to participate.

In Mississippi, there are currently eight accredited independent colleges. Four of these institutions offer degrees beyond the baccalaureate level. Most independent academic institutions in the state are part of the Mississippi Association of Independent Colleges (MAIC). However, no forum exists at the state level for libraries in these institutions. When the MAGNOLIA project started, librarians from the independent colleges began to investigate the possibility of including the independent college libraries as a group within the MAGNOLIA project. Early in 1998, questionnaires were sent to each of the independent academic libraries to determine interest in participation in the statewide project. The surveys also collected information about the level of technology implementation present in each of the libraries as well as current database subscriptions. Librarians were asked in the survey if they were willing to seek technology funding for the independent academic libraries in the state in order to join the MAGNOLIA project.

The progress toward a joint venture between MAGNOLIA and the independent academic libraries came to an end in late 1998 when the independent academic institutions were informed that the CET and the MAGNOLIA Steering Committee had decided against including them in the MAGNOLIA project because the language in the legislation funding MAGNOLIA only included publicly-supported libraries. At the same time, there was an indication the vendors for the MAGNOLIA project would be contacted to find out what it would cost to add the independent academic libraries. Starting to think of themselves as a group, the independent academic libraries began to use the acronym PALMS (Private Academic Libraries of MS) to indicate the informal consortium formed to become part of the MAGNOLIA project.

The following year, up-to-date information was gathered from the PALMS group, particularly full-time equivalent (FTE) enrollment figures from Fall, 1998. At the annual American Library Association conference in June 1999 all MAGNOLIA vendors were contacted and given the FTE information to request a quote for the PALMS group, based on central invoicing for the group through the MAIC office. Later that summer, the library directors of PALMS met to discuss the costs of licensing the equivalent databases in MAGNOLIA as a separate consortium. They also considered the option of working toward amending the legislation to include the independent academic libraries in MAGNOLIA. Unlike cooperative projects in other states, the small number of independent academic institutions made the process of attempting inclusion difficult and ineffective. PALMS librarians were encouraged to make their presidents aware of the need for access to the databases in MAGNOLIA and a PALMS presentation was made to representatives from independent institutions at a leadership meeting of the MAIC.

The amount required to replicate the MAGNOLIA databases for the PALMS group was daunting, especially for some of the libraries of the smaller institutions. Without grant funding, it would be impossible to license all the databases as a separate consortium without creating an excessive burden on both small and large libraries. A few of the larger PALMS libraries were already subscribing to some of the MAGNOLIA databases as individual libraries. Some of the libraries in the PALMS group were already participating in licensing certain databases through another informal consortium of libraries in state institutions of higher education coordinated through Mississippi State University.

One positive result for the PALMS group in the process of trying to become part of the MAGNOLIA project was increased communication between library directors in the independent colleges. Based on previous interactions with one of the MAGNOLIA vendors, the PALMS group secured a quote on a number of databases. Several of the libraries made a decision to go with the vendor for the databases because of the attractive price given to the group. For the last four years, the PALMS consortium has licensed databases as a group. While not all libraries in PALMS choose to participate, the licensing of databases is always open to every library in the group.

The small number of libraries active in the PALMS group is an obstacle for future projects and negotiations with database vendors. Several of the institutions have graduate level programs which require specialized and expanded resources beyond the scope of the databases that are currently licensed. While some databases are licensed through a statewide college and university library consortium coordinated by Mississippi State University, there are other database vendors which do not offer consortial pricing for such small groups.

According to Brooks and Dorst (2002), "a good academic library must accumulate and deliver information resources within a vastly expanded information universe that is available to every student and faculty member. And only libraries that employ consortial affiliations wisely and well will prosper."[2] Academic libraries in all types of institutions, public and independent, must work collaboratively to assure that students and faculty have access to needed information. For smaller independent colleges and universities, the need to collaborate is greater than ever before. The array of electronic resources available for licensing is growing at a rapid pace. In most cases, maintaining current levels of electronic information offerings is a challenge for library budgets. Libraries today cannot have a "go-it-alone" attitude and expect to offer more electronic resources. As Alexander (1999) points out, the cost of scholarly information will continue to rise and the quantity of information produced will continue to increase in the years ahead. Cooperative collection development has never been more important.[3]

There are a number of barriers to forming successful library alliances, either inside or outside a formal organized consortium. For the very small independent college or university, the major barrier seems to be financial. Even if a product can be licensed by a group, the individual institutional price may still be well beyond the affordability point for the library. In some states, there is a considerable difference between the size of the smallest and the largest independent academic institutions. Some institutions may offer graduate programs which require more specialized information resources. Depending on the pricing models used, larger libraries in the independent institutions may not benefit from a consortial pricing model since the pricing depends on the level of participation and some of the smaller institutions may not need the specialized resources.

Another potential barrier is that of political and organizational realities. Unless there is a platform for representation in library or other organizational issues for the independent colleges and universities at the state level, it is difficult to effect changes which can result in better representation. Librarians must see political realities as they are and work through existing structures to inform those in politically influential positions of the importance of including all libraries in state or regional consortia.

A crucial barrier to forming successful alliances is that of a lack of vision for the impact of a shared project on all citizens of a state or region. A provincial attitude is anathema to most librarians, who usually seek to reach out for the good of all of those who will benefit by increased access to information resources. "Consortia, which involve groups of libraries cooperating for mutual benefit," Alberico (2002) points out, "are a natural outgrowth of a spirit of sharing that lies at the foundation of all libraries."[4] Lack of vision hampers planning wisely for the future. In a time of rapid change, libraries and consortia must have a vision of what is truly important and essential in the provision of services to faculty and students. Fortunately for independent academic libraries in most states and regions, library consortia have made some kind of provisions to incorporate the independent academic libraries into the planning processes.

The organizational jurisdiction, political alignment, and involvement of the state library agency are potential barriers to multi-type library consortia. The state library agency in most states is the agency that channels federal money to the public library jurisdictions in the state. Since the state agency has legal parameters for serving public libraries (and by default, libraries in public institutions of higher education), there may be a potential for "illegal" aid to libraries in independent (non-tax-supported) institutions of higher education. This legal status conundrum is sometimes a larger issue than it needs to be. Independent institutions participating in resource-sharing subsidize public libraries and public institutions of higher education by lending materials from their collections. In Mississippi, a significant portion of the enrollment in most of the independent colleges and universities are in-state residents with public library privileges (see Appendix for enrollment figures). Independent institutions contribute significantly to the economic life of the community and the state.

Licensing issues are also potential challenges for smaller independent college or research libraries. Most of these libraries do not have a staff librarian who is well-versed in the finer points of negotiating with vendors of electronic products. Vendor licenses may be filled with fine print often ignored by librarians or others responsible for signing the licenses. It is not necessarily negligence on the part of the librarian or other responsible party, but they simply do not realize all the implications of not understanding the complete terms of the license. The "strength in numbers" principle upon which consortia are founded provides librarians with the added ability to discuss the license negotiation process with others and the assurance that they can rely on those persons in the consortium who are knowledgeable about licensing procedures.

Some vendors of electronic databases have used pricing models based on FTE (full time equivalent) student enrollment counts. These models seem to work well in consortial arrangements where large and small institutions are part of the mix. There are many databases which are priced as a package regardless of an institution's FTE count. These databases are seldom made available through a consortium license. Libraries in smaller colleges and universities may be faced with the dilemma of the high cost of databases when the usage is low. For one institution, a database may be the premier source in a given subject field, but due to a small number of undergraduate or graduate students in the subject field, the low use cannot justify the expense of the electronic resource. Libraries in similar situations must collaborate to bring pressure on vendors to offer consortium pricing based on FTE counts.

In the early days of library consortia a reason to join was the potential cost savings. While some research has documented overall cost savings as a result of consortial affiliations, a more significant reason to join consortia is that libraries are able to offer more databases and electronic information than they could as an individual library. According to Peters (2003), "alternatives to consortial collaboration include: unilateral activity by a library, bilateral agreements between libraries and publishers, aggregators, vendors, and service suppliers, unnecessary redundancy, and missed opportunities."[5] The alternatives to collaboration are invariably negative. Since most libraries seek to affiliate with a consortium or consortia that will best meet the information needs of students and faculty, what are some existing models of cooperation?

There are several factors that seem to contribute to the success of library consortia. First of all, in states where a multi-type consortium has developed, there was already a strong history of cooperation. In Alabama, where the most recent development is the Alabama Virtual Library (AVL), the beginnings of cooperation, particularly between institutions of higher education, started with the Network of Alabama Academic Libraries (NAAL). At NAAL's inception, public and independent colleges and university libraries with graduate programs came together for cooperative projects. Later, independent academic institutions without graduate programs were added to the group. As Morgan (2001) documents, the foundation of the AVL was laid through the successful prior projects of NAAL and the coalition of state agencies brought together to lobby for the AVL.[6]

Another factor in the development of statewide multi-type consortia is special groups formed for libraries in independent higher education institutions. These groups either existed prior to the formation of the multi-type consortium or banded together to participate as a group in the multi-type consortium. There are examples from many states, including the Georgia Private Academic Libraries (GPALS), the Private Academic Library Network of Indiana (PALNI), and Ohio Private Academic Libraries (OPAL). In the cases of PALNI and OPAL, academic libraries also share a common vendor platform for library systems. In Georgia, GPALS secured private foundation funding initially to join the statewide GALILEO project.

The incorporation of independent academic libraries into the LOUIS (Louisiana Online University Information System) project is recorded by Wittkopf (2002).[7] In 1992 a task force of the Board of Regents was reorganized as the Louisiana Academic Library Information Network Consortium (LALINC). All academic libraries, both public and independent, constitute the membership of the consortium. Through initial grant funding, several of the libraries were automated using the software on the Louisiana State University Library mainframe computer. In 1999 LOUIS became the Louisiana Library Network, officially incorporating all public university, community, and technical college libraries as well as the independent colleges and university libraries.

The PASCAL (Partnership Among South Carolina Academic Libraries) project of the South Carolina Virtual Academic Library (SCVAL) is a recent example of the incorporation of public and independent academic libraries into a consortium. The PASCAL/SCVAL project is presently evolving, but information on the website indicates that there is significant progress toward the goals of PASCAL/SCVAL. State funding is being sought for various projects of the consortium. The PASCAL project goes beyond just licensing of databases. A union catalog, delivery service, and patron borrowing privileges from any participating library are also components of the project.

The academic libraries in South Carolina were organized into two groups for several years. The Library Directors Forum (LDF), established by the Commission on Higher Education, represented the public institutions. The Library Directors Council (LDC) represented the libraries of the South Carolina Independent Colleges and Universities. These two groups began to meet together to explore possibilities for cooperation. A Strategic Plan for South Carolina Academic Libraries is a result of the collaboration of these two groups.[8]

The Kentucky Virtual Library (KYVL), launched in 1999, was originated by the State-Assisted Academic Library Council of Kentucky (SAALCK). SAALCK's proposal for a virtual library became part of the planning for a statewide virtual university. The project evolved into a multi-type library consortium which also includes Kentucky's nineteen independent colleges and universities. The libraries of the institutions represented by the Association of Independent Kentucky Colleges and Universities (AIKCU) had participated in other projects with the state institution libraries before KYVL. When KYVL was in the planning process, the executive director of AIKCU and library directors of the AIKCU institutions were invited to participate in the meetings and organization of KYVL. While the AIKCU institutions pay to participate in KYVL, they pay a reduced rate compared to what they would pay to the database vendors as individual institutions because they are a group within the overall project. AIKCU library directors meet twice yearly to work on joint projects and share information.

In Tennessee, the TENNSHARE project started as a resource-sharing group in the early 1990s. One of the early concepts was the idea of electronic databases available to all libraries throughout the state. This concept evolved into the Tennessee Electronic Library (TEL), a project of the Tennessee State Library and Archives, which provides all libraries (public, academic, and school) with access to a number of databases from one vendor. The TENNSHARE project has plans for the joint acquisition of databases for all libraries with a sliding scale so that all libraries, particularly in smaller academic institutions, would be able to participate in the project. The library directors of the Tennessee Independent Colleges and Universities Association, a group of thirty-six institutions, have recently begun to investigate ways to facilitate other cooperative ventures, especially database licensing, in addition to the TEL.

TexShare, the multitype library consortium in Texas, provides an example where the value of the role of independent college and university libraries in the statewide information network is recognized in the legislative language which formed the consortium. Promotion of the public good through efficient and effective information resource sharing is a bedrock value in the formation of TexShare.

> The legislature finds that it is necessary to assist academic libraries at public and private or independent institutions of higher education to promote the public good by achieving the following public purposes through the following methods:
>
> 1. to promote the future well-being of the citizenry, enhance quality teaching and research excellence at institutions of higher education through the efficient exchange of information and the sharing of library resources, improve educational resources in all communities, and expand the availability of information about clinical medical research and the history of medicine;
> 2. to maximize the effectiveness of library expenditures by enabling libraries at institutions of higher education to share staff expertise and to share library resources in print and in an electronic form, including books, journals, technical reports, and databases;
> 3. to increase the intellectual productivity of students and faculty at the participating institutions of higher education by emphasizing access

to information rather than ownership of documents and other information sources; and

4. to facilitate joint purchasing agreements for purchasing information services and encourage cooperative research and development of information technologies.[9]

TexShare is an excellent model of a multi-type library consortium that is organized around core principles, is actively involved in strategic planning, and is vision-oriented.

From the examples above, it is clear that each state has unique situations that have contributed to the formation of consortia. Where there is a history of joint projects and resource-sharing efforts between libraries, there seems to be a willingness to continue to explore options for more effective and efficient ways to gain access to a wider variety of resources as a group than individual libraries could possibly attain on their own. Libraries in state and independent institutions are increasingly forced to make tough decisions about allocation of resources to electronic databases and printed materials. Libraries in state institutions are feeling the effects of cutbacks in funding from state budgets because of economic downturns and growing demands for state funds in the social services areas of government. Economic lean times also cause libraries in many independent institutions to struggle with static or declining budgets.

What are alternatives for independent or private academic libraries when consortial affiliation at the state or regional level is not possible? Operating within the political and organizational realities helps libraries to redefine priorities. In addition to working within the existing system for the larger goal of being a part of a larger and more powerful group to deal with vendors, each library must explore ways to make vendors aware of their predicament. A library could inquire if the vendor will provide a creative option such as joining a group outside a library's geographic area. This may not be an optimal solution, but it could be a way to open new avenues of resource sharing with other libraries. Fact-gathering is another important task for libraries without consortial affiliations. Some questions of immediate relevance must be posed. What is the history of library cooperation in the state or region? Are there other libraries in the state or region in a similar situation without valuable consortial affiliation? How have they approached vendors to license databases or other electronic products?

Political and institutional realities will not change rapidly. Librarians must make their needs known, especially to their presidents and academic officers who may be able to bring the situation to the state organization representing the independent colleges and universities. In many states that have implemented multi-type consortia, the state organization representing independent higher education institutions has been involved to some extent. Libraries without consortial affiliations should continue to explore new avenues of cooperation, even outside their geographic boundaries.

Future developments in library consortia will certainly build on existing consortial arrangements. However, as Kaufman (2001)[10] and Peters (2003)[11] indicate, future library consortia will probably depend less on geography and more on type of library. Many libraries are already involved in multiple consortia. One may be a loosely organized group of small college libraries with one librarian representing the group negotiating with a vendor for the best pricing package. The same libraries may belong to another consortium formed with the sole purpose of dealing with a particular vendor. The libraries may also participate in a formal, statewide union catalog project. As Carlson (2003) points out, in some cases, libraries have a "consortium conundrum."[12] With so many choices for participating in consortia, it becomes á challenge for libraries to sort out all the possibilities.

Library affiliations within consortia will become more crucial in the future. If a library in an independent institution of higher education does not participate in a statewide consortium, it should be represented by a group of libraries from similar institutions, either statewide or in a multi-state arrangement. There will be more consolidation among vendors in the future and libraries must work as groups to assure fair and accurate representation of the interests and needs of individual libraries. Peters (2003) indicates that "a radically new type of organizational structure and vision for consortia will be need to foster, facilitate, manage, and exploit a shifting matrix of interlibrary alliances."[13]

CONCLUSION

Participation in library consortia is valuable and necessary for all libraries and will become more crucial in the future. Development of statewide multi-type consortia is a mosaic of different structures and levels of involvement of various types of libraries. One state may have strong leadership from a central administrative agency. Another state may have groups of libraries active in the planning and development of consortia. The history of library cooperation varies significantly from state to state. State consortia have usually developed based on existing groups created for resource-sharing or other joint projects. Do the models always work? The answer is probably yes and no. Yes, the models work well for the individual states since they are based on existing structures for cooperative projects. Yes, the existing models can be a target of aspiration as one state seeks to learn from the formation and operation of a consortium in another state. A successful model in one state may not be easily transferable to another, however, simply because of the existing climate of co-operation, the political realities of state library agency jurisdiction, and the lack of political clout of groups of libraries, particularly those in independent institutions of higher education.

It is clear that a vision must be created in order for libraries to be able to thrive in the challenging economic landscape of information procurement. Political realities must be faced and strategies must be formed to provide an alternative model of a consortium that will better meet the needs of all participating libraries. Peters believes that libraries must do a better job of calculating the costs and benefits of consortial involvement.[14] While costs and benefits should be calculated within the library organization, librarians, particularly in independent academic institutions, should actively provide information to policy makers showing the economic benefits of students in their institutions to the community and state. Political involvement in existing representative organizations presents an additional avenue for advocacy of a new model of cooperation. In the future, geographical limitations may not hinder the formation of consortia. Librarians must be creative in seeking solutions to the need to provide access to information for students and faculty. It takes work, but it is possible to change existing structures to improve access to information.

NOTES

1. Michael Rogers, "Mississippi Links Libraries to Statewide Periodicals Network." *Library Journal*, 122, no. 16, October 1 (1997): 29.

2. Sam Brooks and Thomas J. Dorst, "Issues Facing Academic Library Consortia and Perceptions of Members of the Illinois Digital Academic Library." *portal: Libraries and the Academy*, 2, no. 1, January (2002): 43-57.

3. Adrian W. Alexander, "Toward 'Perfection of Work': Library Consortia in the Digital Age." *Collection Management*, 28, no. 2 (1999): 1-14.

4. Ralph Alberico, "Academic Library Consortia in Transition." *New Directions for Higher Education*, no. 120, Winter (2002), 63-72.

5. Thomas A. Peters, "Consortia Thinking: Consortia and Their Discontents." *The Journal of Academic Librarianship*, 29, no. 2, (2003): 111-113.

6. Josie Morgan, "Working Together Really Can Turn Dreams into Realities." *Computers in Libraries*, January (2001): 51-55.

7. Barbara J. Wittkopf, "Resource Sharing in Louisiana." *Resource Sharing & Information Networks*, 16, no. 1 (2002), 103-120.

8. "Strategic Plan for South Carolina Academic Libraries," http://pascal.tcl.sc.edu/planning/straplanfinal2.html#intro (accessed June 16, 2004).

9. *Vernon's Texas Code Annotated, Government Code*, sec. 441 (West 2003).

10. Paula Kaufman, "Whose Good Old Days Are These? A Dozen Predictions for the Digital Age," *Journal of Library Administration*, 35, no. 3 (2001): 5-19.

11. Peters, "Consortia and Their Discontents."

12. Scott Carlson, "Libraries' Consortium Conundrum," *Chronicle of Higher Education*, 50, no. 7 (2003): A30.

13. Thomas J. Peters, "Graduated Consortial Memberships and Rogue Facilitators," *The Journal of Academic Librarianship*, 29, no. 4 (2003): 254-256.

14. Peters, "Consortia and Their Discontents."

APPENDIX

Enrollment Figures

Colleges and Universities in
PALMS (Private Academic Libraries in Mississippi) Consortium
2003

Name of Institution	Fall, 2003 FTE Students	Percentage of In-State Students
Belhaven College	2,354	68
Blue Mountain College	389	90
Millsaps College	1,163	58
Mississippi College	2,705	86
Tougaloo College	914	82
William Carey College	2,344	92
Total FTE students	9,869	

Cooperative Library Services in Southeast Florida: A Staff Perspective

Maris L. Hayashi

SUMMARY. This article presents the staff perspective on the advantages of collaboration between a library cooperative in Southeast Florida and one of its member libraries. Collaborative relationships between library cooperatives and member libraries exist primarily to benefit library patrons and community users. Important relationships between cooperatives and their members' employees also exist, yet this aspect is rarely identified and discussed. Cooperatives provide the resources and services to staff that are necessary for the establishment and continuance of lifelong learning. Staff take the skills and knowledge they acquire and learn, and put them to use when providing high quality service to their library patrons. *[Article copies available for a fee from The Haworth Document Delivery Service: 1-800-HAWORTH. E-mail address: <docdelivery@haworthpress.com> Website: <http://www.HaworthPress.com> © 2005/2006 by The Haworth Press, Inc. All rights reserved.]*

KEYWORDS. Library cooperatives, library staff training, Florida libraries, Southeast Florida Library Information Network

---

Maris L. Hayashi is Assistant University Librarian, Florida Atlantic University, S. E. Wimberly Library, 777 Glades Road, Boca Raton, FL 33431 (E-mail: mhayashi@fau.edu). She also serves as the SEFLIN Training Administrator for FAU.

[Haworth co-indexing entry note]: "Cooperative Library Services in Southeast Florida: A Staff Perspective." Hayashi, Maris L. Co-published simultaneously in *Resource Sharing & Information Networks* (The Haworth Information Press, an imprint of The Haworth Press, Inc.) Vol. 18, No. 1/2, 2005/2006, pp. 61-71; and: *Libraries Beyond Their Institutions: Partnerships That Work* (ed: William Miller, and Rita M. Pellen) The Haworth Information Press, an imprint of The Haworth Press, Inc., 2005/2006, pp. 61-71. Single or multiple copies of this article are available for a fee from The Haworth Document Delivery Service [1-800-HAWORTH, 9:00 a.m. - 5:00 p.m. (EST). E-mail address: docdelivery@haworthpress.com].

http://www.haworthpress.com/web/RSIN
© 2005/2006 by The Haworth Press, Inc. All rights reserved.
Digital Object Identifier: 10.1300/J121v18n01_06

INTRODUCTION

Library cooperatives and their member libraries share the common goal of providing the best possible service to their public, academic, school, and special library users. Most often the definition of "library user" is relegated specifically to people such as school children, community citizens, and university students. Yet, the user may also be a staff member of one of those libraries who, like the library patron, makes use of the products and services provided by a library cooperative. This article offers the insights of a staff member who benefits from the cooperative's continuing education services. From this perspective, the article explores the collaborative relationship between the Southeast Florida Library Information Network (SEFLIN) and one of its academic member libraries. It also briefly discusses the role of SEFLIN's Training Administrators as the communication liaisons between SEFLIN and the libraries. Lastly, the article addresses the implementation of SEFLIN's *Community of Learning Program* at the University as well as the continuing education benefits received by library staff using SEFLIN's training and development resources.

COLLABORATIVE RELATIONSHIPS BETWEEN LIBRARY COOPERATIVES AND MEMBER LIBRARIES

The collaborative relationships between a library cooperative and its member libraries are especially built to benefit library users whether the given institution is a public, academic, or special library. Some of the services available to these users include access to cultural information, community lecture presentations, and resource sharing features such as reciprocal borrowing and cooperative database purchasing.

The benefits for library users, rather than the benefits for staff, are usually investigated. In other words, libraries normally focus their attention on how *patrons* benefit from their collaborative relationship with the library cooperative (Curry 1998; Curry 1993). However, the benefits that staff members receive, such as access to continuing education training programs, greatly influence the type of services they are able to offer their users. Bruce Massis (2001), for example, observes how the benefits libraries receive from training programs include "better hires, increased retention of qualified staff, and improved customer service" (49). Once in place, these collaborative relationships also improve staff morale and support staff training through continuing education for member libraries' staff. To better understand these benefits, let us turn to a library cooperative in Southeast Florida.

INTRODUCTION TO FLORIDA LIBRARY COOPERATIVES

Six regional library cooperatives in Florida (see Figure 1) collectively cover the whole state, and play fundamental roles in providing outreach and services to users of public, academic, school, and special libraries throughout the state. These cooperatives were initially created to provide Florida residents with access to book and journal collections and have grown to encompass access to electronic databases, online virtual reference services, and courier delivery of interlibrary loan materials. Many library cooperatives also offer various forms of training for library staff.

SEFLIN members include twenty-six public, academic, and school libraries or library systems that serve over five million residents of Monroe, Miami-Dade, Broward, Palm Beach, and Martin Counties. SEFLIN, like the other cooperatives, receives its budget through local funding and statewide grants. They ensure that all Southeast Floridians receive free and open access to information. One service SEFLIN recently debuted, MyLibraryService.org, is a Web gateway that allows users to search online public access catalogs of other member libraries, browse their borrowing policies, and obtain full text articles from select newspapers, magazines, and journals. Similarly, MiServiciodeBiblioteca.org, the Spanish equivalent to MyLibraryService.org, was recently released for the growing Spanish-speaking community of library users in Southeast Florida. SEFLIN also provides opportunities for employment seekers to conduct library job searches in the Southeast Florida area, hosts library conferences, and offers continuing education and training for staff. To assist with these opportunities there are Training Administrators at the individual libraries who coordinate staff training on behalf of SEFLIN.

FIGURE 1. Regional Library Cooperatives in Florida

Florida Library Cooperatives	Year Founded
Central Florida Library Cooperative	1989
Northeast Florida Library Information Network	1993
Panhandle Library Access Network	1991
Southeast Florida Library Information Network	1984
Southwest Florida Library Information Network	1991
Tampa Bay Library Consortium	1979

Source: Florida Library Association, 1998. Used with permission.

SEFLIN'S TRAINING ADMINISTRATORS

SEFLIN works with Training Administrators (TAs) to assist in the day-to-day task of keeping member libraries' staff informed of the continuous educational opportunities that SEFLIN provides. A TA from each of the member libraries is selected to help with the implementation of SEFLIN's training program for staff. Each TA's responsibilities include serving as the liaison between SEFLIN and the member libraries, distributing information to library staff regarding training and continuing education, and keeping track of staff rosters and contact information. But the TA's principal task is to assist in "marketing" SEFLIN's continuing education program for staff and to make sure that every employee is aware of the importance staff training and life-long learning play in the services libraries provide for their patrons. It is the collaborative efforts of SEFLIN and its TAs that help the cooperative realize its mission.

Thirty-one individuals from twenty-five SEFLIN libraries or library systems currently hold the title of SEFLIN Training Administrator for their respective institutions. Under the guidance of the SEFLIN Associate Director, TAs meet at the SEFLIN headquarters several times a year to discuss trends in and issues related to continuing education and staff training. TAs communicate the information and ideas to the staff of their respective libraries and re-channel prospective feedback and comments to SEFLIN. This is usually accomplished through the dissemination of surveys assessing the needs and wants of library staff and through day-to-day conversations between TAs and staff.

At my library, staff training is implemented usually when new staff are hired or continuing staff need quick answers to questions relating to SEFLIN training. The TA introduces newly hired employees to SEFLIN and its resources in an informal setting, often in a small bibliographic instruction classroom where users have access to computers, thus allowing staff to immediately enroll in continuing education training programs such as Element K or the Community of Learning Program (discussed in the following section). When the instruction classroom is not available an alternative facility that houses a computer, usually the staff person's own office or desktop computer, is used. Introducing training resources to a new staff member soon after hiring provides the opportunity to view the lists of possible training courses that one can take. This can pique the new staff member's interest in pursuing continuing education opportunities early on in that person's tenure at the library.

The main goal of the TA is to ensure that all staff are acquainted with the available educational resources and, most importantly, that staff members at least have a knowledge of whom they can contact when questions or problems arise. The presence of TAs in libraries helps to continue the collaborative relationship with SEFLIN that is central to providing end users, the library patrons, with the best possible service. TAs also assist SEFLIN directors in regularly evaluating the continuing education programs and resources for staff. One of these resources is the Community of Learning Program.

IMPLEMENTATION OF COMMUNITY OF LEARNING PROGRAM

In the fall of 2003, preparations were being made to implement SEFLIN's new Community of Learning Program (CLP) Website which offers learning opportunities for member library staff for early 2004 (http://clp.mylibraryservice. org). SEFLIN TAs were expected to view the CLP site and become familiar with its design and interface so that staff at SEFLIN libraries might seek assistance from their respective TAs when the site became available. Staff at all SEFLIN libraries were encouraged to register for the CLP site upon its debut. However, staff are required to register if and when they decide to take part in a SEFLIN workshop, tutorial, teleconference or other activity. The SEFLIN Associate Director relied on the TAs to promote the site by word-of-mouth as a place where staff can access a variety of resources necessary to pursue continuing education goals. Anyone can navigate throughout the site and view course listings, calendar events, and other resources, but it is designed so that users must register with "MyCLP," the customizable arm of the site, before enrolling in a workshop, tutorial, or web-based course, or attending a SEFLIN conference.

Created in part by funds received through provisions of the Library Services and Technology Act, the CLP Website serves as a portal for staff continuing education and training. It provides access to listings of SEFLIN Blended Learning Opportunities such as workshops, tutorials, and teleconferences as well as a gateway to computer and technology training courses paid for through SEFLIN memberships. The site also supplies additional information such as links to SEFLIN newsletters and reports and upcoming SEFLIN-related events. "MyCLP" allows users to explore and keep track of their own continuing education opportunities available through SEFLIN.

Five categories make up the Blended Learning Opportunities: instructor-led workshops; library-specific videos on demand; teleconferences; video tutorials; and web-based courses. Within these categories, training opportunities are created for specific areas of interest: cataloging, children and young adults, collection development, customer service, disabilities and access, diversity, information literacy, introduction to the library, library advocacy, library development, library management, library security, preservation and conservation, reference, and technology. Courses falling into one or several of these areas are offered through the CLP site (see Figure 2).

Instructor-led courses, tutorials, and workshops take place either at various SEFLIN member libraries or at one of the five Comp USA stores and training centers throughout the SEFLIN region, and are usually half-day or full-day in length. Instructor-led sessions cover a number of topics such as teamwork, advanced Web searching, and finding graphics on the Internet. At the beginning of each fiscal year, SEFLIN allocates a certain number of Comp USA vouch-

FIGURE 2. Types of Blended Learning Opportunities

Blended Learning Opportunities Courses by Areas of Interest[1]	
Area of Interest	Course Name
Instructor-Led Courses, Tutorials, and Workshops	
Children and YA	Young Adult Resources on the Internet
Library Development	Grant Writing for Libraries
Preservation & Conservation	Book Repair Made Easy
Reference	Art Research Using the Web
	Virtual Reference Services in the 21st Century
Technology	Access 2000 Level 1
	Powerpoint 2000 Level 1
	Technostress: Adopting Technology Successfully
Library-Specific Video on Demand	
Information Literacy	Find, Evaluate, and Organize
	This Changes Everything
Library Management	How to Keep From Glazing Over . . . Assessment
Reference	Digital Reference
Video Tutorials	
Children and Young Adults	Leading Kids to Books
Customer Service	Is the Customer Always Right?
Disabilities & Access	Serving and Employing People with Disabilities
Library Advocacy	For Freedom's Sake: Intellectual Freedom
Library Security	Be Prepared: Security & Your Library
Web-Based Courses, Tutorials, and Workshops	
Cataloging	OCLC ILL Web Tutorial
Collection Development	Collection Development for Small Public Libraries
Introduction to the Library	Research 101–Basic Library Searching Skills
Library Management	Conflict Intervention
Reference	Conducting the Reference Interview

Source: Southeast Florida Library Information Network Community of Learning Program (CLP) Website, June 2004. Used with permission.
[1]This is not a comprehensive list. The CLP Website contains the names of all courses currently offered.

ers to its libraries which staff can then use to take courses related to computer and technology training such as Macromedia Flash MX 1 and Introduction to Digital Imaging. These courses are taught by certified Comp USA instructors.

Videos on demand are Webcast presentations available on the World Wide Web and are produced by organizations such as OCLC and ACRL. Video tutorials are sent as VHS cassette tapes from the SEFLIN offices to library staff and usually contain documentaries specific to librarianship and libraries. SEFLIN encourages staff to view a video with other staff members and to then spend time discussing the topic afterwards.

Web-based courses, tutorials, and workshops are self-paced and accessible on the World Wide Web. Examples of course topics include copyright, grant writing, and library marketing and are often produced by academic and public libraries and library organizations. Other Web-based courses connect to Element K, an online learning environment that gives users the opportunity to gain expertise in computer software programs, leadership skills, and project management (http://www.elementk.com). Element K courses are either taught virtually by an instructor over a period of four or five weeks, or are self-paced which allows staff to complete courses online when time allows. Titles of some recent courses include DHTML, Crystal Reports 9.0, FileMaker Pro 5.0, and Adobe Acrobat 6.0.

During July 2004, SEFLIN's schedule included approximately 17 instructor-led courses, 8 library-specific courses, 20 video tutorials, and 50 Web-based courses that were to be offered through September 2004.

In June 2003, the SEFLIN Associate Director sent out a needs assessment survey to all library staff who had previously participated in SEFLIN's continuing education programs. The results suggested that SEFLIN create several Training Tracks in different subject areas from which library staff can select and become proficient. These areas include workshops and classes that fall into two areas: library-specific and technology. The library specific training track includes management, reference, and customer service, while technology focuses on Microsoft Excel, Access, or PowerPoint. These are the topics that staff who took the SEFLIN survey said were most relevant to their continuing education needs. To complete a training track, staff members must take a specific number of courses from the Blended Learning Opportunities categories. For example, a staff member who wants to complete a library specific training track in management, such as Staff and Staffing Issues, needs to complete any four courses, tutorials, or workshops that are listed on the CLP site. The Advanced Management Issues track requires completion of only three courses (see Figure 3).

Once a staff member completes a designated number of courses within a training track and discipline, that person receives a certificate of completion.

FIGURE 3. Community of Learning Program Management Training Tracks

Management Track Name	Course, Tutorial, or Workshop Name
Basic Library Management[1]	The Practical Library Manager
	Basic Toolkit–Good Library Manager/Employee Skills
	Teamwork in Your Library
	Ranganathan's Five Laws of Library Science Looking to the Past to Help Shape the Future
	Managing Change
	Teamwork Basics
	Time Management
Staff & Staffing Issues[2]	Interviewing Job Candidates
	A Professional Toolkit
	Communication Skills for Your Library's Frontline
	Professional Development Skills for Library Staff
	Recognizing Employee Performance
	Conflict Intervention
	Disciplining and Redirecting Employees
	Providing Effective Feedback
	Motivating Employees
	Preventing Sexual Harassment for Employees
	Delegating
Advanced Management Issues[3]	Developing a Strategic Plan
	Be Prepared: Security & Your Library
	Leading Effective Teams
	Managing Multiple Library Locations
Leadership[4]	Applying Leadership Basics
	Creating a Strong Leadership Team
	Solving Performance Goals & Expectations
	Preventing Sexual Harassment for Leaders
	Professional Ethics

Source: Southeast Florida Library Information Network Community of Learning Program (CLP) Website, June 2004. Used with permission.
[1]Requires completion of four courses in this track.
[2]Requires completion of four courses in this track.
[3]Requires completion of three courses in this track.
[4]Requires completion of three courses in this track.

Yet, it is not required that users complete a specific training track or discipline before receiving certificates. SEFLIN also provides them to staff who may only complete one course or attend one workshop. The CLP site uses an honor system approach to allow staff to access their transcript, keep track of both completed and upcoming courses, and receive documentation of course completion. To do this, a staff member logs into the "MyCLP" account and views the transcript. Once a course is completed, the staff member can click a linked button that says "Course Completed" and print out a certificate for that course. This process allows library administrators and managers to place trust in their staff while providing staff with the opportunity to have a say in the types of workshops they can attend, thus empowering them to be in control of their continuing education objectives.

The TAs sometimes face the difficult task of convincing staff to register for the CLP site. This is especially the case if registration is not required by respective library directors. Often if the immediate incentive is not provided at the onset of registration, i.e., receiving instant continuing education credits for signing up, staff may feel that the time spent on registering for "MyCLP" is best spent on other, more pressing activities and tasks, with registration being saved for when the need arises. SEFLIN offers a free gift as an incentive to staff members who register for "MyCLP," but there is no evidence available as to whether this affects the registration rate.

EVALUATING SEFLIN'S SERVICES FOR STAFF

SEFLIN relies on the comments of library staff who have participated in the continuing education programs to help them evaluate SEFLIN's services. This allows SEFLIN staff to identify program strengths and weaknesses and to determine how they can provide the necessary resources that let staff reach their goals.

A staff member from a SEFLIN library states that the training opportunities provide her with the chance to improve in areas she might not otherwise have access to if she were not employed at the library: "I have taken advantage of the continuing education opportunities offered by SEFLIN, particularly Element K and the CompUSA courses and I find these opportunities very helpful and practical in gaining and updating a variety of skills for my current position."

Within the last few years, surveys have been conducted that ask users to evaluate SEFLIN's continuing education opportunities. The response rates are as follows: 22% response rate in 2001; 40% response rate in 2002; 31% response rate in 2003. Despite the fact that the majority of users who were surveyed did not respond, those who did reacted positively to continuing education training.

Responses to a number of open-ended questions that appeared in the "Training Outcomes Evaluation Survey Report–2001" showed that staff greatly benefited from technology courses on topics such as Microsoft Access and Excel. Thirty-two percent of the respondents said that they work better with their patrons as a result of taking technology courses, 27% increased their confidence level in assisting patrons, and 14% rated the voucher program, such as the Comp USA courses, as excellent (SEFLIN 2001).

In the 2002 "SEFLIN Element K Survey Report" that focused solely on Element K usage, 95% of the staff who responded found that "learning on their own" was an enjoyable experience and approximately 85% said that using Element K provides a "positive impact on job performance and delivery of service" (SEFLIN 2002).

The "Blended Learning Questionnaire" that SEFLIN conducted in 2003 found that 66% of the respondents wanted to acquire further training in computer skills, specifically Microsoft Excel, Access, and PowerPoint (SEFLIN 2003). With regards to the types of staff development courses offered, staff believed that the areas most helpful for them were customer service, reference services, and library management. The challenges that staff members face in taking courses include lack of time, scheduling conflicts, and lack of staff.

The results from these surveys provide ample evidence that continuing education training for staff of SEFLIN libraries positively influences the types of services they provide to their patrons, and gives them confidence in performing their library duties. It also suggests that staff will continue to enroll in continuing education training courses.

CONCLUSION

Many benefits of continuing education for staff can be acquired through the collaborative relationships between SEFLIN and library TAs. This ongoing process requires TAs to keep track of what their fellow staff members want and need from the SEFLIN training and education programs. TAs and the SEFLIN Associate Director collaborate to determine what works best for staff members and base their continuing education plan on the needs expressed by staff and management, as well as on the types of resources available whether they are in the form of capital or technology. The plan is not something that can be developed overnight, nor is it expected to be set in stone. Changes are bound to take place, but such changes can sometimes work to the benefit of all involved. In the end library cooperatives, library members, library staff, and library patrons come out as winners when all parties work together to provide the resources and services necessary for long-term staff continuing education needs and ultimately for more efficient patron service.

REFERENCES

Curry, Elizabeth. "Stone Soup Collaboration: SEFLIN Examples." *Florida Libraries* 41, no. 7 (1998): 142-145.

_____. "Costs and Benefits of Library Networking and Cooperative: A SEFLIN Example." *Florida Libraries* 36, no. 1 (1993): 9-11.

_____. "Southeast Florida Library Information Network (SEFLIN) Strategic Planning in a Cooperative Environment." *Florida Libraries* 37, no. 3 (1994): 253-256.

Element K: The Knowledge Catalyst. Retrieved 2 June 2004. <http://www.elementk. com>.

"Fact Sheet Number 2: Multitype Library Cooperatives." *Florida Libraries* 41, no. 2 (1998): 31-34.

"Multitype Library Cooperatives." Retrieved 5 April 2004 <http://www.flalib.org/ library/fla/fscoop.htm>.

Massis, Bruce E. "Planning for International Library Exchange and Cooperation: The IFLA/SEFLIN International Summit on Library Cooperation in the Americas." *Resource Sharing & Information Networks* 16, no. 2 (2002): 239-253.

_____. "How to Create and Implement a Technology Training Program." *American Libraries* 32, no. 9 (2001): 49-51.

Southeast Florida Library Information Network. *Community of Learning Program.* Retrieved 5 April 2004 <http://clp.mylibraryservice.org>.

_____. "Blended Learning Questionnaire, 2003." *Community of Learning Program.* Retrieved 29 June 2004 <http://clp.mylibraryservice.org/index.cfm?fuseaction= pages.BlendedLearningOpportunitiesQuestionnaire>.

_____. *Member Services.* Retrieved 5 April 2004 <http://www.seflin.org/>.

_____. "SEFLIN Element K Survey Report–2002." *Community of Learning Program.* Retrieved 29 June 2004 <http://clp.mylibraryservice.org/index.cfm?fuseaction= pages.SEFLINelementkSurveyReport>.

_____. "Training Outcomes Evaluation Survey Report–2001." *Community of Learning Program.* Retrieved 29 June 2004 <http://clp.mylibraryservice.org/index.cfm? fuseaction=pages.TrainingOutcomesEvaluationSurveyReport>.

Watkins, Christine. "Grassroots Report: New Study to Shed Light on Library Cooperatives." *American Libraries* 33, no. 2 (2002): 13.

Wylie, Neil R., and Tamara L. Yeager. "Library Cooperative." *New Directions for Higher Education*, no. 106 (1999): 27-35.

Library Assessment
as a Collaborative Enterprise

Martha Kyrillidou

SUMMARY. This paper focuses primarily on the collaborative partnerships that have shaped the ARL Statistics and Measurement Program, which currently serves the objective of "describing and measuring the performance of research libraries and their contribution to teaching, research, scholarship, and community service." Over the last ten years, the ARL Statistics and Measurement Program has continued to engage in active collaboration at the national and international level, enabling libraries to enhance assessment. *[Article copies available for a fee from The Haworth Document Delivery Service: 1-800-HAWORTH. E-mail address: <docdelivery@haworthpress.com> Website: <http://www.HaworthPress.com> © 2005/2006 by The Haworth Press, Inc. All rights reserved.]*

KEYWORDS. Library assessment, collaboration, library associations, new measures initiative, LibQUAL+™, E-Metrics, MINES, Association of Research Libraries, library statistics

INTRODUCTION

The Association of Research Libraries (ARL) works in an extensive and intensive collaborative environment, building consensus and defining the col-

---

Martha Kyrillidou is Director, ARL Statistics and Measurement Program, 21 Dupont Circle, Washington, DC 20036 (E-mail: martha@arl.org).

[Haworth co-indexing entry note]: "Library Assessment as a Collaborative Enterprise." Kyrillidou, Martha. Co-published simultaneously in *Resource Sharing & Information Networks* (The Haworth Information Press, an imprint of The Haworth Press, Inc.) Vol. 18, No. 1/2, 2005/2006, pp. 73-87; and: *Libraries Beyond Their Institutions: Partnerships That Work* (ed: William Miller, and Rita M. Pellen) The Haworth Information Press, an imprint of The Haworth Press, Inc., 2005/2006, pp. 73-87. Single or multiple copies of this article are available for a fee from The Haworth Document Delivery Service [1-800-HAWORTH, 9:00 a.m. - 5:00 p.m. (EST). E-mail address: docdelivery@haworthpress.com].

Digital Object Identifier: 10.1300/J121v18n01_07

lective actions that libraries undertake to shape and influence the forces affecting the future of research libraries in the process of scholarly communication. ARL is a not-for-profit membership organization comprising the leading research libraries in North America. ARL programs and services promote equitable access to and effective use of recorded knowledge in support of teaching, research, scholarship, and community service. The Association articulates the concerns of research libraries and their institutions, forges coalitions, influences information policy development, and supports innovation and improvements in research library operations.

Within ARL, a set of eight strategic objectives has defined the organization's activities throughout the 1990s. ARL is currently undergoing a strategic planning process and a new vision will be emerging in the coming months. This rapidly approaching change creates a timely pressure to document the extensive and intensive collaborative partnerships that have shaped library assessment within the ARL Statistics and Measurement Program during the last decade. This paper focuses primarily on the collaborative partnerships that have shaped the ARL Statistics and Measurement Program, which currently serves the objective of "describing and measuring the performance of research libraries and their contribution to teaching, research, scholarship, and community service."

INTERNAL AND EXTERNAL COLLABORATIONS

One can view collaboration within ARL at many different levels, starting from within the organization and among the various programmatic areas that are served by the eight ARL strategic objectives.[1] One of the most prominent opportunities for internal collaboration involves the Statistics and Measurement Program. All program staff are actively interested in promoting the overall mission of the organization and frequently work together. For example, the ARL Statistics and Measurement Program often contributes evidence that is used by the Federal Relations Program[2] to inform testimony for legislative purposes. Data collected through the ARL Statistics are used to inform the "Create Change" campaign[3] and sensitize external constituencies through SPARC.[4] The ARL Statistics and Measurement program monitors trends in economic indicators affecting libraries, especially tracking the journal costs that cause tensions in the scholarly communication system.[5] In the preservation area, the ARL Preservation Statistics[6] are a reflection of the close collaboration between the Preservation Program and the assessment capability within ARL. Through the New Measures Initiative, the interlibrary loan/document delivery (ILL/DD) cost study builds a similar bridge between the assessment capability and the collections and access area.[7] Finally, a close relationship has also evolved through the New Measures Program[8] between the Office of Leadership and Management Services and the ARL Statistics and Measurement Program, as we engage in helping libraries move in a more seamless way from assessment to management.[9]

The primary thrust of ARL collaborative activities, though, lies not with internal collaborations but rather with the external ones each program establishes with different constituencies. ARL has an structure of committees and task forces that monitor programmatic areas of the association, support specific projects, and often guide the program in establishing collaborative relations with external constituencies. External collaborations whether among the ARL member libraries, subgroups, or a mix of member and non-member libraries often make collaboration a very exciting and productive strategy. The rest of the article examines external collaboration activities in terms of how each programmatic area defines collaborative actions and services among (a) *all* ARL member libraries, (b) select subgroups of ARL member libraries, and (c) a mix of ARL member libraries and other libraries external to ARL. These overlapping circles of influence interact with one another in new ways as the external environment is enhanced with new technological applications and increased competition for attention.

Assessment by Consensus

Some collective actions are supported by all ARL member libraries. In the policy area, where timely topics arise, the political process usually involves the interaction of program staff, committee involvement, and ARL Board involvement. The ARL Statistics and Measurement Committee has grown from its beginning as the oversight committee for two long-term assessment activities that have become operationalized as established services for all member libraries. Those two activities involve the data collection of (a) the *ARL Annual Salary Survey*[10] and (b) the *ARL Statistics*,[11] which now have well-formed processes that require advisory oversight from the committee and adjustments as new needs arise. These activities are primarily valued for the long-term stability and reliability the services provide to the members, by allowing members to benchmark against one another in familiar and well-established ways.

In terms of performance measures, the two general areas that have sustained support and interest from member libraries over decades of collecting and describing the environment of research libraries reflect (a) the area of human resources and (b) the area of institutional qualitative and quantitative indicators. These areas are represented by annual data collection activities in the form of the *ARL Annual Salary Survey* and the *ARL Statistics*. All member libraries are actively contributing data for institutional benchmarking in both sets of annual publications.

The *ARL Statistics*, in particular, has strong roots in defining membership for the association over a number of years. A set of five variables (volumes held, volumes added gross, current serials, total expenditures, and professional plus support staff) from the larger pool of variables collected through the ARL Statistics has been reduced into a weighted index of the level of investment the parent institution has historically made in its library operation.[12] Although the ranking of this index has been used for comparative purposes, the main thrust of the index is to emphasize the similarity of these institutions, given the historically large investments that have been made in them.

The political process of defining membership criteria has evolved over the years to emphasize more qualitative aspects of a library's operations, yet the historical reality of the ARL membership criteria index still is a powerful unifying force for these institutions. As Kendon Stubbs noted in the conclusion of an address to the ARL directors: "Look around the room at the dozen people in your group, and ask: what do we have in common, and how can we describe it? Is it volumes held? Added volumes? Number of professionals? Interlibrary loan turnaround time? Success rates of reference transactions? Or even a combination of variables like the ARL Index?"[13] Yet as libraries are moving into increasingly competitive environments, the issue of increasing diversity in the interests of the various institutions as they deploy their resources into different collaborative arrangements has brought forward another model of engaging in assessment activities: sponsoring projects by subgroups of interested member libraries, or what is called "assessment by affinity subgroups" in the next section.

Assessment by Affinity Subgroups

In 1999, a small group of directors of ARL libraries under the leadership of the newly elected chair of the ARL Statistics and Measurement Committee, Carla Stoffle, Dean of Libraries at the University of Arizona established what has historically come to be known as the New Measures Initiatives. With the establishment of eight areas of investigation outlined in the original Tucson retreat, it was clear that the developing assessment agenda was growing in complexity and diversity. As a result different models for exploration and experimentation were adopted by different groups of libraries. There were varying levels of readiness to articulate the issues related to each one of these areas, as well as a different set of strategies deployed in some areas. For example, in some of the areas of investigation, such as the areas of learning and research outcomes, a more conceptual and theoretical investigatory approach was followed. For others, a robust mix of a conceptual research design and pragmatic technical applications was developed such as the work in the area of measuring library service quality that resulted in the establishment of the LibQUAL+™ service.

Select subgroups of ARL member libraries have come together since the Tucson retreat to experiment in specific areas and develop "new measures" that are not necessarily of interest to all member libraries. Measuring service quality, assessing information literacy skills, and measuring the impact of networked information resources are some examples of such areas of investigation. These areas of investigation resulted into the development of various assessment tools respectively, such as LibQUAL+™, SAILS, E-Metrics, and MINES. These tools have been used by different groups of libraries from year to year.

An interesting example of a New Measures pilot project that is being successfully operationalized is the ARL E-Metrics[14] project, which originally started as a pilot area of investigation by a group of 24 interested ARL libraries. This group has grown since 2000 to 50 ARL libraries and, following an assessment of the importance of the data elements proposed for collection through the project, the move to establish this pilot activity as the new *ARL Supplementary Statistics*[15] for 2003-04 was supported by the ARL Statistics and Measurement Committee. As a result, the forthcoming *ARL Supplementary Statistics* survey that will be mailed to all member libraries will ask them to consider reporting new data elements such as electronic journal subscriptions, searches, sessions, and items downloaded, which primarily attempt to describe electronic resources beyond the expenditures that have been successfully captured with earlier supplementary surveys. The maturation of E-Metrics is an example of a successful pilot activity that has moved from the support of an affinity subgroup to a consensus assessment activity for all ARL member libraries.

Beyond ARL Membership

Another model of developing and deploying assessment tools through the New Measures Initiatives is supported by a combination of ARL member libraries and other libraries external to ARL. These groups come together to test new approaches to collecting evidence for decision making. Two of the New Measures Initiatives, LibQUAL+™ and Standardized Assessment of Information Literacy Skills (SAILS) secured external funding from U.S. federal agencies that supported their expansion and application development to non-ARL member libraries. LibQUAL+™ was awarded a three-year grant by the Fund for the Improvement of Post-Secondary Education (FIPSE) in 2001[16] and SAILS is in its last year of grant support from the Institute of Museum and Library Services (IMLS).[17] Both projects have been applied extensively to settings outside of the immediate ARL community, often with enthusiastic support for meeting important needs at the institutions that deployed these new tools.

A recent New Measures Initiative, known as Measuring the Impact of Networked Information Services (MINES), is under development in partnership with a consortium of libraries that involves both ARL and non-ARL member libraries in Canada, the Ontario Council of University Libraries (OCUL). MINES has evolved from an earlier methodology, applied to a variety of settings by Brinley Franklin and Terry Plum for measuring library usage patterns in the electronic information environment involving 15,000 users. The authors discover use of electronic sources shifting from in-library to remote use and argue that this phenomenon is going to increase rapidly.[18] MINES has used the experience of these earlier studies and is currently being applied for evaluating the electronic resources that have been acquired through a centralized purchasing consortium, OCUL. OCUL has established a centralized portal through which it provides access to a rich array of licensed electronic resources. The MINES methodology provides a framework for collecting data from the users of these electronic resources through a pop-up user survey. Currently, data collection is ongoing and is expected to be completed by summer 2005.

Interest in LibQUAL+™ from consortia has also been apparent, since the scalability of the total market survey approach makes it attractive to libraries that want to evaluate their users' perceptions and expectations in ways that are consistent across libraries. Often these consortia are partnering to offer enhanced access to electronic resources.[19] Needing to move beyond the boundaries of a local institution in deploying assessment tools is, to some extent, related to the globalization[20] elements that are affecting the library marketplace today.

At least some of the New Measures Initiatives, including LibQUAL+™, SAILS, and MINES, have evolved into collaborative activities where both ARL member and non-member libraries are coming together to engage in different assessment protocols and learn from one another. For example, LibQUAL+™, which now involves many non-ARL libraries, is designed so that libraries can share results and learn from each other. So, collaborative participation is highly valued assuming that it will lead to the identification of best practices and improvement in local service. We are all eagerly awaiting the next point of development, the movement into actions beyond the local level, based on the results that are gathered at various macro levels of consortia and group organizations.

ADVISORY STRUCTURES

The ARL Statistics and Measurement Committee

A complex set of issues like the ones addressed by the ARL Statistics and Measurement Program is affected by a variety of spheres of influence, ranging from the direct guidance provided by the directors of the various ARL member libraries who serve on the ARL Statistics and Measurement Committee, to the people who actually carry forward the data collection activities at the various libraries; in addition, these are internal staffing resources available at ARL. The development of the ARL Statistics and Measurement Program is directed by the ARL Statistics and Measurement Committee, a focused, programmatic committee that provides advice and guidance regarding existing and emerging operations. The chair of the committee, in collaboration with program staff, is working on developing the agenda for the biannual committee meetings, which usually take place in conjunction with the May and October ARL Membership Meetings. Information about the agenda, the issues discussed, and the ways in which they are resolved is also posted on the Web site along with the committee minutes and agendas.[21]

Often, approaches that may have been discussed in earlier years are given renewed emphasis and impetus as changing leadership and environmental conditions provide more fertile ground for addressing specific assessment protocols. For example, discussions about the need to measure service quality from a user-based perspective took place at the ARL Statistics and Measurement Committee's meeting in October 1995, when Danuta Nitecki was invited to present results of her award-winning dissertation.[22] Nitecki subsequently worked with ARL and drafted a proposal for application of a protocol across different libraries, but the proposal was not funded at that time. A few years later, however, the various New Measures Initiatives provided the impetus for further action, and LibQUAL+™ was developed through a new partnership with Texas A&M University libraries. The interaction of member library leaders and staff is of key importance in the effective deployment of new projects.

ARL Survey Coordinators

Staff working in ARL member libraries are closely involved with the activities of the ARL Statistics and Measurement Program if they work on the ARL Annual Salary Survey, the ARL Statistics, ARL Law Library Statistics, ARL Health Sciences Library Statistics, or a well-established service like LibQUAL+™. They often meet in person in conjunction with ALA annual meetings.[23] Through these five data collection services, the ARL Statistics and Measurement Program interacts with (a) human resources specialists, (b) administrative and collection development specialists, specialized staff in (c) law libraries and (d) health sciences libraries, and (e) public services teams who tend to lead the LibQUAL+™ survey at the local level. For example, human resources coordinators often provide support for data collection efforts relating to the ARL Salary Survey, and they often develop proposals for modifying the survey's various data elements. In 2003, members of the ACRL Personnel Administrators and Staff Development Officers Discussion Group examined the Functional Specialist category of the ARL Salary Survey and recommended changes to clarify the positions included in the category in order to ensure more comparability among the resulting data. These recommendations were accepted by the ARL Statistics and Measurement Committee and implemented in the 2004-05 ARL Annual Salary Survey.[24]

Visiting Program Officer

Sometimes specific projects are conducted by staff members who are appointed as Visiting Program Officers (VPOs) at ARL. For example, Stanley Wilder collaborated with ARL twice as a VPO to finish his analysis of the age demographics of academic librarians.[25] Another example of a VPO appointment that fostered the subsequent development of the ARL E-Metrics project was Tim Jewell's work in 1997-98, when he helped to clarify the issues related to the characterization of expenditures for electronic resources.[26]

Expert Advice

In addition to working with the various survey coordinators and Visiting Program Officers, ARL often brings experts and advisors to various projects. Examples of such collaborations include the reviewing services and advice provided by the well-known demographer Murray Gendell regarding the studies of age demographics. More recently, ARL has established close collaborative relations with leading qualitative and quantitative researchers through joint grants with Texas A&M University. Yvonna Lincoln and Bruce Thompson from the School of Education at Texas A&M University have served as qualitative and quantitative experts, respectively, on the LibQUAL+™ project.

Technology Support for Collaborative Assessment

It is worth making a special note about the kind of collaboration that the LibQUAL+™ process brings to the large and complex research library environment. A team generally leads the local LibQUAL+™ process, with one person designated as a primary contact for communications on ARL's. This collaborative relationship is supported by a Web-based management center that allows each institution to define six points of contact at each institution (three primary liaisons and three assistants). Communications among the various contacts is not only supported by related listservs, but also by the availability of an online directory that allows participating libraries to identify appropriate contact names for further dialogue, discovery, and learning about the interpretation of the LibQUAL+™ results.

Another important aspect of the LibQUAL+™ service's collaborative environment is the ability to work through groups of libraries with a common purpose, and yet get evidence that is useful and granular enough for planning at the local level. In promoting LibQUAL+™, we emphasize the benefits provided to various consortia, including:

- Analysis of group results and a group results notebook that is provided to all consortium participants
- The ability to add five additional questions to the survey as a unified group; data from those questions will be presented in the group notebook
- The opportunity for a locally hosted, customized results meeting (depending on the number of consortium participants and the availability of staff)
- The ability to benchmark user perceptions and expectations across different library settings within the peer group defined by the consortium.

During 2003 and 2004, we worked successfully with a diverse group of consortia from all over the globe (see Table 1). A total of thirteen different consortia, ranging from state-defined groups to other types of institutional associations, indicate that the majority of participating institutions during the last three years have joined this assessment activity as part of a larger group.

COOPERATIVE RELATIONS WITH OTHER ORGANIZATIONS

ARL has a strong tradition of collaborative relations with other associations, both in North America and the larger international environment. Some of the collaborations have taken place to promote standards and policy-related work. ARL itself does not develop standards in the same way that other library associations do. ARL tends to be involved through partnerships with other organizations that support the development of standards through the official standards-setting bodies of the library marketplace (NISO and ISO).

TABLE 1. Consortium Participants by Year of Participation in LibQUAL+™

Consortium	Years				
	2000	2001	2002	2003	2004
Association of Academic Health Sciences Libraries (AAHSL)			35	21	12
American Jesuit Law Colleges and Universities (AJCU)					19
Church Education System (CES)					6
European Business School Librarians Group (EBSLG)					5
Hospital/MLA					7
Independent Participants with no official consortium affiliation	*13*	*41*	*72*	*118*	*107*
Military Educational Research Libraries Network (MERLN)				6	
Network of Alabama Academic Libraries (NAAL)				10	1
NY3Rs (New York)				76	
Oberlin				12	8
OhioLINK			57	45	1
SCONUL				20	16
State Universities of Florida					6
University of Wisconsin System					14

Standards

ARL often works with other associations at the international and national level to promote the establishment of standards that are useful to the library marketplace and the implementation of policies that promote library values in relation to information access. The ARL Statistics and Measurement Program and Committee members have been actively involved in supporting the development of the revised NISO Z39.7-2004, "Information Services and Use: Metrics and Statistics for Libraries and Information Providers–Data Dictionary." Member leaders are representing ARL perspectives in the process of revising the library statistics and performance measures standards both at ISO and NISO. More recently, ARL has supported the development of COUNTER Online, which, although not an official standard-setting body, is promoting work that will help the establishment of standardization and good practices in the reporting of networked usage statistics.

Policy

In the area of policy development, ARL has been an active participant at the Academic Libraries Advisory (ALS) Committee to the National Center for Education Statistics (NCES) that has historically been staffed by the ALA Office of Research and Statistics under the leadership of Mary Jo Lynch and whose work has been supported by the National Commission on Library and Information Science (NCLIS). The ALS committee provides feedback to NCES in relation to the biennial academic libraries survey. Program staff at ARL have also been actively involved in the adjudication process of the Academic Libraries publication at NCES, a quality control mechanism that ensures that the publications produced by NCES have been thoroughly reviewed by external reviewers. More recently, a strong partnership has evolved between ARL and ACRL as the latter organization, a division of ALA, has supported the implementation of the ARL Statistics survey to all academic libraries in the U.S. and Canada. Similar partnerships exist between ASERL and ARL and other smaller organizations. As a result, *ARL Statistics* is becoming an important instrument beyond simply describing those research libraries that are members of ARL, and it is being applied in more diverse and complex environments.

At the international level, ARL closely follows developments regarding the collection of annual statistics across the Atlantic, where SCONUL is currently introducing new data elements for describing and measuring electronic resources. Exchanges of information are also taking place between ARL and other library statistical units in other countries in Europe (Spain and Greece in particular). Furthermore, some thinking has taken place about the need to foster stronger Franco-American relations in the area of library assessment.[27] Much of this important work relating to library assessment is presented at a specialized forum known as the Northumbria Conference. ARL was an official sponsor of the 3rd Northumbria meeting, which took place in Pittsburgh, Pennsylvania as an official IFLA preconference activity.[28] LibQUAL+™ is also expanding internationally with the increasing representation of languages and countries.[29]

STRATEGIC BOUNDARIES

In thinking retrospectively about assessment activities within the research library community, it is evident that the ARL Statistics and Measurement Program has effectively moved from simply describing, as is mostly done by the *ARL Statistics* and the *ARL Annual Salary Survey*, to offering interpretive frameworks, fostering action, and supporting collaborative assessment. In 1996, Sarah Pritchard eloquently described the plight of assessment: "The difficulty lies in trying to find a single model or set of simple indicators that can be used by different institutions, and that will compare something across large groups that is by definition only locally applicable–i.e., how well a library meets the needs of its institution. Librarians have either made do with oversimplified national data or have undertaken customized local evaluations of effectiveness, but there has not been devised an effective way to link the two."[30] In 2004, we have moved beyond locally applicable assessment into more collaborative and global assessment frameworks. However, some may still question whether this provides, by necessity, better library service to the diverse users of libraries around the globe since we need more evidence of action and relation to learning, teaching, and research outcomes.

Two verbs are included in the objective served by the ARL Statistics and Measurement Program: to "describe" and "measure"–both of which have been active in the last decade. In terms of what we need to measure, i.e., "the performance of research libraries"–there continues to be some ambiguity as to whether our current tools, even as they are enhanced by the New Measures Initiatives, are meeting the true needs of describing library organizational performance. Every method and tool has inherent limitations that tend to lead to further development and enhancements.

CONCLUSION

There continues to be a healthy search for identity and purpose on behalf of research libraries, as ARL's currently unfolding strategic planning process attempts to articulate and define the research library of the next decade. In an occasional paper published by the University of Illinois at Urbana-Champaign, Krummel describes the seven ages of librarianship and articulates that the currently unfolding age of libraries will be for future generations to characterize and articulate its significance.[31] In venturing to predict the future, this author believes that the importance of the collaborative community that comes together to share common values, organizational purpose and/or geography, and the need for that community to maintain a center for preserving the collective memory, are three aspects of the currently unfolding age.

Libraries as collaborative enterprises and librarians as collaborators will need to be more focused and diffused in the community they serve, engaged in maintaining and serving the community needs, and alert in understanding the need to break or raise boundaries. Librarians are operating in increasingly intensive collaborative environments. There is always a fine balance to achieve between maintaining community and furthering action. Similarly, library assessment is becoming an increasingly intensive collaborative enterprise, and the need to maintain this fine balance between understanding community needs and moving beyond understanding into action is a healthy tension that characterizes all the activities described above.

It is the fine psychology of the emerging library "user," and our collaborative engagement in assessing with this "user" the collective and individual worth of our value as libraries and librarians, that will dominate the next age of libraries. In the words of the French philosopher and moralist François de La Rochefoucauld (1613-1680) and sounding as heretical as he probably did, we may indeed "need to study the people more than the books."[32]

NOTES

1. ARL Program Plan 2003 (Washington, DC: Association of Research Libraries, 2003).

2. Federal Relations and Information Policy <http://www.arl.org/info/index.html>.

3. Create Change <http://www.createchange.org/home.html>.

4. SPARC <http://www.arl.org/sparc/>.

5. Mary M. Case, "A Snapshot in Time: ARL Libraries and Electronic Journal Resources." *ARL*, no. 235 (August 2004): 1-10. <http://www.arl.org/newsltr/235/snapshot.html>.

6. ARL Preservation Statistics. (Washington, DC: Association of Research Libraries, annual) <http://www.arl.org/stats/pres/>.

7. Mary E. Jackson, "Assessing ILL/DD Services Study: Initial Observations." *ARL*, no. 230/231 (October/December 2003): 21-22. <http://www.arl.org/newsltr/230/illdd.html>.

8. Julia C. Blixrud, "Mainstreaming New Measures." *ARL*, no. 230/231 (October/December 2003): 1-8. <http://www.arl.org/newsltr/230/mainstreaming.html>. Also, see New Measures Initative page at <http://www.arl.org/stats/newmeas/index.html>.

9. Steve Hiller and James Self, "From Measurement to Management: Using Data Wisely for Planning and Decision-Making," *Library Trends* (forthcoming 2004).

10. Martha Kyrillidou and Mark Young, *ARL Annual Salary Survey* 2003-04 (Washington, DC: Association of Research Libraries, 2004).

11. Martha Kyrillidou and Mark Young, *ARL Statistics* 2003-04 (Washington, DC: Association of Research Libraries, 2004).

12. ARL Membership Criteria Index <http://www.arl.org/stats/factor.html>.

13. Kendon L. Stubbs "On The ARL Library Index," Research Libraries: Measurement, Management, Marketing: Minutes of the 108th Meeting, May 1-2, 1986, Minneapolis, Minnesota. Washington, DC: Association of Research Libraries, 1986. p. 18-20.

14. Rush Miller, Sherrie Schmidt, and Martha Kyrillidou, "New Initiatives in Performance Measures," in *Global Issues in 21st Century Research Librarianship* (Helsinki: NORDINFO Publication 48, 2002): 161-177.

15. Association of Research Libraries *ARL Supplementary Statistics* (Washington, DC: Association of Research Libraries, annual).

16. Colleen Cook, Fred Heath, and Bruce Thompson, "Users' Hierarchical Perspectives on Library Service Quality: A LibQUAL+™ Study," *College & Research Libraries* 62 (2001): 147-153; and Bruce Thompson, Colleen Cook, and Fred Heath, "How Many Dimensions Does it Take to Measure Users' Perceptions of Libraries?: A LibQUAL+™ Study," *portal: Libraries and the Academy* 1 (2001): 129-138. For detailed bibliography regarding LibQUAL+™, see: <http://www.libqual.org/Publications/index.cfm>.

17. Lisa G. O'Connor, Carolyn J. Radcliff, and Julie A. Gedeon, "Applying Systems Design and Item Response Theory to the Problem of Measuring Information Literacy Skills," *College & Research Libraries*, 63, no. 6 (2002): 528-543; and, Lisa G. O'Connor, Carolyn J. Radcliff, and Julie A. Gedeon, "Assessing Information Literacy Skills: Developing a Standardized Instrument for Institutional and Longitudinal Measurement." In H. A. Thompson (Ed.), *Crossing the Divide: Proceedings of the Tenth National Conference of the Association of College and Research Libraries* (Chicago: 2001), 163-174.

18. Brinley Franklin and Terry Plum (2004), "Library usage patterns in the electronic information environment," *Information Research*, 9(4) paper 187 [Available at http://InformationR.net/ir/9-4/paper187.html].

19. A set of annual group reports are produced by the LibQUAL+™ research team. In 2004, the available reports are for the following groups: ARL, AAHSL, Association of Jesuit Colleges and Universities Law Libraries, CES Library Consortium, European Business School Librarians Group, Hospital/MLA, Oberlin Libraries Group, SCONUL, State University Libraries of Florida, and University of Wisconsin System.

20. Martha Kyrillidou, "New Collections, New Marketplace Relations," *Resource Sharing & Information Networks*, 14 (1) (1999): 61-75, Preprint version available at: http://www.arl.org/stats/ifla83.html.

21. ARL Statistics and Measurement Committee <http://www.arl.org/stats/program/meeting.html>.

22. ARL Committee on Statistics and Measurement Minutes from the 127th ARL Membership Meeting, Wednesday, October 18, 1995 <http://www.arl.org/stats/program/min1095.html>.

23. ARL Survey Coordinators' Meetings <http://www.arl.org/stats/arlstat/coord_mtgs.html>.

24. ARL Committee on Statistics and Measurement Minutes from the 143rd ARL Membership Meeting, Wednesday, October 15, 2003, Item 10 <http://www.arl.org/stats/program/2003/agnd1003.htm>.

25. Stanley J. Wilder, Demographic Changes in Academic Librarianship (Washington, DC: Association of Research Libraries, 2003) and Stanley J. Wilder, *The Age Demographics of Academic Librarians: A Profession Apart* (Washington, DC: Association of Research Libraries, 1995).

26. Timothy D. Jewell, "The ARL Investment in Electronic Resources Study: Final Report to the Council on Library and Information Resources," December 24, 1998 <http://www.arl.org/stats/specproj/jewell.html>.

27. James H. Spohrer, "*Dossier: Regards étrangers sur les bibliothèques françaises: Les bibliothèques universitaires françaises et nord-américaines*," BBF 2002–Paris, t. 47, n° 5, p. 32-35 (Avril 2002). <http://bbf.enssib.fr/bbf/html/2002_47_5/2002-5-p32-spohrer.xml.asp>.

28. Joan Stein, Martha Kyrillidou, and Denise Davis, eds. *Proceedings of the 4th Northumbria International Conference on Performance Measurement in Libraries and Information Services.* Pittsburgh, Pennsylvania, August 12-16, 2001 (Washington, DC: Association of Research Libraries, 2002).

29. Martha Kyrillidou, Toni Olshen, Fred Heath, Claude Bonnelly, and Jean-Pierre Cote, *"Cross-cultural implementation of LibQUAL+™: The French language experience,"* Paper presented at the 5th Northumbria International Conference, Durham, UK, July 29, 2003.

30. Sarah Pritchard, "Determining Quality in Academic Libraries," *Library Trends* (January 1, 1996).

31. Donald Krummel, *Fiat Lux, Fiat Latebra: A Celebration of Historical Library Functions.* Occasional Papers 209 (Urbana, IL: Graduate School of Library and Information Science, 1999).

32. François de La Rochefoucauld's quote in original French: "Il est plus nécessaire d'étudier les hommes que les livres." Source: *Maximes Posthumes* page 51, line 106. Note: we were able to locate the original version of the quote through the kind service provided to us by the University of Virginia library.

Civic Partnerships:
The Role of Libraries
in Promoting Civic Engagement

Nancy Kranich

SUMMARY. Schools, colleges and universities, and local communities now recognize the key role they play to encourage citizen participation and promote civic engagement. New civic engagement initiatives underway offer perfect opportunities for libraries to fulfill their traditional roles of promoting civic literacy and ensuring an informed citizenry. Today, libraries undertake a vast array of innovative programs that bring citizens together to share common concerns. These programs are most successful when libraries forge civic partnerships to extend their reach and work with other organizations and individuals to strengthen participation in democracy. *[Article copies available for a fee from The Haworth Document Delivery Service: 1-800-HAWORTH. E-mail address: <docdelivery@haworthpress.com> Website: <http://www.HaworthPress.com> © 2005/2006 by The Haworth Press, Inc. All rights reserved.]*

KEYWORDS. Civic engagement, public forums, civic librarianship, civic literacy, civic partnerships

Nancy Kranich is Past President, American Library Association.
Address correspondence to Nancy Kranich at: 580 Galen Drive, State College, PA 16803 (E-mail: nancy.kranich@nyu.edu).

[Haworth co-indexing entry note]: "Civic Partnerships: The Role of Libraries in Promoting Civic Engagement." Kranich, Nancy. Co-published simultaneously in *Resource Sharing & Information Networks* (The Haworth Information Press, an imprint of The Haworth Press, Inc.) Vol. 18, No. 1/2, 2005/2006, pp. 89-103; and: *Libraries Beyond Their Institutions: Partnerships That Work* (ed: William Miller, and Rita M. Pellen) The Haworth Information Press, an imprint of The Haworth Press, Inc., 2005/2006, pp. 89-103. Single or multiple copies of this article are available for a fee from The Haworth Document Delivery Service [1-800-HAWORTH, 9:00 a.m. - 5:00 p.m. (EST). E-mail address: docdelivery@haworthpress.com].

Digital Object Identifier: 10.1300/J121v18n01_08

For the first two-thirds of the twentieth century a powerful tide bore Americans into ever deeper engagement in the life of their communities, but a few decades ago–silently, without warning–that tide reversed and we were overtaken by a treacherous rip current. Without at first noticing, we have been pulled apart from one another and from our communities over the last third of the century.[1]

Americans increasingly live disconnected lives from each other and from the institutions of civic life. According to Robert Putnam, author of *Bowling Alone*, many citizens stopped voting, curtailed their work with political parties and service organizations, and attended fewer community meetings and political events over the last thirty years. They have even diminished their pleasurable get togethers, with fewer people entertaining friends at home. Americans are also less public spirited, giving fewer dollars to charities. It is unlikely that our civic culture will be reclaimed without a sustained, broad-based social movement to restore civic virtue and democratic participation in our society.[2]

Americans face a variety of economic, moral, and political dilemmas such as improving their schools, expanding job opportunities, combating crime, reducing poverty, and determining their role in the world–dilemmas that in a healthy democracy require the public to engage in democratic discourse in order to understand the issues, determine options for action, and choose among competing policy alternatives. But too often, the public has abrogated its responsibility to participate in this process, delegating this role to politicians and professionals, and relegating themselves to passive spectators in the political process.

Public institutions can make a difference when they help citizens understand these issues and find effective ways to act on public problems. For, it is in the public realm where common political understandings emerge, where political will arises, and where public trust is built. It is there that private individuals connect their self-interests with those of others, where people form public perspectives on problems, and where they can make choices about what society should do. And it is within the public realm that people join together to act with a common purpose.

Libraries are among the most trusted public institutions. As the place where citizens turn for neutral information about common problems, many work closely with their communities to find new means to connect citizens and boost civic participation. Indeed, because libraries uphold and strengthen some of the most fundamental democratic ideals of American society, they not only make information freely available to all citizens, but also foster the development of civil society. Throughout the nation, libraries facilitate local dialogue, disseminate local data, conduct public programs, and boost civic literacy by building community partnerships. When successful, these efforts rekindle civic engagement, promote greater citizen participation, and encourage increased involvement in community problem-solving and decision-making, while garnering greater community support and positioning libraries as even more essential community-based institutions.

AN OVERVIEW
OF THE CIVIC ENGAGEMENT MOVEMENT

To Vaclav Havel, "Civil Society . . . means a society that makes room for the richest possible self-structuring and the richest possible participation in public life."[3] Over the last two decades, civil society began to blossom in Havel's Czech Republic. But in America, the associations and activities that create the glue that strengthen civil society, notably described by Alexis de Tocqueville in *Democracy in America*[4] in 1835, have ensured a structure and climate for more than two centuries of active citizen participation in this country's democratic system. By the late 20th century, however, journalists, political scientists, philanthropists, and citizens alike were documenting a declining public sphere, diminishing civic engagement, and eroding social capital. In a widespread acknowledgement of the crisis, social scientists proposed new models to invigorate a weakened democracy and to encourage more active citizen involvement with governance.

Among the leading voices proposing new models, Benjamin Barber prescribes "strong democracy" as a remedy to incivility and apathy, where "active citizens govern themselves in 'the only form that is genuinely and completely democratic.'" Barber claims that "community grows out of participation and at the same time makes participation possible," and that "strong democracy is the politics of amateurs, where every [person] is compelled to encounter every other [person] without the intermediary of expertise." From his perspective, "citizens are neighbors bound together neither by blood nor by contract but by their common concerns and common participation in the search for common solutions to common conflicts."[5] In a later work, Barber calls for "a place for us in civil society, a place really for us, for what we share and who, in sharing we become. That place must be democratic: both public and free."[6]

Another proponent of citizen participation, David Mathews, has applied practical techniques to this active citizenship model, engaging lay citizens in deliberation about issues of common concern. As president of the Kettering Foundation, he has developed a national network for civic forums, teaching citizens to frame issues, make choices, find common ground, and act in their community's best interest.[7] Others contributing to the civic renewal chorus include James Fishkin, who has also helped pioneer this framework for citizen deliberation,[8] Daniel Yankelovich and his colleagues at Public Agenda, who have analyzed issues and created choices for public deliberation,[9] and political scientist Harry Boyte, who has advanced new models for reinvigorating communities by creating free spaces or commons for public discourse and deliberation.[10] But not until Robert Putnam published his bestselling book *Bowling Alone*[11] did the importance of reviving community and increasing civic engagement transcend academic discourse and gain widespread public attention.

Many of the theorists who focus their scholarship on new forms of citizen participation recognize the central role of information to bolster civic engagement. Boyte devotes a chapter of his book on the return to citizen politics, *Commonwealth*, to the information age, elaborating the importance of schooling citizens in democracy by informing them about issues and using public spaces to listen, negotiate, exchange, act, and hold officials accountable. Others, like Lawrence Grossman, Anthony Wilhelm, and Douglas Schuler, accentuate how access to cyberspace presents both promises and challenges for wider participation in a 21st century democracy.[12] More recently, Boyte has worked with colleagues Lewis Friedland and Peter Levine to test pilot projects that use new technologies to build citizen spaces in partnership with community organizations.[13]

Echoing these theorists are a new cadre of librarians advocating a broader new "civic librarianship" where libraries build community and solve local problems.[14] Recent books such as R. Kathleen Molz and Phyllis Dain's *Civic Space/Cyberspace: The American Public Library in the Digital Age*; Kathleen McCook's *A Place at the Table: Participating in Community Building*; Ronald McCabe's *Civic Librarianship: Renewing the Social Mission of the Public Library*; and Nancy Kranich's *Libraries and Democracy: The Cornerstones of Liberty* all advance the notion that libraries provide both real and virtual civic spaces that engage citizens and renew communities.[15]

CIVIC ENGAGEMENT INITIATIVES
IN SCHOOLS, COLLEGES, AND COMMUNITIES

Today, scholars, teachers, journalists, and foundation leaders explore new opportunities to rekindle civil society in schools, colleges and local communities. For example, the Carnegie Corporation of New York has funded a 2003 report recommending that schools renew their civic mission by helping "young people acquire and learn to use the skills, knowledge, and attitudes that will prepare them to be competent and responsible citizens throughout their lives."[16] In addition to promoting civic engagement, the report also encourages communities and local institutions to collaborate to provide civic learning opportunities. Another report that year issued by the Albert Shanker Institute promotes the adoption of state standards for civic education.[17] Also in 2003, the Kettering Foundation published a document demonstrating how public engagement can improve education and strengthen democratic participation in communities.[18] A year later, Kathryn Montgomery and her colleagues completed a study of youth civic culture on the Internet and recommended models that nourish the web for youth by increasing their access to civic information, teaching civic literacy skills, and reserving spaces for a youth voice.[19]

Like schools, colleges and universities have also rediscovered the once vital tradition of civic education.[20] Many colleges now actively promote public engagement as a critical part of their overall institutional mission–with faculty incorporating civic content into their curricula and students participating in socially responsible extracurricular activities. Eager to connect liberal learning more directly with service and civic responsibility, the Association of American Colleges and Universities and Campus Compact launched the Center for Liberal Education and Civic Engagement in 2003.[21] To date, 450 college presidents have committed their institutions to educating students as active and knowledgeable citizens.[22] Recognizing that a robust democracy and the public welfare depend on an engaged and informed citizenry, colleges and universities are now willing and eager to strengthen both the study and practice of civic engagement in a diverse democracy and interdependent world.

The National Issues Forums Institute (NIFI), in conjunction with the Ohio-based Kettering Foundation,[23] develops discussion guides for deliberative forums hosted in community centers, libraries, and churches. Citizens use these NIF guides to tackle topics such as the environment, terrorism, immigration, public education, health care, and the Internet.[24] Over 30 institutions across America, including colleges and universities, civic and other grass-roots organizations, conduct NIF Public Policy Institutes to train citizens to convene and moderate forums and to frame issues of local concern.[25] A number of other organizations also sponsor forums to engage the public in issues of the day; among them are national programs like Study Circles and the Choices Program at Brown University, as well as local programs such as Community Conversations based in Owensboro, Kentucky, Texas Forums in Austin, and the Peninsula Conflict Resolution Center Civic Engagement Initiative in Northern California.[26]

THE ROLE OF LIBRARIES IN CIVIC ENGAGEMENT

Free and open access to information is essential to civic participation because it encourages the development of civil society. When people are better informed, they are more likely to participate in policy discussions where they can communicate their ideas and concerns freely. Most importantly, citizens need civic commons where they can speak freely, discern different perspectives, share similar interests and concerns, and pursue what they believe is in their and the public's interest. Members of the community must have the real and virtual spaces to exchange ideas–ideas fundamental to democratic participation and civil society. Ultimately, discourse among informed citizens assures civil society; and civil society provides the social capital necessary to achieve sovereignty of the people, by the people, and for the people.

Within this calculus, libraries serve as pivotal community institutions upholding, strengthening, and realizing some of the most fundamental democratic ideals. Quintessentially American, libraries make knowledge, ideas, and information available to all citizens by serving as the public source for the pursuit of independent thought, critical attitudes, and in-depth information. They prepare citizens for a lifetime of civic participation and encourage the development of civil society. Effective citizen action is possible when citizens develop the skills to gain access to information of all kinds and to put such information to effective use.

Civic engagement initiatives underway in schools, academic institutions, and local communities offer perfect opportunities for libraries to fulfill their traditional roles of promoting civic literacy and ensuring an informed citizenry. Many libraries already present thoughtful, engaging programs about community concerns–programs that encourage more active citizenship. Librarians also help citizens learn how to identify, evaluate, and use information essential for making decisions about the way they live, work, learn, and govern. In short, libraries play a critical role in rekindling civic spirit not only by providing information, but also by expanding opportunities for dialogue and deliberation that are essential to making decisions about common concerns.

EXAMPLES OF CIVIC PARTNERSHIPS

Today, libraries throughout the country undertake a vast array of innovative programs that bring citizens into a commons where they share interests, concerns, and decision making. In addition to hosting community-wide reading programs, libraries are: convening groups to consider local issues and teach civic skills; creating digital neighborhood directories and community information services; educating voters; serving as polling places; and partnering on civic projects with local museums and public broadcasting stations. These collaborative efforts benefit individual citizens as well as increase the community's social capital–the glue that bonds people together and builds bridges to a pluralistic and vibrant civil society. The challenge for libraries in the information age is to extend their reach well beyond educating and informing into a realm where they increase social capital, rekindle civil society, and expand public participation in democracy. To that end, libraries accomplish these goals not by working alone, but by building strong partnerships–partnerships that establish new constituencies, widen public support, broaden and diversify sources of funding, and strengthen public involvement with local affairs.

The Library as Civic Space. Libraries abet social capital by providing a space, or commons, where citizens can turn to solve personal and community problems. Over the past decade, communities, schools, colleges, and universities have refurbished or built exciting new spaces for their libraries–spaces that also serve as public gathering spots. They anchor neighborhoods, downtowns, schools, and campuses. They provide inviting, comfortable, and attractive commons for residents to reflect and converse. They offer an exciting line up of programs that increase the use of all their resources. More people come to the library when they perceive it as a desirable place that beckons them inside and glues their communities together. And partners depend on the library to offer a comfortable, neutral space conducive to civic activities.

The Library as Public Forum. When libraries serve as public forums, they also encourage civic engagement. Many libraries host public programs that facilitate the type of discourse that offers citizens a chance to frame issues of common concern, deliberate about choices for solving problems, create deeper understanding about others' opinions, connect citizens across the spectrum of thought, and recommend appropriate action that reflects legitimate guidance from the whole community. Librarians moderate forums in conjunction with such groups as the Kettering Foundation's National Issues Forums, Study Circles, Choices, and others that seek community sites and involvement in their promotion of participatory democracy.

In Bartlesville, Oklahoma, the public library has co-sponsored a standing-room only, award-winning series of forums about the First Amendment. At the Columbus, Ohio, Metropolitan Library, staff trained as moderators have hosted forums about the future of the community's public schools in conjunction with the Council for Public Deliberation and the Mayor's Office; they have also conducted a series on racial and ethnic tensions with the United Way Vision Council on Race Relations and framed issues around environmental quality with the local Health Department. Similarly, the Hennepin County, Minnesota, Library System, with funds from the Hennepin County Foundation, has teamed up with the Twin Cities Public Television Station and the Star Tribune to launch a forum series, beginning with a pilot on terrorism held at the Mall of America. In addition, the Johnson County, Kansas, Library has joined with the Kettering Foundation to sponsor a forum on U.S./Russian Relationships, and the LaPorte County Public Library has partnered with the Democratic Women's Club and the League of Women Voters to enhance its longstanding study circles series with dialogue about the county jury system and voting. In Virginia Beach, the public library is proposed as the lead agency in a Civic Academy project aimed toward expanding the community's civic capacity for leadership, collaboration, and problem solving in order to develop and nurture a whole new generation of community partners.[27]

Academic and special libraries are also hosting forums. At Ripon College in Wisconsin, McDaniel College in Maryland, and Franklin Pierce College in New Hampshire, librarians have joined with faulty, clubs, and the student radio station to promote campus forums. And at the Lyndon Baines Johnson Presidential Library, staff have worked with the Kettering Foundation, state humanities council, and the Texas Library Association to launch Texas Forums in 2002 in order to help Texans deliberate about issues of common concern.

The Library as Civic Information Center. When libraries provide civic and government information to the community, they build social capital and encourage civic involvement. Thanks to new technologies, libraries now deliver numerous local databases and web sites to citizens eager to find and use vital services within their communities. Citizens can look at meeting agendas and actions of local boards and commissions, seek social services, and identify emergency contacts. Joan Durrance and her colleagues at the University of Michigan School of Information have identified and evaluated successful civic library projects that guide citizens to government, and job information sites in Onondaga County, New Haven, Chicago, and Multnomah County; help immigrants and minorities in locales ranging from Queens, Austin, and San Jose; and teach youth to participate in community problem solving in Harlem, Newark, Oakland, and Detroit. They have also highlighted library-based collaborative community networking efforts in Tallahassee, Pittsburgh, and suburban Chicago that pull together essential information and communication resources that might otherwise be difficult to identify or locate.[28] All of these civic information projects require libraries to collaborate and build partnerships with the organizations that are listed in their databases if they are to foster civic education and community development.

The Library as Community-Wide Reading Club. In a phenomenon sweeping the country, public, school, and academic libraries are hosting community-wide One Book/One Community reading clubs. Launched initially by the

Seattle Public Library, the idea has caught fire in cities from Rochester, New York, to Greensboro, North Carolina, where 125 facilitators were trained to moderate 200 discussions with 12,000 people that came out to consider issues surrounding racism. Like many of the communities undertaking these efforts, Chicago went well beyond promoting reading by "giving a 'public voice' to what is usually considered a private activity . . . to discover or build unity in a diverse city."[29] And in Kentucky, the State Library linked up with Kentucky Educational Television (KET) to launch a highly successful statewide reading effort with outreach and engagement activities that took on a mix of partners that numbered more than 130 educational institutions, bookstores, public and school libraries, businesses, media outlets, adult education centers and arts, civic and social service organizations.[30]

The American Library Association Public Programs Office has joined with libraries in promoting this highly successful collaborative experiment to engage citizens in community-wide dialogue by co-sponsoring with the Public Library Association a One Book/One Conference discussion series at its 2003 Annual Conference in Toronto and publishing a CD-Rom planning guide for members.[31] Each of these efforts has included numerous cosponsors, giving libraries the opportunity to spread involvement and interest throughout the community.

The Library as Partner in Public Service. After Pennsylvania State University hosted a conference on the importance of developing partnerships between public broadcasters and other public service organizations in 1999, it launched the Partners in Public Service (PIPS) initiative to demonstrate how collaborative projects between public broadcasting stations, libraries, museums, and educational institutions could enhance services to the eight participating communities. With support from the Corporation for Public Broadcasting and the Institute of Museum and Library Services (IMLS), PIPS produced a useful guide with case studies on how to undertake these institutional partnerships in order to help communities revitalize through reinventing themselves by using digital technologies and fulfilling unmet needs.[32] Considered a vision for a "community as a learning campus," IMLS built upon the PIPS idea by launching its 21st Century Learning Initiative, which included a conference, "Exploring Partnerships for 21st Century Learning," publication of a report, and the funding of numerous collaborative civic projects around the country.[33] Likewise, the Urban Libraries Council has endorsed similar initiatives, recognizing that they enhance the capacities and opportunities for member libraries to contribute to civic agendas.[34]

The Library as Enabler of Civic Literacy. Children and adults alike must learn a broad range of 21st Century literacy skills if they are to become smart seekers, recipients, and creators of content, as well as effective citizens. Reflecting the growing concern for such skill development as early as 1989, a special ALA presidential committee issued a report stating that "to be information literate, a person must be able to recognize when information is needed and have the ability to locate, evaluate and use effectively the needed information."[35] Since that time, both the American Association of School Librarians (AASL) and the Association of College and Research Libraries (ACRL) have developed standards, showcased best practices, and promoted the development of partnerships to enhance 21st century literacy in schools and colleges.[36] Information literacy partnerships equip citizens for full participation in the digital age. Partnerships focusing on civic literacy ensure that the public has the political knowledge and skills to serve as active informed citizens. Libraries can join with other civic-literacy institutions like Study Circles, newspapers, and organizations such as the League of Women Voters to extend their information literacy initiatives as well to elevate the competency of citizens and enhance civic engagement.[37]

LIBRARIES AS BUILDERS OF CIVIC PARTNERSHIPS

Efforts abound that encourage more active citizenship. They offer libraries ideal opportunities to get more involved with promoting civic engagement in their communities and to join forces with the many organizations and institutions already committed to strengthening participation in democracy. Public, school, academic, and special libraries can forge civic partnerships with other organizations and individuals that extend their reach and help them achieve their mission. They can benefit from new relationships that provide expertise, financial support, experience, and good public relations. Civic partnerships that establish new constituencies can widen public support, broaden and diversify sources of funding, and strengthen public involvement with local affairs.

Libraries and librarians can participate in rekindling civic engagement from many venues. College and university librarians should consider working with the Association of American Colleges and Universities and Campus Compact to promote community service and develop student citizenship skills and values, encourage collaborative partnerships between campuses and communities, and assist faculty with integrating public and community engagement into teaching and research. School librarians should consider participating in projects such as the Campaign for the Civic Mission of Schools grants sponsored by the Carnegie Corporation of New York and the Knight Foundation to renew and elevate civic education in America's schools,[38] and First Amendment Schools grants, aimed at helping teach students the rights and responsibilities of citizenship that frame civic life in a democracy.[39] Public librarians should consider partnering with a long list of civic organizations to develop civil society programs, guide citizens to community information, and host reading clubs and other public forums. All libraries should participate in the September Project, a September 11th effort to bring people together in libraries for talks, roundtables, public forums, and performances in towns and cities across the country.[40]

Nonetheless, committing the library to forging civic partnerships requires political savvy. Libraries need to identify individuals and groups with common concerns, looking far beyond the normal sources for allies. Building a broad base of support for civic engagement not only ensures participation from many segments of a community, but also serves to spread the workload and prevent burnout of committed volunteers. For their civic efforts, libraries should recruit steering committee members who can strengthen partnerships through their professional or civic involvement–individuals such as school administrators and teachers, faculty with subject or experience building civil society, and leaders of local civic organizations like the League of Women Voters. One partner not to overlook is the media. Like librarians, journalists are deeply concerned with civic involvement and they can add significant benefits by covering activities and highlighting a positive image of libraries undertaking these endeavors. Furthermore, the library can extend its outreach efforts by encouraging partner organizations to showcase joint efforts through their newsletters, Web sites, and other public relations tools.

In the words of Robert Putnam, "Citizenship is not a spectator sport."[41] If libraries are to fulfill their civic mission in the information age, they must find active ways to engage citizens in order to encourage their involvement in democratic discourse and community renewal. Working closely with a rich and diverse array of partners, libraries of all types must help rekindle civic engagement, promote greater citizen participation, and increase community problem solving and decision making.

NOTES

1. Robert Putnam, *Bowling Alone: The Collapse and Revival of American Community*, New York: Simon and Schuster, 2000, p. 27.

2. Putnam, 2000, pp. 15-47.

3. Vaclev Havel, "State of the Republic" Presidential address to the Parliament and Senate of the Czech Republic, December 9, 1997, as quoted in: Jean Bethke Elshtain, "Families and Civic Goods: Connecting Private Lives and Civic Goods," http://www2.duq.edu/familyinstitute/templates/features/conference/elshtain.html.

4. Alexis de Tocqueville, *Democracy in America*, New York: Vintage Books, 1990 ed.

5. Benjamin Barber, *Strong Democracy*, Berkeley, CA: U. of California Press, 1984, p. 148, 152, 219.

6. Benjamin Barber, *A Place for Us: How to Make Society Civil and Strong*, New York: Hill and Wang, 1998, p. 38.

7. Among the many works authored by Mathews, see: "The Public in Practice and Theory," *Public Administration Review*, 44, special issue (March 1984): 120-125; "After Thoughts," *Kettering Review*, (Winter 1994): 89; *Politics for People*, 2nd ed., Champagne, IL: University of Illinois Press, 1999; and *Making Choices Together: The Power of Public Deliberation*, with Noelle McAfee, Dayton, OH: Charles F. Kettering Foundation, 2001.

8. See James Fishkin, *The Voice of the People: Public Opinion and Democracy*, New Haven, CT: Yale U. Press, 1995; and *Democracy and Deliberation: New Directions for Democratic Reform*, New Haven, CT: Yale U. Press, 1997.

9. See Daniel Yankelovich, *Coming to Public Judgment: Making Democracy Work in a Complex World*, Syracuse, NY: Syracuse U. Press, 1991; *The Magic of Dialogue*, New York: Simon and Schuster, 1999. See also the Public Agenda web site: http://www.publicagenda.org/, particularly the Civic Engagement and Issue Guides pages.

10. See Harry C. Boyte, *The Backyard Revolution: Understanding the New Citizen Movement*, Philadelphia: Temple U. Press, 1980; *Citizen Action and the New American Populism*, with Heather Booth and Steve Max, Philadelphia: Temple U. Press, 1986; *Commonwealth: A Return to Citizen Politics*, New York: The Free Press, 1989; *Free Spaces: The Sources of Democratic Change in America*, with Sara M. Evans, New York: Harper and Row, 1986, rev. ed. Chicago: U. of Chicago Press, 1992; and *Building America: The Democratic Promise of Public Work*, with Nancy N. Kari, Philadelphia: Temple U. Press, 1996.

11. Putnam, 2000; Robert Putnam, "Bowling Alone: America's Declining Social Capital," *Journal of Democracy* 6 #1(January 1995): 65-78, and Robert Putnam and Lewis M. Feldstein, *Better Together: Restoring the American Community*, New York: Simon and Schuster, 2003.

12. Several recent titles focusing on electronic democracy include: Lawrence Grossman, *The Electronic Republic: The Transformation of American Democracy*, New York: Viking, 1995; Roza Tsagarousianou, Damian Tambini, and Cathy Bryan, eds., *Cyberdemocracy: Technology, Cities and Civic Networks*, New York, Routledge, 1998; Anthony G. Wilhelm, *Democracy in the Digital Age: Challenges to Political Life in Cyberspace*, New York: Routledge, 2000; Peter Levine, "Can the Internet Rescue Democracy? Toward an On-line Commons," in *Democracy's Moment: Reforming the American Political System for the 21st Century*, edited by Ronald Hayduk and Kevin Mattson, Lanham, MD: Rowman and Littlefield Publishers, 2002, pps. 121-137; Douglas Schuler and Peter Day, eds., *Shaping the Network Society*, Cambridge, MA: MIT Press, 2004; and Bruce Bimber, *Information and American Democracy: Technology in the Evolution of Political Power*, NY: Cambridge U. Press, 2003.

13. See, "The New Information Commons: Community Information Partnerships and Civic Change," by Lew Friedland and Harry Boyte, University of Minnesota Hubert Humphrey Institute, Center for Democracy and Citizenship, January 2000, http://www.publicwork.org/pdf/workingpapers/New%20information%20commons. pdf; Peter Levine, "Building the Electronic Commons," *The Good Society*, vol. 11, #3, 2002: 4-9, http://www.peterlevine.ws/goodsociety.pdf; Peter Levine, "Civic Renewal

and the Commons of Cyberspace," *National Civic Review*, vol. 90, #3, (Fall 2001): 205-12, http://www.ncl.org/publications/ncr/90-3/chapter1.pdf; and Carmen Sirianni and Lewis Friedland, *Civic Innovation in America: Community Empowerment, Public Policy, and the Movement for Civic Renewal*, Berkeley: U. of California Press, 2001. Projects testing these ideas include: St. Paul Community Information Corps, http://www.stpaulcommons.org, which uses technology tools to involve young people in work on different types of community projects like mapping, creating a learning directory, and computer training; and The Prince Georges County Information Commons, http://www.princegeorges.org, a democratic, participatory, nonprofit association that produces Web sites, e-mail discussions, databases, digital maps, streaming or broadcast videos, tutoring services, Internet access, free software, and local policy initiatives as a service to the community.

14. Ronald McCabe, "Civic Librarianship," in *Libraries and Democracy*, edited by Nancy Kranich, Chicago, IL, American Library Association, 2001, pp. 60-69.

15. Redmond Kathleen Molz and Phyllis Dain, *Civic Space/Cyberspace: The American Public Library in the Digital Age*, Cambridge, MA: MIT Press, 1999; Kathleen de la Pena McCook, *A Place at the Table: Participating in Community Building*, Chicago: American Library Association, 2000; Ronald B. McCabe, *Civic Librarianship: Renewing the Social Mission of the Public Library*, Lanham, MD: Scarecrow Press, 2001; and Nancy Kranich, *Libraries and Democracy: The Cornerstones of Liberty*, Chicago: American Library Association, 2001.

16. Cynthia Gibson and Peter Levine, *The Civic Mission of Schools*, New York: Carnegie Corporation and CIRCLE, February 2003, http://www.pewtrusts.org/pdf/public_policy_circle_mission_schools.pdf.

17. Paul Gagnon, *Educating Democracy: State Standards to Ensure a Civic Core*, Washington, DC: Albert Shanker Institute, September 2003, http://www.shankerinstitute.org/Downloads/gagnon/contents.html.

18. Collaborative Communications Group, *New Relationships with Public Schools: Organizations That Build Community by Connecting with Public Schools*, Dayton, OH: Kettering Foundation, May 2003, http://www.publicengagement.com/practices/publications/newrelationshipssummary.htm.

19. Kathryn Montgomery, Barbara Gottlieb-Robles and Gary Larson, *Youth as E-Citizens: Engaging the Digital Generation*, Washington, DC: American University, Center for Social Media, March 2004, http://www.centerforsocialmedia.org/ecitizens/youthreport.pdf.

20. Harry C. Boyte, "The Struggle Against Positivism," *Academe* 86, no. 4 (July/August 2000): 46.

21. For more information about Center for Liberal Education and Civic Engagement, see: http://www.aacu.org/civic_engagement/objectives.cfm.

22. An up-to-date list of signatories to the Declaration is available at: http://www.compact.org/presidential/plc/signatories.html.

23. More information about the Kettering Foundation is available at: http://www.kettering.org.

24. For a complete listing of available discussion guides as well as recent network news, events and other information, see the NIF web site at http://www.nifi.org/.

25. For a useful manual about deliberation, see: *Missouri Deliberates, Discovering Common Ground–Deliberation and Your Community: How to Convene and Moderate Local Public Forums Using Deliberative Decision-Making* (training manual), Colum-

bia, MO: Community Development, University of Missouri Outreach and Extension, 2003. http://www.ssu.missouri.edu/commdev/pubdelib/trainmat.htm.

26. Study Circles Resource Center, http://www.studycircles.org/; The Choices Program, Brown University Watson Center for International Studies, http://www.choices.edu/index.cfm; Community Conversations, Inc., http://www.nifi.org/news/news_detail.aspx?itemID=1403&catID=24; Texas Forums, http://www.texasforums.org/; and the Peninsula Conflict Resolution Center Civic Engagement Initiative, http://www.pcrcweb.org/civicengagement/civic.asp.

27. Virginia Beach, Citizen Communication and Interrelationships Workgroup, *Connections for a Lifetime: Building Community Trust and Relationships*, Final Report, Virginia Beach, VA: March 2001, http://www.vbgov.com/city_hall/docs/communitytrust.pdf.

28. Joan Durrance et al., "Libraries and Civil Society," in *Libraries and Democracy*, edited by Nancy Kranich, Chicago, IL, American Library Association, 2001, pp. 49-59.

29. Putnam and Feldstein, 2003, p. 53.

30. Pennsylvania State University Public Broadcasting, *Digital Alliances–Partnerships in Public Service: Models for Collaboration*, Washington, DC: Benton Foundation, 2002, http://www.benton.org/publibrary/partners/pips.pdf, p. 12.

31. American Library Association, Public Programs Office, *One Book, One Community*, (CD-Rom), Chicago, IL: American Library Association, 2003.

32. Pennsylvania State University, 2002.

33. Institute for Museum and Library Services, *The 21st Century Learner*, Washington, DC: IMLS, 2001, http://www.imls.gov/pubs/pdf/pub21cl.pdf. See also IMLS, *The 21st Century Learner Resource Listing*, (web site), http://www.imls.gov/whatsnew/21cl/21clrsc.htm.

34. Urban Libraries Council. Urban Libraries/Urban Assets Strategy Group, http://www.urbanlibraries.org/standards/cassets.html.

35. American Library Association, *Presidential Committee on Information Literacy: Final Report*. Chicago, IL: American Library Association, 1989, http://www.ala.org/Content/NavigationMenu/ACRL/Publications/White_Papers_and_Reports/Presidential_Committee_on_Information_Literacy.htm.

36. American Association of School Librarians (AASL) and the Association for Educational Communication and Technology, *Information Power: Building Partnerships for Learning*, Chicago, IL: American Library Association, 1998; American Library Association, *A Library Advocate's Guide to Building Information Literate Communities*, Chicago, IL: American Library Association, 2000, http://www.ala.org/Content/ContentGroups/Advocacy/informationliteracy.pdf; Association of College and Research Libraries (ACRL), Instruction Task Force, *Information Literacy Competency Standards for Higher Education*, 2000, http://www.ala.org/Content/NavigationMenu/ACRL/Standards_and_Guidelines/Information_Literacy_Competency_Standards_for_Higher_Education.htm.

37. For more background about the civic literacy movement, see Michael H. Parsons and C. David Lisman, (eds), *Promoting Community Renewal through Civic Literacy and Service Learning*, San Francisco: Jossey-Bass, 1996; Henry Milner, *Civic Literacy: How Informed Citizens Make Democracy Work*, Hanover, NH: University Press of New England, 2002; and Elizabeth Marcoux, "Information Literacy for the Twenty-First Century Citizen, in *Libraries and Democracy*, edited by Nancy Kranich, Chicago, IL, American Library Association, 2001, pp.70-80.

38. Council for Excellence in Government, "Carnegie Corporation of New York and the Knight Foundation Fund New Campaign to Put Civic Education Back in the Schools," Press Release, May 2004, http://excelgov.org/displayContent.asp? NewsItemID=5198.

39. First Amendment Center and Association for Supervision and Curriculum Development, *First Amendment Schools: Educating for Freedom and Responsibility,* http://www.firstamendmentschools.org/.

40. The September Project, "What's Your Library Doing on September 11?" http://www.theseptemberproject.org/index.htm.

41. Putnam, 2000, p. 341.

Another Kind of Diplomacy:
International Resource Sharing

Kenning Arlitsch
Nancy T. Lombardo
Joan M. Gregory

SUMMARY. Over the past six years, the University of Utah libraries have developed an extensive international presence through digital resource sharing. Services include instruction, electronic document delivery, shared catalogs, and full-text databases. This paper will describe the process of establishing, extending, and improving these services through international cooperation and collaboration. The benefit to the smaller library with limited funding is dramatic and the impact on the larger library providing the service is minimal. *[Article copies available for a fee from The Haworth Document Delivery Service: 1-800-HAWORTH. E-mail address: <docdelivery@haworthpress.com> Website: <http://www.HaworthPress.com> © 2005/2006 by The Haworth Press, Inc. All rights reserved.]*

Kenning Arlitsch, MLIS, is Head, Information Technology, J. Willard Marriott Library, 295 South 1500 East, Room 463, University of Utah, Salt Lake City, UT 84112-0860 (E-mail: kenning.arlitsch@library.utah.edu).

Nancy T. Lombardo is Systems Librarian (E-mail: nancyl@lib.med.utah.edu) and Joan M. Gregory is Technical Services Librarian (E-mail: joang@lib.med.utah.edu), both at Spencer S. Eccles Health Sciences Library, 10 North 1900 East, University of Utah, Salt Lake City, UT 84112-5890.

[Haworth co-indexing entry note]: "Another Kind of Diplomacy: International Resource Sharing." Arlitsch, Kenning, Nancy T. Lombardo, and Joan M. Gregory. Co-published simultaneously in *Resource Sharing & Information Networks* (The Haworth Information Press, an imprint of The Haworth Press, Inc.) Vol. 18, No. 1/2, 2005/2006, pp. 105-120; and: *Libraries Beyond Their Institutions: Partnerships That Work* (ed: William Miller, and Rita M. Pellen) The Haworth Information Press, an imprint of The Haworth Press, Inc., 2005/2006, pp. 105-120. Single or multiple copies of this article are available for a fee from The Haworth Document Delivery Service [1-800-HAWORTH, 9:00 a.m. - 5:00 p.m. (EST). E-mail address: docdelivery@haworthpress.com].

Digital Object Identifier: 10.1300/J121v18n01_09

KEYWORDS. Resource sharing, international cooperation, library networks, document delivery, interlibrary loan, international programs, Middle East Cancer Consortium (MECC), American Library Association (ALA), Council of American Overseas Research Centers (CAORC), shared library resources, health sciences libraries

INTRODUCTION

American librarians often think of themselves as underfunded and underappreciated. We lament our falling budgets, the unconscionable cost of serials, and the ever-increasing formats of information resources that we are asked to organize and manage. We decry the lack of insight of our elected leaders when they assert that everything can be found on the Internet and that libraries are outdated. We fend off attacks from those who, driven by one credo or another, would demand control over the materials in our collections.

Our problems are real, but they are relative to our expectations and to the general opulence of the United States. Compared to libraries in many countries our wealth is fabulous. Our holdings are measured in the millions, our computers are replaced every three years, our networks are fast and increasingly wireless, and our potential for serving our patrons is nearly unlimited. American libraries stand as models for libraries in developing countries.

Our library philosophy is that access to information is the key to success for any free society, and in some small way we have been able to provide that access. The following pages offer an overview of the services that the libraries at the University of Utah have provided to libraries, institutions, and individuals in other countries, usually at minimal cost and effort. By sharing expertise and resources, the medical library and main library have launched several successful document delivery, instruction, digitization, indexing, and catalog creation projects that have greatly improved access to information resources in and by other countries.

Working on these international projects for the past six years has made it clear to us that we can help improve the lives of entire groups of people, and that by slightly altering and extending the services we offer to our own patrons we can bring information–crucial and timely in the case of medical information–to people who want and need it. Our libraries and patrons have benefited from the valuable resources and expertise that lie outside our borders. In the process of extending our services, we also find new ways to better serve our campus and community.

The projects described include:

1. Cyprus Medical Libraries Project
   a. Electronic document delivery service
   b. Full-text database of Cypriot medical publications
2. Extension of the document delivery service to numerous other countries
3. American Overseas Digital Library (AODL) catalog
4. Internet Navigator online information literacy course
5. Videoconferencing experiments for instruction purposes

ALA FELLOWSHIPS FOSTERED INTERNATIONAL AWARENESS

In the mid 1980s, the American Library Association (ALA) and the United States Information Agency (USIA) established an international fellowship program[1] whose aim was to send American librarians abroad as consultants. The program was an extension of the American foreign policy that established USIA (formerly USIS) libraries as a literary weapon in the Cold War.[2] USIA libraries were often the only exposure international communities had to American culture, and they were generally appreciated because there was little other access to information resources. The International Fellows program was funded by USIA and administered by the ALA, and "over the course of the eleven years of the program 118 U.S. librarians provided expertise and assistance to colleagues in 83 countries while serving as emissaries of American culture, society, and technology."[3] The program also provided selected international librarians with opportunities to visit libraries in the U.S.[4] In 1998, the USIA was folded into the State Department and funding for the International Fellows program was rescinded. The ALA made efforts to secure funding from other government and private sources, but in the end the program collapsed.[5]

One of the authors of this article, Kenning Arlitsch, was awarded a fellowship in this program during its final year, along with eleven other American librarians who were sent to such diverse nations and territories as El Salvador, Estonia, Germany, Japan, Moldova, Russia, Sri Lanka, Uganda, Vietnam, and the West Bank. Mr. Arlitsch was sent to Cyprus for six months, where he worked with the Cyprus Library Network (CLN) and reported to the Public Affairs Officer at the American Embassy.[6] Besides teaching and consulting with individual libraries he helped the CLN establish its first cooperative Web-based database purchase. Ten academic, public, and special libraries joined forces to purchase four SearchBank™ databases from Information Access Company.

MECC GRANT

During his stay in Cyprus, Mr. Arlitsch met Andreas Savva, the medical librarian at the Nicosia General Hospital. Like many libraries in Cyprus the medical library at the hospital was underfunded and understaffed. Despite such challenges Mr. Savva had a vision for the library services he could provide to Cypriots, and he enlisted Mr. Arlitsch's help in applying for a grant from the Middle East Cancer Consortium (MECC).[7]

The grant proposal identified two major needs:

- *Electronic document delivery of health sciences literature*
    While document delivery was available through the British Lending Library, processing time was painfully slow and costs exceeded the budget of the Cypriot medical libraries.
- *Scanning and indexing of health related materials originating in Cyprus*
    Health-related literature produced in Cyprus and published in journals, conference proceedings, and government documents was generally inaccessible due to lack of systematic collection and indexing.

The $15,000 grant was awarded in the spring of 1998, and renewed in 2001. After notification of the funding award, Mr. Arlitsch enlisted the help of Nancy Lombardo, Systems Librarian, and Joan M. Gregory, Technical Services Librarian at the University of Utah's Spencer S. Eccles Health Sciences Library. Their experience with health science resources and practices proved invaluable in developing the Cyprus Medical Library Project.[8]

CYPRUS MEDICAL LIBRARY PROJECT

Solutions for the two major components of the grant proposal, the document delivery service and the indexing of Cypriot health materials, were developed by taking advantage of existing tools and practices at the Eccles Health Sciences Library (see Figure 1). In the electronic environment, adding services for a library in another country is nearly as simple as adding services for an individual patron. Physical boundaries are truly irrelevant and designing these solutions required a mere extension of services. Extending existing services allowed the team to build the project infrastructure and test all procedures at the University of Utah. Mr. Arlitsch and Ms. Lombardo traveled to Cyprus in early 1999 to implement the project.

FIGURE 1. Cyprus Medical Libraries <http://medlib.med.utah.edu/cyprus/>

Cyprus Medical Libraries

Through funding from the Middle East Cancer Consortium and a partnership with the Spencer S. Eccles Health Sciences Library at the University of Utah, Cyprus medical libraries now have access to the PubMed *Loansome Doc* document delivery system and to a database of Cypriot cancer and health literature. This page is intended as a starting point for those and other services.

Cyprus Medical Literature
Database - Include *Cyprus* as a keyword to
limit the search to Cypriot materials.

General Medical Links

- ‣ Spencer Eccles Health Sciences Library
- ‣ US National Library of Medicine
- ‣ US National Institutes of Health
- ‣ US Centers for Disease Control and Prevention
- ‣ US National Cancer Institute
- ‣ World Health Organization

DOCUMENT DELIVERY
THROUGH THE LOANSOME DOC PROGRAM

The solution to the document delivery issue was found through PubMed, Loansome Doc, and traditional Interlibrary Loan (ILL) services using electronic delivery. With PubMed, (http://www.ncbi.nlm.nih.gov/PubMed/), the National Library of Medicine's free Web access to MEDLINE, PREMEDLINE, and molecular biology databases, biomedical literature searching is available to the worldwide Internet community. While only citations and abstracts are available in the MEDLINE database, PubMed includes the Loansome Doc service, which allows users to order complete articles directly from their on-line search results. The user must establish an account with a participating health sciences library, and requests are automatically routed to the participating library.

A Loansome Doc account was established for the Medical Librarian, Andreas Savva, to serve the four government hospital libraries in Cyprus. The account allows online ordering of articles and document delivery through the Eccles Health Sciences Library at the University of Utah. A free trial period was established allowing up to 50 free documents per month from March through May of 1999. The trial period helped the borrowing and lending institutions establish effective procedures and communication.

Using this service, Mr. Savva is able to search the free PubMed service on the Internet and place orders directly from the online literature search results. Physicians and health professionals submit their own PubMed searches to the Librarian who places requests for the articles selected. For materials not found in PubMed, Mr. Savva is able to place requests using the Eccles Library electronic ILL request forms on the Library Web site. While it is technically possible for the individual health professionals to place their orders directly, a centralized ordering procedure has been established to allow Mr. Savva to track usage and costs and to ensure accurate accounting.

Documents were originally delivered electronically from the Eccles Library to the Nicosia General Hospital Library via e-mail. Now, the articles can also be made available on a password protected website. Print articles are scanned using the Research Libraries Group's Ariel software (http://www.rlg. org/ariel/), a flatbed scanner, and networked computer at the Eccles Library. The Ariel software is easily configured to deliver the scanned material through e-mail or the Web, and the process is fast and efficient. The articles are converted to graphic TIF format or in Portable Document Format (PDF). Once displayed, the article is printed on a laser printer and distributed. Mr. Savva is responsible for tracking the orders and delivering the articles as they arrive. After the trial period, a per-article charge was established.

INDEXING CYPRIOT HEALTH MATERIALS

The second part of the Cyprus Medical Libraries project involved scanning and indexing medical literature published in Cyprus, and not included in any other periodical index. Andreas Savva identified several journal titles, along with conference proceedings and government health reports for inclusion in the database. The materials were shipped to the Marriott Library at the University of Utah, where they were scanned and converted to PDF files. The files were then transferred to a server in the Eccles Library, where they were indexed.

The solution to the indexing of Cypriot health materials was found through the use of the Eccles Health Sciences Library's existing integrated library system, Dynix Horizon.[9] For over 10 years, Eccles Library has partnered with health sciences libraries in the Utah Health Sciences Library Consortium

(UHSLC)[10] to provide integrated library system services. Librarians and library managers at these libraries have installed the Horizon software on workstations at their libraries, have been trained on the use of the cataloging, circulation, and serials management modules, and as a result are able to offer web-based access to their collections via Horizon's web-based online catalog. Partnering with Cypriot medical libraries was an easy extension of our integrated library system service.

Library catalogs are typically not used to index beyond the title of a journal. Indexing individual articles stretches the limits of a catalog's purpose. But the materials being indexed in this project were to be digital resources accessible on the Internet and Eccles Library had long been involved in cataloging digital resources with images from the "Slice of Life" Project,[11] web resources, and electronic journals. Again, it was an easy extension from this service to indexing electronic Cypriot health materials.

The Horizon system allows the creation of "locations" and "collections," which enables limiting a search to a specific group of materials. A new location and seven new collections were established to allow Cypriot users to search their own collection, if desired. Scanning procedures were developed based on the electronic reserves scanning procedures at the Eccles and Marriott libraries. Procedures based on those used by UHSLC hospital libraries and in cataloging electronic resources were established for indexing the Cypriot electronic monographs, journal articles, conference proceedings, government documents, and pamphlets. MARC-based templates (Horizon work forms) were developed for articles, pamphlets, and proceedings, which simplified the indexing process, helping novice indexers to more easily identify the required indexing information (i.e., MARC fields). Procedures for Horizon client software installation were documented, and a manual was prepared for use in training. Mr. Savva was trained on entering records into the system during a training visit made by Mr. Arlitsch and Ms. Lombardo.

Materials are now scanned and loaded onto the Eccles Library web server in portable document format (PDF) from Cyprus. Records are entered from Cyprus directly into Horizon with 856 field hyperlinks providing direct access to the full text of the literature. Quality control is provided by the electronic resources cataloger at Eccles Library who checks the records entered and adds Medical Subject Headings (MeSH).

Some challenges that were anticipated never materialized. For instance, it was thought that many of the articles would be written in Greek. This was not the case, and transliterations and translations of titles and translations of abstracts were necessary for only a small number of items. A cataloger at Marriott Library was able to assist with this effort. However, an unanticipated challenge was that of finding time in the Cypriot medical librarian's schedule to work on scanning material and entering records into the catalog. The solution came when a former member of the Marriott Library staff learned that she was going to be living in Cyprus for five years. Before leaving Utah, she was trained in both scanning and cataloging and is now in Cyprus coordinating this part of the project with the goal of training additional members of the Cypriot medical library staff in order to sustain the project.

As more articles, pamphlets, and proceedings are scanned and records are added to the Eccles Library Horizon catalog, health care professionals worldwide will have web-based access to the previously inaccessible Cypriot medical literature. In the future (following an upgrade to Horizon Information Portal), the web interface will be customized to present a unique look for the Cypriot user, allowing the Cyprus libraries to have a distinct catalog, or index, to local materials.[12]

Since the inception of the project to index Cypriot health materials, opportunities have arisen to partner with local Utah health care organizations (The Utah AIDS Foundation's Resource Library Project and The Utah Department of Health's Online Public Health Library Project) to provide similar access to their electronic resources and publications. Our experience with the Cyprus project laid the groundwork for these two Utah projects, bringing the extension of services full circle back to Utah.

DOCUMENT DELIVERY

Since the inception of the Cyprus project, the international document delivery concept has become quite popular.

- In late 1999, the medical librarian from the University Sts. Cyrill and Methodius Medical Library in Skopje, Macedonia visited the Eccles Health Sciences Library. Upon hearing of the Cyprus document delivery program, she immediately enrolled her own library in the program. Macedonia continues to be an active participant.
- During the spring of 2000, a returned medical missionary from The Church of Jesus Christ of Latter Day Saints read an article in the Eccles Library newsletter and contacted Ms. Lombardo about establishing a service in Sofia, Bulgaria.
- Later in 2000, another medical missionary with ties to the University of Utah who was stationed in Nepal contacted Ms. Lombardo about the possibility of establishing services with a number of institutions there.

With virtually no promotion, the service has now grown to include 14 sites in 9 countries and discussions have begun with medical schools in Ghana and

Papua New Guinea[13] (see Table 1). The Eccles Library has found that offering services to these widely dispersed locations is no more difficult than offering services to active faculty in their own institution. The amount of activity at each site varies considerably, with sites requesting anywhere from 1 to 265 articles per month.

AMERICAN OVERSEAS DIGITAL LIBRARY

While in Cyprus during the 1997-98 fellowship, Mr. Arlitsch lived at the Cyprus American Archaeological Institute (CAARI), one of nineteen such research institutes spread throughout the world. As members of the Council of American Overseas Research Centers (CAORC),[14] the institutes offer residential facilities and research libraries for scholars from all countries. Two hundred and eighty American universities, colleges, museums, and research institutes and societies hold 513 institutional memberships in the overseas re-

TABLE 1. International Sites Supported by Eccles Library Document Delivery

Institution	Country	Location	Service Start Date
National Hospital Health Sciences Libraries	Cyprus	Nicosia	February 1999
University Sts. Cyrill and Methodius Medical Library	Macedonia	Skopje	November 1999
Pirogov Hospital	Bulgaria	Sofia	May 2000
Tribhuvan University Teaching Hospital	Nepal	Kathmandu	September 2000
Belarus Medical Libraries	Belarus	Minsk	February 2001
Patan Hospital	Nepal	Kathmandu	March 2001
Lalitpur Hospital	Nepal	Kathmandu	March 2001
Higher Medical Institute Library	Bulgaria	Plovdiv	May 2001
KAT-Medical Library	Greece	Athens	November 2002
Individual Client	Cyprus	Larnaca	May 2003
Centros Médicos Docente Adaptógenos	Venezuela	Caracas	October 2003
Individual Client	Peru	Santa Marina Callao	January 2004
Clients at Universidad de Buenos Aires (UBA)	Argentina	Buenos Aires	January 2004
InterCollege	Cyprus	Nicosia	January 2004

search centers.[15] In 1998, the libraries were in varying states of automation: some had commercial catalog software, some had small databases built in-house, and some were still using card catalogs. Access to their holdings, which were often rich with local materials, was limited.

At CAARI, a friend of the institute had built a small library database in the early 1990s, using Dbase IV software. While clearly an improvement over a card catalog, the Dbase catalog was a stand-alone system that could not be accessed from anywhere else, and the software and the hardware it ran on were aging. This catalog was representative of the situation in many CAORC institutes; a physical visit to the library was usually required to determine its holdings. A solution was needed, but individually the research institutes could not muster the resources to do the work.

In 1999, CAORC was awarded a grant[16] from the U.S. Department of Education to begin providing online access to the resources of its member institutes. An ORPAC (Overseas Research Public Access Catalog) was only one component of the overall plan for the American Overseas Digital Library (AODL). Other components included dissertation, journal, photograph, map, and ethnomusicology databases. But it was the ORPAC that most directly addressed the problem of making the CAORC institutes' library holdings accessible to a wider audience.

Upon hearing of this grant, Mr. Arlitsch contacted David Magier, the Columbia University librarian who was the lead consultant on the project. The plan was to convert existing library records to MARC format, but beyond that there was uncertainty about how or where the records could be hosted. The Marriott Library offered to host the records on its existing Horizon catalog, and that offer was accepted by CAORC. It was estimated that the combined records of the CAORC institutions would not exceed 500,000 unique bibliographic records.

Rather than add CAORC records to its existing catalog the library decided to implement an entirely new Horizon catalog. Most CAORC institutions sent their catalog data as tab-delimited files, with ISBN, Author, Title, Call Number, Date of Publication, and other pertinent fields included. Some institutions sent their formatted MARC records for direct import into Horizon.

The condition of cataloging records from the CAORC institutions ranged in quality from "dirty data" to "beautifully cataloged records." A process to parse these records and achieve high-quality MARC records for the AODL catalog was developed. The incoming records were classified as five data types:

1. *OK records*–these were fully cataloged records with AODL call numbers and did not require any additional processing prior to import.

2. *ISBN matches Utah's Horizon database*–these items existed in the University of Utah's collection and the MARC record could be matched with the AODL call number.

3. *No ISBN matches*–these items were not in the University's collection, and data were therefore sent to OCLC so that a programmed search by ISBN and Year of Publication could be conducted for a matching MARC record.

4. *No ISBN matches in OCLC or no ISBN number*–in this case item data were sent to India, where catalogers conducted manual searches in OCLC. If matches were found, properly formatted MARC records were sent back to Utah with AODL call numbers.

5. *No records in OCLC*–these data were sent to India where original catalogers created properly formatted MARC records and sent them to Utah with AODL call numbers.

Properly formatted MARC records were imported into the AODL catalog as they became available. As of July 2004, the AODL catalog hosted by the Marriott Library contains approximately 240,000 bibliographic records from fourteen CAORC institutions (see Figure 2). The Marriott Library donated staff time, software, and part of the hardware, while CAORC contributed toward the cost of a new server.

INTERNET NAVIGATOR–INFORMATION LITERACY ONLINE

Another area where the University of Utah has extended its reach through international collaborations is instruction. In spring of 1995, Nancy Lombardo, Systems Librarian, and Wayne Peay, Director of the Eccles Health Sciences Library at the University of Utah, developed a grant proposal in cooperation with the Utah Academic Library Council, for the Internet Navigator course project.[17] Funded by Utah Higher Education Technology Initiative (HETI), this project enabled approximately 13 librarians, representing each of the eleven college and university libraries in the state, to work together to develop the course, with Ms. Lombardo as the project director. The course was initially developed to teach Internet skills, and was first offered for one college credit at ten Utah colleges and universities in Spring of 1996. The content has since evolved into an information literacy curriculum, covering essential skills required for college-level students doing research in the electronic environment. The course was designed with the academic institutions of Utah in mind; however, it has always been open to the world via the Internet (see Figure 3).

FIGURE 2. American Overseas Digital Library Public Access Catalog <http://aodl.lib.utah.edu/ipac-cgi/ipac>

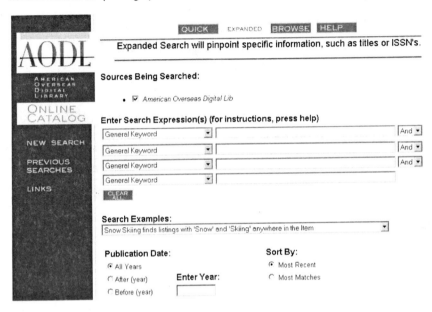

In 1997, Ms. Lombardo was contacted by Jennifer Oakley from the University of Tasmania, University Preparation Program (UPP). Ms. Oakley was interested in using sections of the Internet Navigator to help prepare mature age (over 21 years) students in becoming successful in the University environment. With no hesitation, the Utah librarians accepted their new colleague and Ms. Oakley was added as an instructor with the freedom to use all or part of the Internet Navigator with her Australian students. Since then, instructors have participated from international sites including: Griffith University, Queensland, Australia; NHTV Breda, Netherlands; the French International School in Hong Kong; and the American University in Cairo, Egypt.

Because the course is entirely Web based, widely divergent instructor locations are not a limiting factor in offering the course. All student work is submitted online, using either e-mail-based forms or auto-grading quizzes. Adding instructors is a simple HTML coding procedure. Including an international list of instructors gives students a sense of the global recognition of the value of information literacy skills.

FIGURE 3. Internet Navigator Online Course <http://www-navigator.utah.edu/>

VIDEOCONFERENCING FOR INSTRUCTION

Most recently, the Eccles Health Sciences Library has been experimenting with videoconferencing tools to facilitate instruction. These technologies can potentially provide local instruction to learners at remote locations, and can bring remote instructors to local learners. The experiments at the Eccles library have involved use of videoconferencing technologies ranging from desktop units which allow data sharing, conference room units connecting to a multi-port bridge, and use of an Access Grid node, using the high speed Abilene (Internet 2) network. These technologies offer enormous potential, though there are also many obstacles to overcome to ensure their functionality. With ever increasing network security, the issue of maintaining open ports on the firewall has become the most frustrating issue in implementation.

Initial experiments with Polycom Via Video desktop videoconferencing units were promising. Because the software allows for data sharing, an instructor is able to present course materials in many formats, including PowerPoint, a Web browser, and most other common desktop applications. Additionally, the software includes a chat function, allowing communication without interrupting the class. In the experimental classes, Nicola Gaedeke, PhD, a former Eccles Library faculty member who now resides in Berlin, Germany, presented workshops on a variety of databases produced by the National Center for Biotechnology Information (NCBI). Dr. Gaedeke holds a doctorate degree in Molecular Biology, and her expertise and interest in teaching information retrieval skills are in great demand. Using the Polycom technology, the Eccles

Library was able to retain her specialized expertise without the cost and inconvenience of international travel. The time difference presents some difficulty, but in this case the instructor was willing to present the class in the evening in order to allow students in Utah to attend in the early afternoon. However, after successful trial classes, the connection between the two locations became increasingly difficult. The German instructor's connection was a 128K DSL line; connectivity was slow, and video connections were often impossible. Despite extensive trouble shooting with Polycom technical staff, no solutions were found and the classes have been discontinued until the technical problems are resolved.

On a more successful front, the larger Polycom viewstation equipment was used to connect students in Utah, Texas, Sweden, and Iceland to conduct a Nursing Informatics course. The Eccles Library, in collaboration with the University of Utah Telehealth Network, provided the equipment and conference room for the course. Instructors at the various locations took turns presenting material, and students and faculty were able to interact in real time. Data sharing is more limited using this technology. PowerPoint displays reasonably well and a Web browser will display, but the image is not ideal. In this case, all sites had high speed Internet connectivity and were higher education institutions, allowing for high quality videoconferencing and consistent connectivity.

The authors believe that this technology offers great potential for sharing of instructional expertise. The Eccles Library has been in discussions with a medical school in Egypt, which may not have library staff to provide essential database searching, literature evaluation, and other instruction. Eccles Library is discussing using this technology to extend online instruction from Utah to Cairo using videoconferencing technologies. In this way, the medical school in Cairo will receive expert instruction, despite the lack of local instructional resources.

CONCLUSION

In most cases, these international projects and services are extending valuable and timely information services to libraries, individuals, and institutions where resources and funding are scarce. In Macedonia, the library services continued to be delivered during outright war. The ability to deliver vital documents to physicians and health care workers during such dramatic local strife is not only satisfying, but may be saving lives. While each example presented in this paper may not achieve that level of value, the bonds created do improve the perception of American libraries outside our borders. Even further, those bonds may improve the perception of the United States in general, at a time when our international image is at an all time low. Resources are not distributed evenly throughout the world, but libraries can make information accessible to almost any site using current technologies.

The projects described in this article were developed through creative application of technologies and services already offered in American libraries. The extra step of offering those services requires a willingness to share our relative wealth. It also requires that U.S. Libraries be willing to share their intellectual property and design products for open inclusion. In the case of the Internet Navigator information literacy course, the library consortium chose to open the course to all interested instructors, rather than retain all intellectual property and close the course to outside faculty. Libraries should be evaluating projects and looking for ways to adapt for broadest application, abandoning archaic models of intellectual property which lead to hoarding of resources and exclusion. U.S. libraries can also benefit from the wealth of resources and expertise around the world. By helping others create the American Overseas Digital Library and the digital Cypriot medical literature database, we also created resources that our own patrons will find useful for many years to come. With a mindset of sharing so much can be accomplished.

REFERENCES

1. "Overseas fellowships open in new USIA-ALA program." *International Leads* v. 1 (Spring 1987) p. 1.

2. Berry, John. "Propaganda, the USIA, and ALA" [editorial]. *Library Journal*, (December 1986).

3. ALA '97-'98 Library Fellows: http://www.ala.org/ala/iro/awardsactivities/9798library.htm.

4. Ibid.

5. Kniffel, Leonard. "Abandoning overseas fellowships is penny-wise, pound foolish." *American Libraries*, (April 1997), Vol. 28 Issue 4, p. 30.

6. Arlitsch, Kenning. "Report on Activities in Cyprus: 1997-98 USIA/ALA Library Fellows Program": http://www.ala.org/ala/iro/awardsactivities/cyprus97-98.pdf.

7. The Middle East Cancer Consortium was established through an official agreement of the Ministries of Health of Cyprus, Egypt, Israel, Jordan, and the Palestinian Authority. It is based in Haifa, Israel: http://mecc.cancer.gov.

8. Lombardo, N.T., Arlitsch, K., Gregory, J.M. (2000, Summer), "Cyprus Medical Libraries Project: International Collaboration for Electronic Document Delivery and Full Text Database Development." *Issues in Science and Technology Librarianship*, 27. Published online: http://www.istl.org/00-summer/.

9. Dynix Inc.: http://www.dynix.com/.

10. Utah Health Sciences Library Consortium: http://medstat.med.utah.edu/uhslc/.

11. Slice of Life website: http://www-medlib.med.utah.edu/sol/.

12. Cyprus Medical Libraries website: http://medstat.med.utah.edu/cyprus/.

13. Hansen, C. and Lombardo, N. (1997). Toward the Virtual University: Collaborative Development of a Web-Based Course. *Research Strategies*, 15(2), pp. 68-72.

14. Council of American Overseas Research Centers website: http://www.caorc.org.

15. American Overseas Digital Library–Detailed Overview–The Partners: http://www.aiys.org/aodl/public/partners.php.

16. American Overseas Digital Library–Program Funding: http://www.aiys.org/aodl/public/funding.php.

17. Internet Navigator course: http://www-navigator.utah.edu/.

Preparing Ethnic Non-Profits
for the 21st Century

Romelia Salinas
Richard Chabrán

SUMMARY. As librarians involved with various technology initiatives, we have harnessed new technologies to create information systems and services to increase access to digital information for marginalized communities. The focus of this article is to share information about our work with two technology projects, the Chicano/Latino Network and the Community Digital Initiative, and the partnerships that were formed with organizations beyond the library in the process. In this discussion, reflections on the lessons learned from these experiences will be provided as well as the strategies used for forming successful partnerships with community institutions such as non-profit organizations, professional associations, local governments, and schools. *[Article copies available for a fee from The Haworth Document Delivery Service: 1-800-HAWORTH. E-mail address: <docdelivery@haworthpress.com> Website: <http://www.HaworthPress.com> © 2005/2006 by The Haworth Press, Inc. All rights reserved.]*

Romelia Salinas is Social Science Librarian, California State University, Los Angeles, 5151 State University Drive, Los Angeles, CA 90032 (E-mail: RSalina@exchange.calstatela.edu).

Richard Chabrán is Chair, California Community Technology Policy Group, 606 South Olive Street, Suite 2400, Los Angeles, CA 90014 (E-mail: chabran@cctpg.org).

[Haworth co-indexing entry note]: "Preparing Ethnic Non-Profits for the 21st Century." Salinas, Romelia and Richard Chabrán. Co-published simultaneously in *Resource Sharing & Information Networks* (The Haworth Information Press, an imprint of The Haworth Press, Inc.) Vol. 18, No. 1/2, 2005/2006, pp. 121-136; and: *Libraries Beyond Their Institutions: Partnerships That Work* (ed: William Miller, and Rita M. Pellen) The Haworth Information Press, an imprint of The Haworth Press, Inc., 2005/2006, pp. 121-136. Single or multiple copies of this article are available for a fee from The Haworth Document Delivery Service [1-800-HAWORTH, 9:00 a.m. - 5:00 p.m. (EST). E-mail address: docdelivery@haworthpress.com].

KEYWORDS. Chicano/Latino Network, Community Digital Initiative, community partnerships, Eastside Intercambios, Infopeople, information literacy, library collaboration, library outreach, library partnerships, REFORMA

The convergence of increased information production with emerging technological advances positioned libraries in a new social space with innovative tools. This in turn made it necessary to re-envision collections and services.[1] As librarians involved with various technology initiatives over the course of the last few decades, we have harnessed these new technologies to create new information systems and services in order to increase access for marginalized communities. It has been some time since we played a leadership role in these initiatives so this paper provides an opportunity for reflection on the role of partnerships. Early in our endeavors, we learned that partnerships and collaborations were essential for success in such activities.

For the present discussion, we selected two projects where partnerships, information systems, and technology were at the heart of our work. We reflect on the lessons learned from these experiences and share strategies used to form successful partnerships with community institutions such as non-profit organizations, professional associations, local governments, and schools. We have also attempted to share not just what worked but what did not work. It is important to note that these interventions emerged from our work in a university-based ethno-specific library.[2] It is also important to note that these interventions were not aimed at changing public library practices, but investigating how high technologies might be incorporated in efforts to develop new public spaces powered by information systems that could be useful to underserved communities.

We began these projects by acknowledging the global forces that provided the context for our work. In particular, we attempted to keep our eye on the rapidly changing global economy and the dramatic role that immigrants and immigration were playing in the transformation. The new economy has transformed how we think about information. While information has a long history of being bought and sold, a look at licensed databases available in our libraries illustrates how information is now treated as a commodity rather than a social good. Like other commodities there are demands that it be available just in time–anytime–anywhere. This has deep implications for libraries, which traditionally have viewed information as a social good and have been for the most part place-based institutions. The introduction of networked information and communication technologies into libraries called for the re-articulation of many traditional library concepts and services. For instance, the concept of a library collection needed to be expanded to be inclusive of items beyond the immediate physical location. Technology innovations also allowed for collections to digitally include items in formats such as photographs, maps, and music without the need to deal with issues of physical storage or preservation.

While this period generated much excitement as to the possibilities and benefits afforded by electronic networks, it also introduced challenges, many stemming from the need to rethink concepts such as access, collections, and reference. We found it useful to reaffirm traditional library values such as those expressed in The Library Bill of Rights. According to The Bill, libraries should provide information for the interest of all people, from all points of view, to oppose censorship, support freedom of expression and access to ideas for all regardless of origin, age, background, or views.[3] These changes also required re-conceptualizing the librarian's role in these transformations. Bonnie Nardi and Vicki O'Day's work on information ecologies reaffirms the role of librarians as a keystone species in the new economy, but also note that libraries are not the only places that have their own information ecology; so do other institutions, associations, and organizations.[4] Their work considers how new high technologies are impacting all of these different ecologies. Their inquiry in turn provides us with a framework to examine and make strategic decisions about where interventions can be most effective.

As the social implications of the integration of information technologies, like the Internet, have come to be explored it has become evident that inequities in access and use which exist for certain communities posed a serious dilemma for libraries as institutions devoted to information equity for all.

During the Clinton Administration the popular metaphor that represented the lack of equity in the way emerging technologies were being experienced was the "digital divide." Keith Fulton, from the National Urban League, states that "In a very rapid way, the term digital divide began to emerge as a leading phrase for describing a range of disparities between those who enjoy the benefits of information and communications technology and those who do not."[5] Blanco Gordo coined the term "enhanced access" to expand the discourse of the digital divide. She cautions us that as we consider such items as computer ownership and Internet access, which tend to focus on consumption, that we need to refocus on under what conditions people can use high technologies to become producers.[6] This has led us to consider Sakia Sassen's term "cyber-segmentation" as a better way of describing what is popularly known as the digital divide.[7] We have reformulated cyber-segmentation as *the inequalities that exist with regard to the material capacity, acquired skills, and differential use of digital technologies.*

In an effort to address this cyber-segmentation, we have worked on several technology projects that have led us to form numerous partnerships with organizations and institutions beyond the library. While libraries incorporated new technologies into their maintenance and delivery systems, and in building digital collections, they have generally concentrated on doing this within the bounds of their physical space. While it is now common to see public workstations in public libraries this was not always the case. Early on libraries were slow to develop programs aimed at addressing the technology gap. Computers if they existed in libraries were generally out of public view. This changed dramatically with the Bill and Melinda Gates Foundation Library program.[8] While there have been important exceptions, generally libraries have not been involved in the development of community information networks.[9] Thus, at that time the work of our projects was highly innovative and unique. Our work was driven by the following objectives: to provide and facilitate Internet access, Internet training, and content relevant to marginalized communities. These objectives were pursued within a community informatics framework, which seeks to use information and communication infrastructures, applications, and services to empower and sustain the social capital of communities.[10] Thus, the ultimate goal of these projects was to provide support and a channel for the self-empowerment of these communities.

The first project was the Chicano/Latino Network (CLNet), established in 1993 and the second was the Community Digital Initiative (CDI), established in 1997. Although technology was a central component for both of these projects, they were in many ways very different from each other as will be discussed.

CHICANO/LATINO NETWORK (CLNet):
A RELEVANT INFORMATION SYSTEM

Before 1992, the presence of Latino content on the Internet was minimal.[11] This gap in representation and lack of relevant content provided the space for the Chicano/Latino Electronic Network (CLEN) to be established in 1993. CLEN was a project of the University of California that proposed to create a comprehensive database and electronic services for those interested in Chicano/Latino and linguistic minority issues and research through the use of the Internet. The major goals of CLEN were to develop Internet access, services, and training, which would facilitate and promote Latino and linguistic minority research beyond the University of California. CLEN was the umbrella unit for a joint project between the UCLA Chicano Studies Research Library and University of California (UC) Linguistic Minority Research Institute (LMRI) headquartered at the University of California Santa Barbara (UCSB). The UCLA Chicano Studies Library created and maintained the CLNet, while the UCSB Institute developed LMRINet, a project that focused on education and language minority issues. Both of these projects began as gopher sites and became websites as the technology evolved. Eventually, CLNet was moved to the University of California Riverside in 1997.[12]

As founders of CLNet and as librarians, we used the metaphor of a library as a means for identifying, selecting, and organizing the digital information that became the base for this information system. During the 1960s and 1970s, Chicano Studies libraries were developed across the United States as a strategy for supporting emerging Chicano Studies teaching and research initiatives.[13] The fundamental goal of all of these initiatives was the identification, selection, and inclusion of a corpus of work that had been largely excluded in American libraries. CLNet's development was grounded in this history and functioned in virtual space in ways similar to those in which Chicano Studies libraries had in real space. In this sense it sought to be a Latino Studies library without walls.

Although we were academic librarians, our ideas of outreach extended beyond our campus and our university system. In order for CLNet to be used and to function as envisioned, we needed to reach out beyond the academic community. Empirical findings indicated that the Latino community was not involving itself with this technology at the same rate that dominant society had embraced it.[14] With this reality in mind, CLNet committed itself to increasing its role in encouraging the Latino community to partake of the resources the Internet offered.

Since CLNet was headquartered in Los Angeles it became the place for us to initiate our work. However, outreach to the Latino community in the Los Angeles area posed a substantial number of challenges due to its large size and diversity. Los Angeles County has the largest population, 10,047,300 as of July 2003, of any county in the nation and 44.6% of that population is of Latino origin. It covers 4,084 square miles and has 88 cities, each with its own city council.[15] The realization of the immensity of the task we intended to pursue quickly became evident. Thus, we sought out community institutions as partners to collaborate on work towards meeting CLNet's objectives of fostering Internet access, Internet literacy, content production, and policy awareness within the Latino community.

This community, like other marginalized groups, needed to increase participation not only in terms of use and as information providers, but also in the politics of community networking. Therefore, every presentation made to organizations included a discussion on policy issues related to information technology. This included a discussion on the possible ramification of being technology illiterate within an economy that was quickly mandating such skills and displacing labor-intensive, industrial-age work. For instance, Latino children would find it difficult to compete for success in a technology-dependent society without these skills. Information technology was transforming political communication and the delivery of services, and without private and public access points, many Latinos could be further marginalized from public life.[16] Reasons such as these were presented to illustrate the importance for Latinos to address access barriers such as cost and literacy and to develop efforts that would motivate infrastructure investment in Latino-dominant neighborhoods by the technology industry.

CLNet worked with at least thirty non-profit organizations. The vast majority were located in the Los Angeles area, but as other organizations learned about our services we were sought out and came to work with organizations located throughout the nation. These partnerships were established through various methods. Initial contacts were made via techniques such as:

- Participating in business meetings or conferences
- Mailing out invitations to organizations to become information providers
- Meeting with key individuals in organizations
- Televising presentations on local community shows
- Interviews on local Latino radio, cable, and television programs

Our approach of incorporating multiple methods of outreach was essential as we found that use of just one tactic was not very effective. Each strategy had its weaknesses; however together they proved to be effective for reaching the community. For instance, a disadvantage in mailings was a high rate of undeliverable letters. In a community as large and dynamic as Los Angeles organizations changed physical locations, changed names, or even dissolved quite frequently. Also, radio interviews proved to be limiting since we were working with a visual technology like the World Wide Web. Therefore, creative alternatives of describing the Web over an audio medium had to be developed. We developed Internet training sessions around vignettes that included everyday life experiences such as reading a newspaper from the home country, eating at a local Mexican restaurant, talking to Dona Maria, the Latino version of Ann Landers, or buying a book at the local bookstore. In this manner we introduced new high technologies with familiar examples. This allowed them to see and imagine themselves in these new technologies.

At times, those presentations taught us more about the challenges of the Internet than we taught organizations about the use of the Internet. We came to appreciate how disconnected low-income Latino communities were to new high technologies. This motivated us to engage in a pilot project with a coalition of Latino community-based organizations in East Los Angeles known as Eastside Intercambios. The following premises guided our work in this CLNet project. The first was that many in these communities, including the community-based organizations, lacked access to the Internet; second, that because they had no access they needed to become aware of the power of the Internet, the resources available, and the skills and knowledge necessary to navigate it (we now call this information literacy); and third, and just as important, we wanted to challenge these community-based organizations to establish their own web presence; thus we created initial web sites for many of these organizations to get them started. Some might see this kind of activity as being beyond the role of the library, but for us it was part of the reconceptualization of library services for that period.

Intercambios consisted primarily of organizations in the areas of health, education, and job skill development. This collaboration was ideal since we were able to reach many organizations at once rather than attempting to reach each one individually. In this particular situation, the coalition had an interest in learning how to integrate the Internet into their workflow. However, they knew little about what it was and how they could use it. Intercambios has a vision to increase and improve their services by collaborating with each other through the use of technology. They planned to share technical expertise and training materials, as well as to exchange computer parts to help those organizations that lacked the needed equipment. They also intended to use the Internet to improve communication among themselves and to train clients to be able to help themselves. Although this partnership was successful in creating a web presence for many local organizations we were not as successful in other venues. For instance, since most of the organizations were understaffed CLNet had to take on more responsibility then was expected in the coordination of activities for the coalition, which made it difficult to develop self-reliance among the group. Also, many of the key leaders in some of the organizations were resistant to integrating the technology into their workflow, which limited the value of the tools. Nevertheless, CLNet was able to play a key role in directing these organizations to embrace technology as a tool for empowerment. In there own time, they incorporated the new technologies.

Another CLNet partnership, and one of our oldest, has been with the library service association, REFORMA, The National Association to Promote Library and Information Services to Latinos and the Spanish-Speaking. This partnership has evolved through various stages. We began by working with a local chapter of REFORMA. Initially, we trained librarians and other library staff on Internet basics so they could in turn go back to their libraries and use their newly gained skills in answering reference questions, conducting training workshops, implementing community programs, etc. A large portion of these individuals work in public libraries that serve predominantly Latino populations; thus through this partnership we had indirectly reached a vast number of people. This partnership coupled with the Infopeople Project was very effective.[17] Infopeople provided access to the Internet for the REFORMA librarians we worked with and taught about Internet resources for serving the Latino community.

Beyond the training described above we began to develop a website for the Orange County chapter of the organization. At the same time as members of the organization we began to advocate for the national association to develop a website. Eventually REFORMA National adopted the Orange County chapter website as the national site. In addition, REFORMA established a national web team to maintain the site and CLNet provided support for the team. Also at that time REFORMA formed a national Information Technology Committee, which focused on not only how the organization could use technology but set an information technology agenda for the association.[18] The Information Technology Committee also spearheaded an effort to incorporate information literacy in a draft of the American Library Association's "The Role of Libraries in the Networked World."[19]

Eventually, CLNet established a formal partnership with REFORMA National and continues to host its website and discussion list. As an organization, REFORMA has become a strong information provider of web content on how to serve the Latino community, useful not only to its members, but also to other librarians who work with large Latino and Spanish-speaking populations. Gradually, CLNet faded into the distance and the high technologies we advocated and worked to implement became part of the organization.

Our partnership with REFORMA National can be characterized as work with what we call a distributed community, one where its members are located throughout various geographic placess, but bound by formal structures. Our partnerships with distributed communities brought a different set of challenges than those encountered working with place bound communities as later discussed.

The work achieved through CLNet forced us to rethink our initial assumptions. Even while creating good and relevant community content we needed to get more people connected and to become strategic users of new technologies. This was not something that could be accomplished by giving presentations in the community and hosting web pages; it demanded a prolonged and engaged presence. This conclusion led us to the establishment of the Community Digital Initiative.

COMMUNITY DIGITAL INITIATIVE (CDI):
A NEW COMMUNITY PUBLIC SPACE

In 1997, The California Wellness Foundation awarded a major grant to the University of California, Riverside that allowed us to develop the first community technology center in the Riverside area. CDI is one of eleven sites funded by The California Wellness Foundation's Computer in our Future (CIOF) Program that was part of a larger Work and Health Initiative. CIOF represented a unique attempt to develop community technology centers throughout California. The essential elements of the CIOF model consisted of a physical computer center, which provided open Internet access, educational and training programs, links to employment services to its residents, and a nascent effort to engage the local communities in policies which would support community computing.[20]

CDI is located in the heart of a predominantly Latino and African American community in the eastside of Riverside, California. It targets youth and in partnership with local community-based organizations and institutions, it provides access to computer and information literacy training to a sector of society that might not otherwise have access. CDI is housed in the Cesar Chavez Community Center, an active place where different sectors of the local community meet and engage in a variety of social, educational, political, and cultural activities. The Center is a historic building that sits on the Bobby Bonds Park Complex. The City of Riverside Department of Parks and Recreation runs the community center and the park.

Establishing a Digital Learning Place: A Collective Effort

From the beginning CDI was conceived as a collaborative project with multiple community-based organizations. We knew that the success of CDI hinged on the support from and the integration of the community. Drawing from our experience with CLNet, we sought out partners prior to the establishment of the center.

Establishing CDI was a collective process that included a host of partners. The city of Riverside committed resources for electrical and rewiring and cabling of the room where the CDI Lab is located. Using CDBG funds, the county provided resources for two air conditioning units. A local state assembly person was able to raise over $300,000 of state funds for electrical and air conditioning upgrades for the Chavez Center. While CDI was not responsible for all of this revitalization it did serve as a catalyst.

The creation of a state of the art lab was also accomplished through the establishment of philanthropic partners. The Pacific Bell Foundation and outreach department provided funds for ergonomic chairs, tables, and computing equipment that included: a local area network of 22 Pentium computers workstations running Windows NT, a data projector, scanners, digital cameras, digital video cameras, and printers. CDI also acquired a variety of software to support our programs, many from generous donations by Microsoft, Adobe, and Macromedia. We formed partnerships within the university that provided T1 Internet access to the CDI. Through a partnership with the University Library we qualified for the California Teleconnect Fund that provided a telecommunication discount on our T1 service. The UCR Communication Office installed and configured the routers. The UCR Micro Support Office assists with NT support and hardware repair.

While these partnerships were overwhelmingly positive they at times created challenges. In hindsight, the biggest obstacle we faced in opening the CDI lab was working with university and city officials to secure a lease. Key issues were the university's mandate that it not lease space in buildings that are not earthquake proof and the university's objection to the city's indemnification clause within the lease agreement. Initially, it was also a challenge to explain why we were buying so much equipment that was to be located off campus at a community center. These challenges were overcome by hard work, diligence, and support of a forward-looking dean who cut through the red tape. Towards the end of our work in Riverside neither we nor the community were able to convince another dean of the value of the project.

Training Partnerships

Our initial plan was to provide a new comfortable wired place for different community-based organizations to develop individualized uses of high technologies that could support their existing youth programs. As we will note later this view was problematic for a variety of reasons.

We formed several training partnerships with a variety of university and community-based organizations. At the University, we partnered with a local AmeriCorps program. We provided it with technical training and it provided tutors and mentors in our program. We also established a partnership with Upward Bound where we provided training on computer basics, word processing, spreadsheets, information literacy, and Internet basics as well as a more advanced multimedia component where students were instructed on graphics design and video production. We also established partnerships with several community-based job-training efforts including the Greater Riverside Urban League, and a local Campfire Boys and Girls organization. We trained the participants in these programs on computer basics, word processing, spreadsheets, information literacy, and Internet basics. We also provided similar training for a local 21st Century Community Learning Center, People Reaching Out, an anti-violence youth program, the Community Settlement Association (CSA), a long-standing community support organization, which was established in 1911, and the Park Avenue Baptist Church. CDI also developed a training partnership with Easter Seals to train disabled participants. It was a wonderful group for whom technology has opened new doors.

We have heard and read the statistics of unequal access to technology for low-income minority communities, but at CDI we actually met the individuals that represented those numbers. We witnessed the impact that centers, such as CDI, have had not only on technological fluency and critical literacy, but also on building a lived space that promotes a sense of self-empowerment. CDI offers a space that is different from a library or school because it is not constrained by the same limitations that exist in many public institutions. For example, participants spent an average of almost two hours each time they visited CDI. CDI strives to teach youth how to empower themselves and their local communities by providing them with a place where they can use technology to create different types of projects to express themselves. They are encouraged to explore methods of self and community documentation through technology. Outcomes of such projects have resulted in the creation of personal web pages that provide a virtual representation of their lives and communities on the Web. These products and expressions have a clear connection to who they are and where they live. CDI has provided the forum for people who otherwise would not have the means for contributing content to the World Wide Web.

LESSONS LEARNED

Programs First, Technology Second

As we stated earlier, our initial plan was to provide a new comfortable wired place for different community-based organizations to develop individualized uses of high technologies that could support their existing youth programs. The development of a place and space in the community has been highly successful not just in programs offered but as a catalyst for other efforts. However, we failed to understand that the full success of our approach necessitated a revamping of the existing youth programs we sought to include. While we were able to work around this, in hindsight it may have been better to work with fewer organizations and revamp the programs we were attempting to infuse with technology.

Administration Buy-In

The literature on partnerships mentions the importance of administrative buy-in. We have come to appreciate the importance of administrative support. We understand that prerequisites for garnering this support are the responsibility of the program leader. It is vital that administrators understand the program objectives and why they are important. We view the level of administrative buy-in as an indicator of a critical institutional partnership.

Over the nine years we worked on these efforts there was a dramatic variation in the administrative support that our efforts enjoyed. As academic librarians, we enjoyed the freedom to initiate the programs we worked on, as well as the responsibility to generate the funding necessary to carry out our work. Early on one of the directors that had supervisory responsibility over us seemed to be unhappy not to be in charge and able to direct the program. This person went so far as to talk with our funder. Fortunately, the funder was supportive of our efforts and let the director know that if he wanted a project he should summit a proposal. However, over time it became clear that without more administrative support the project would not receive proper attention and would not flourish. At the other extreme, at one point we had the total support of a dean of a college. He opened every door, showcased our programs, and facilitated fund-raising and program implementation for our community-based effort. He got it! Our lesson here is that you need to continually nurture administrative buy-in, but there are times that no matter what you do that support may not be forthcoming. If this occurs, consideration to moving or terminating the effort is in order.

Collaboration Requires Sharing

We were able to establish a wide range of partnerships with community-based organizations. We attempted to develop what might be called a third space. That is a space not controlled by the university or the city but by community-based organizations. We found that while community technology offers an opportunity for unprecedented collaboration within communities, existing institutional loyalties often hinder collaboration. We have found that while we have had success in bringing different entities together, existing and new resources were generally not shared beyond existing institutional boundaries. We worked against this tendency but had only marginal success.

Meaningful Change Requires Sustained Intervention and Incremental Development

Developing a third space that addresses community-based organizations' inadequate access and equipment and training needs is a long-term process. Our earlier efforts that relied on sporadic meetings could not address the equipment, connection, and training needs of community-based organizations. Since we envisioned CDI as a collaborative effort, we spent a good amount of time nurturing those partnerships. In one case, we found that a key partner had serious organizational issues that made it impossible for it to play the role we had jointly envisioned. In this instance, we came to realize that our original goal of adding a technology component to an existing youth-based programs in Riverside, while necessary, was not sufficient because the larger programs we worked with often need to be rethought.

Difference Between Place-Based versus Distributed Communities

We have found a distinct difference in our partnership efforts that are place-based from those which are distributed communities. Our work in developing a community technology center which is by definition place-based called for partners that would collaborate with us in providing access to the Internet and providing information literacy training. Our distributed communities effort which were reflected in our work with REFORMA focused on facilitating this professional association's presence and use of the Web. It assumed that professional association members had access via the libraries they worked in. This distributed community was successful because the members seized an opportunity and over time integrated it into the workings of the association.

Recognizing the Power of Large Institutions

In all of our work, we were mindful that we were often perceived as agents of a large university. Part of the partnership development was articulating a clear understanding of what our goals were, what we could do, and what we could not do. This was often a challenge because several of the community-based organizations that we had worked with had had mixed experiences in working with a large university. They often felt that they were at the mercy of the university. One of the goals in our work was to deliberately engage in efforts that developed the capacity of the community-based organization rather than develop dependency. At the same time, the positive presence and power of a large university often opened doors and created opportunities that may not have been present otherwise.

Importance of Formal Agreements

In the digital world, the definition of ownership is still very fluid especially at the onset of the Internet. This fluidity created some disappointment for us over the years. For example, on occasion, pages from our website were copied by another site without permission or giving CLNet any type of credit. In another incident, we had scanned over fifty color images of artwork for a Web page after receiving permission from the artists that held copyright. Many hours of work went into scanning, re-sizing, and converting these images as well as into the organization of the images. Months after the project had been completed we discovered that someone else had created a web page using all the images we had scanned, including the way we had organized the images, without recognizing CLNet's work. Although we encounter such challenges we believe that creating public websites is important to the development of the infrastructure of Latino Internet resources. However, these growing pains have caused us to establish more formal agreements with our partners.

CONCLUSION

Working beyond the library walls has been both a privilege and an honor. The experience transformed us in many ways. We have come to appreciate that good partnerships are not born but nurtured. We also have learned to appreciate the wide range of resources available in community-based organizations. They are part of the fabric that makes low-income communities information rich. Many of them, like the people they serve, deserve more resources to serve their communities. We want to end by urging more librarians to form new partnerships that address technology gaps in their communities. As Cesar Chavez used to say, "Si Se Puede!"

NOTES

1. Sul H. Lee, *Impact of Digital Technology on Library Collections and Resource Sharing* (Binghamton, NY: The Haworth Press, Inc., 2002) and Fred M. Heath, "Libraries, Information Technology, and the Future," *Resource Sharing & Information Networks* 10 (1995): 1-20.

2. The Chicano Studies Research Library at the University of California at Los Angeles.

3. American Library Association, *The Library Bill of Rights*, (Chicago: ALA, 1948, Amended February 2, 1961, and January 23, 1980, inclusion of "age" reaffirmed January 23, 1996), <http://www.ala.org/ala/oif/statementspols/statementsif/librarybillrights.htm> (July 6, 2004).

4. Bonnie Nardi and Vicki O'Day, *Information Ecologies: Using Technology with Heart*. Cambridge, MA: MIT Press, 1999.

5. Keith Fulton, CTCNet electronic list, April 14, 1999 <http://www2.ctcnet.org/lists/members99/0410.htm> (July 19, 2004).

6. Blanca Estela Gordo, "The 'Digital Divide' and the Persistence of Urban Poverty," *Planners Network Newsletter*, (May-June 2000), <http://www.plannersnetwork.org/htm/pub/archives/141/gordo.html> (July 19, 2004).

7. Saskia Sassen, "Electronic Space and Power," *Journal of Urban Technology* 4 (1997): 9-11. Examples of cyber-segmentation focus on mergers, deregulation and the drive to be the sole data, voice and digital pipe into home that will increase market share.

8. See The Public Access Computing Project. *Evaluation of the U.S. Library Program*. (Seattle, WA: Bill & Melinda Gates Foundation, 2004), <http://www.gatesfoundation.org/Libraries/USLibraryProgram/Evaluation/default.htm> (July 19, 2004). and *Toward Equality of Access: The Role of Public Libraries in Addressing the Digital Divide* (Seattle: WA: Bill & Melinda Foundation, 2004). <http://www.gatesfoundation.org/nr/Downloads/libraries/uslibraries/reports/TowardEqualityofAccess.pdf> (July 19, 2004).

9. For a discussion of library best practices efforts see Joan C. Durrance and Karen E. Pettigrew, "Toward Context-Centered Methods for Evaluating Public Library Networked Community Information Initiatives," *First Monday*, Volume 6, Number 4 (April 2001), <http://www.firstmonday.org/issues/issue6_4/durrance/index.html> (July 19, 2004).

10. Peter Day, "Community Information and Community Technology: Policy, Partnership and Practice," in *Using Community Informatics to Transform Regions*. Edited by Stewart Marshall, Wal Taylor and Xinghou Yu. (Hershey, PA: Idea Publishing, 2004): 18-36.

11. See Wendy Lazarus and Francisco Mora, *Online Content for Low-Income and Underserved Americans: The Digital Divides New Frontier*. (Santa Monica: The Children's Partnership, 2000), <http://www.childrenspartnership.org/pub/low_income/low_income.pdf> (July 19, 2004).

12. Romelia Salinas, "CLNet: Redefining Latino Library Services in the Digital Era," In *Latino Librarianship*, (Jefferson, North Carolina: McFarland, 2000): 228-240 and Romelia Salinas, "Building Virtual Communities: Latino Organizations in an Urban Setting," *Community Networking Conference Proceedings*, (Taos, NM, May 1996), 121-124. <http://www.laplaza.org/about_lap/archives/cn96/salinas.html> (July 19, 2004).

13. Richard Chabrán, "Mapping Emergent Discourses: Latino Bibliographic Services in Academia," *Alternative Library Literature 1986-87: A Biennial Anthology*. Edited by Sanford Berman and James P. Danky (Jefferson, NC: McFarland & Company, 1988): 116-119.

14. Louis G. Tornatzky, Elsa E. Macias, and Sara Jones, *Latinos and Information Technology the Promise and the Challenge*. (Claremont: Tomas Rivera Policy Institute, 2002), <http://www.ibm.com/ibm/ibmgives/downloads/Latinos_and_IT.pdf> (July 19, 2004).

15. Los Angeles County Online, <http://lacounty.info/overview.htm> (July 8, 2004).

16. Ibid., executive summary.

17. Infopeople <http://www.infopeople.org/> (July 19, 2004). Infopeople is a California State Library project geared to providing Internet access in public libraries. Although CLNet never developed a formal partnership with Infopeople it was a project that assisted us in our work.

18. For examples of ITC's work see <http://www.reforma.org/ITC> (July 19, 2004).

19. Salinas, Romelia, "Reforma Adds its Voice to ALA's Principles of the Networked World," *Reforma Newsletter* 21 (2002): 7, 14.

20. Linda Fowells and Wendy Lazarus, *Computers In Our Future: What Works in Closing the Technology Gap?* (Los Angeles: Computers In Our Future, 2000), <http://www.ciof.org/report-rls.htm> (July 19,2004). Also see Albert Fong and Josh Senyak, *Ten Lessons for Your New Community Technology Center Getting a New Perspective on Your CTC* (San Francisco: CompMentor, June 20, 2000), <http://www.techsoup.org/howto/articlepage.cfm?ArticleId=163&topicid=12>.

Community Collaborations
at Work and in Practice Today:
An A to Z Overview

Julie Beth Todaro

SUMMARY. This paper provides background and practical suggestions for creating and nurturing community partnerships. *[Article copies available for a fee from The Haworth Document Delivery Service:
1-800-HAWORTH. E-mail address: <docdelivery@haworthpress.com> Website:
<http://www.HaworthPress.com> © 2005/2006 by The Haworth Press, Inc. All
rights reserved.]*

KEYWORDS. Community collaborations, partnerships, community
partnerships

Community collaborations abound in the professional literature of social
work, adult education, basic literacy education, religious or church work, and
among governing entities to name just a few environments. Collaborations
and partnerships are, in the broadest sense, connections between and among
people and groups to share interests and concerns, and create visions for the
future.

Julie Beth Todaro is Dean, Library Services, Austin Community College, 1212 Rio
Grande, Austin, TX 78701 (E-mail: jtodaro@austincc.edu).

[Haworth co-indexing entry note]: "Community Collaborations at Work and in Practice Today: An A
to Z Overview." Todaro, Julie Beth. Co-published simultaneously in *Resource Sharing & Information Networks* (The Haworth Information Press, an imprint of The Haworth Press, Inc.) Vol. 18, No. 1/2, 2005/2006,
pp. 137-156; and: *Libraries Beyond Their Institutions: Partnerships That Work* (ed: William Miller, and
Rita M. Pellen) The Haworth Information Press, an imprint of The Haworth Press, Inc., 2005/2006, pp. 137-156.
Single or multiple copies of this article are available for a fee from The Haworth Document Delivery Service
[1-800-HAWORTH, 9:00 a.m. - 5:00 p.m. (EST). E-mail address: docdelivery@haworthpress.com].

http://www.haworthpress.com/web/RSIN
© 2005/2006 by The Haworth Press, Inc. All rights reserved.
Digital Object Identifier: 10.1300/J121v18n01_11

Historically, collaborations and partnerships have been formed to educate, open discussion, and address and solve problems among all parties involved and affected as well as stakeholders in all parts of the problems/issues and solutions.

Collaborations are created when:

- there appears to be no one person or group responsible for the issue
- it doesn't seem possible to solve the problem or address the situation by just one group due to magnitude, lack of knowledge, or amorphic nature of the issue
- there is a high cost of solving the problem or addressing the issue, and/or
- it is important to have a large number of people involved to educate and have good buy-in to the process.

The best collaborations are those (either formal or informal) that:

- Have an organization or a structure to them
- Have a vision, mission, and goals
- Are designed to change as issues evolve and problems are solved
- Find ways to involve people face-to-face but make maximum use of emerging and existing technologies
- Build in a sustained maximum activity and involvement by stakeholders and other participants
- Provide necessary plans such as business plans, marketing plans and communication plans
- Promise and produce a product or results which benefit all group/process members
- Design an active and interactive initial learning period and maintain ongoing learning for stakeholders and participants
- Establish and maintain effective communication and ongoing dialog.

Collecting examples of community collaboration and community partnerships in libraries has always included a wide variety of definitions and examples, but in the last five to seven years the genie has escaped from the bottle. Definitions are being expanded and "redefined." Examples are almost too many to list and are certainly an extensive range for study for benchmarking and best practice. While this growth in collaborative initiatives and environments is exciting and at the same time, daunting, library managers are concerned that some parameters and measurements are established to provide communities and librarians a ground floor for discussion. This ground floor might attempt to establish definitions, benefits for collaborators, benchmarking elements, and best practices to begin looking for, the possible downside to collaboration, corner-stones to use as building blocks, and resources to provide, promote, and support success.

DEFINITIONS/TERMS

One can consult an attorney or pick up a law book for the most formal of language. And, outside the legal interpretations, a multitude of definitions apply. In general however, the more *informal* terms are:

- Outreach
- Cooperation
- Liaison
- Facilitators/facilitated, facilitations
- Arrangements
- Relationships

Outreach

An older term, outreach in both public and academic libraries has historically meant identifying, locating, and reaching out to serve typically eligible clients or patrons but non-users. Contemporary use in public libraries remains primarily the same; however, in academic libraries it is now used more for identifying, reaching out, and establishing partnerships to serve potential users heretofore unable to access or use resources. Outreach K-12 or K-16 responsibilities are being articulated by colleges and universities and articulations include assigning outreach to specific departments or individuals and/or hiring someone to coordinate or complete those responsibilities.

Cooperation

The term cooperation meaning a "common effort" or an "association of persons for common benefits" (Merriam-Webster 2004) is often used to establish a foothold for future more formal arrangements and to assuage fears of a more formal restrictive environment. Only when the term is linked to "agreement" or "arrangement" does it typically denote the formal situations.

Liaison

The term liaison means "communication for establishing and maintaining mutual understanding and cooperation" (Merriam-Webster 2004). An organization establishing a liaison relationship has established specific communication responsibilities for someone in the organization to work with someone in another organization or partnership. Typically, this is not a formal agreement of *mutual* behavior, but rather behavior of only one "side." Liaison relationships, however, often lead to more formal agreements.

Facilitators/Facilitated, Facilitations

Facilitators or facilitated services are designed "to make easier" and to "help bring about" (Merriam-Webster 2004). As an informal term they often indicate an initial commitment on the part of an organization to offer a resource or service or streamline access that might not be easily accessible to users or non-users.

Arrangements

Arrangements are considered informal relationships between or among organizations or partners. Having an arrangement for use of a service or an access point often denotes no written paperwork but just a "handshake" that solidifies what is to occur. Defined as "an informal agreement or settlement" in *Merriam-Webster Online*, arrangements, if successful, often lead to formal agreements.

Relationships

Defined as "connecting or binding participants in a relationship" (Merriam-Webster 2004), relationships are used as informal arrangements. They also often denote an unwritten or handshake situation where organizations are communicating about the issue and deciding how to proceed, but not formalizing activities.

More *formal* terms include:

- Collaborations
- Consortia/consortium
- Agreements
- Contracts
- Partnerships
- Joint use

Collaborations

One of the oldest terms used in the profession is collaboration. This term is used to denote a formal process that includes working jointly with others "especially in an intellectual endeavor" or "cooperating with an agency or instrumentality with which one is not immediately connected" (Merriam-Webster 2004). Collaboration as a term is used for a wide variety of things including "librarians collaborating with classroom faculty for integrated information literacy instruction" which certainly wouldn't be a process that would need a Memorandum of Understanding or a contract; however, when organizations articulate that they are "collaborating" with another group, it indicates a formal process of exchanging information, resources, or services.

Consortia/Consortium

A very formal term, a consortium indicates an "agreement, combination, or group (as of companies) formed to undertake an enterprise beyond the resources of any one member" (Merriam-Webster 2004). Consortia, in existence in libraries for many decades, are formal business agreements for sharing or providing resources and services. Often using "consortia" as a term means partners or members might be of unequal status while cooperatives indicate more equal status.

Agreements

In an agreement there is "harmony of opinion, action, or character," or "an arrangement as to a course of action" (Merriam-Webster 2004). The more formal agreements are "a contract duly executed and legally binding." The term agreement is often linked to both formal and informal descriptors or terms such as a "cooperative agreement" or a "consortia agreement." This use most often refers to the actual paperwork executed that outlines the rules of order for behavior.

Contracts

The most formal of terms, a contract is "a binding agreement between two or more persons or parties; *especially*, one legally enforceable," or "a business arrangement for the supply of goods or services at a fixed price" (Merriam-Webster 2004). Contracts are the cornerstone of formal arrangements and are found most often when arrangements involve money and resources and ownership. Money issues can also be tangential. For example, an initial service may not involve money but may eventually entail user fees, or fines collected. Contracts can be written *exclusive* of money being expended or outlined as part of the process for the use of goods or services.

Partnership

Partnership is the "more friendly" and more often used word both in the professional literature and in practice for the more formal arrangements. A partnership can be defined as any project in which someone "partnered with another organization on programs or activities to accomplish a common goal" (Merriam-Webster 2004). As a more positive term, it implies by its very nature an equal footing for all involved. Not all formal agreements denote equal footing or even need to denote equal footing.

Joint Use

Joint use is also referred to as *shared space* and *co-location*. This (typically dreaded) partnership is becoming more common and examples include:

- Community college and 4-year university which build one library
- Co-design and funding of multiple higher education environments to serve distributed or distance learning students
- Public and academic libraries built to serve two (or more) population bases
- Public and school libraries built to serve two (or more) population bases
- Public and academic or public and school which partner to provide one service within another existing building.

In review of the literature what is most commonly found and what is described as working the best is when one organization takes the lead in design and financial arrangements and responsibility for the project and the other organizations "contract" or purchase services that they assist in designing. In the past two years, however, several longer-term projects have reached fruition and represent organizations take a dual/balanced set of roles/responsibilities.

Memorandum of Understanding

The MOU is a method of establishing and documenting partnerships, most commonly those in a consortial arrangement. It can be a document of incorporation or a method of outlining agreements between or among libraries or institutions. It is an umbrella for other vital documents including:

- vision and goals
- organization
- governance

- member responsibilities
- group responsibilities for services
- resources (more specific articulation of objectives and strategies)
- e-resource and data rights and responsibilities
- documents relating to access of information as well as borrowing/access
- fiscal rights
- responsibilities and obligations
- other elements such as local, state, regional or federal laws that apply.

Other terms that may be used synonymously for discussing serving patrons from one library in another include articulation agreements, guidelines for service, patron/client support agreements, universal service agreement, affiliation agreements, statement of service, service commitments, cooperative service agreements, and service plan.

WHAT'S IN IT FOR THEM AND WHAT'S IN IT FOR US?

There are literally dozens of reasons to partner or collaborate. Reducing the ideas to a few key phrases creates a simple list that includes:

- Maximize resources
- Economize
- Solve a problem
- Make money for the umbrella institution
- Indicate worth for services within an environment
- Give good/better customer service
- Create an information literate community
- Meet a need
- Change an image
- Create a need that should be there
- Do a good deed
- Provide access to . . . information . . . resources . . . buildings . . . services . . . experts
- Serve the un-served . . . the underserved (new and existing service and non-service populations)
- Build community.

Although all professionals would like to believe that all collaborations are established to most importantly and ultimately benefit the customer, user, and/or patron, the reality is that collaborations *must* provide benefits to all collaborators and partners either sooner or later in the process of designing and maintaining relationships. In listing benefits, however, one should note the following statements:

- Not everyone views or values "benefits" in the same way. What is a benefit to one environment or type of library or in one part of the country may not be a benefit elsewhere.
- Just as political agendas, administrations, services, and members of the community or public change, so do benefits. That is, what works well and what benefits are realized under one leader may not work or be realized under another.
- Projects have "lives," that is a project may live and be successful and grow and then the project, activity, service or partnership, the benefit, may die a natural death.

That said, what *are* some of the benefits? For purposes of this overview, the content has been arranged by sections that include the library itself, the libraries' umbrella institution and the community or patron/users/potential users. The reality is that many benefits are the same in each area.

LIBRARY BENEFITS (ALL TYPES OF LIBRARIES)

- An increase in the network of institutional/library supporters (grassroots support) for activities and future needs (bond issues, funding battles, legislation, etc.) as well as support for the partnership activities themselves.
- An increase in the information network that increases/improves services for library/information patrons.
- Visibility for library services/activities as well as visibility for partnership and collaborative activities.
- Energize library staff with new activities, new recognition, new services, and possible new skills.
- Greater knowledge base of people who "know" what the library is and what it can do.
- Increased dollars to, for example, increase access for new partners, expand collections for different patrons, etc.
- Public relations and marketing opportunities for "new" or "cutting edge" approaches to solving problems.
- A possible opportunity to discover and access new services and unique collections which in turn would increase collection size and design and create new collections and ways to access.

- Possible increase in staff to handle new arrangements/temporary or permanent.
- Gaining new skills for staff such as opportunities to gain leadership and management skills.
- Expanding and enhancing staff roles.
- Expanding a volunteer base.
- Expanding a fundraising base.
- Expanding a base for trustee, board, friends positions and relationships.
- Possible access to a high profile demographic customer base.
- Expanded extensive communication systems.
- Possible gains in expertise that may have been lacking in such areas as marketing, technology, and finance.
- Prized relationships with community leaders and other influential people.

LIBRARY UMBRELLA INSTITUTION
(CITIES, COUNTRIES, ACADEMIC INSTITUTIONS,
BUSINESSES, K-12 ENVIRONMENTS)

- Recognition of the variety of roles that libraries play, both traditional and non-traditional, in the life of the organization as a whole.
- Opportunity to form internal partnerships and collaborations as well as external roles.
- In higher education, increased enrollment in the institution as families view higher education as more accessible and "possible."
- In K-12 environments, the opportunity for staff to learn about, work with, and bring "in" the parents of children as well as to meet them in other parts of the community and workplace.
- Forming a base to justify local/statewide funding as others view partnerships as efficient and effective use of money.
- Consistent and effective instruction in 21st century learning/skills needed.
- Opportunity to access unique collections/services and information.

COMMUNITY

- A smarter, more prepared 21st century community.
- Economic and efficient expenditure of public money and/or realized cost savings through shared facilities, services or activities (a benefit possibly realized by all environments involved).

- A more knowledgeable community who see opportunities in information environments and maximizes resources.
- A more solidly networked and informed community and everyone now knows what the others are "doing."
- Creation of network of people to "make things happen."
- Opportunities for one-stop shop approach for providing community resources.
- Discover of what organizations and institutions have in common and shared values.

WHAT ARE IDENTIFIED AREAS OF CONCERN IN COLLABORATIONS? WHEN DOESN'T IT WORK?

Although the professional literature typically focuses on collaboration and partnership successes, professional e-lists and conference discussions, among others, indicate that for every success there are just as many failures. Failures can include:

- Projects that don't go anywhere
- Projects that come from ignorance (think of ALL the money and time we'll save)
- Projects that are forced on one partner or collaborator
- Projects that are delivered as ultimatums (you won't get what you need or you won't get anything unless you take this)
- Projects that began and fizzled out due to lack of interest
- Projects that began but organizational elements such as management failed
- Projects that began but collaborator/partner leaders changed and new leadership was not committed to continuation or success
- Projects that failed because patrons/customers didn't use all or part of the services or activities offered
- Projects that began but support from partners was pulled such as financial support.

AND WHAT ARE THE ELEMENTS OF FAILURE?

A Bad Fit

Some organizations are the right fit and some are the wrong fit. Wrong or bad fits are often immediately apparent but climates, politics, or available resources force the connection. For example, don't form a partnership if the organizational missions don't coincide at least in some part. Don't form a partnership to "cash in" on available grant monies if the grant guidelines are too directive. The project may not be sustainable post grant and building a partnership or cooperative relations on, for example, soft money that is more restrictive than permissive is not worth the effort. Consider informal cooperative small projects with no long-term commitments to see if your partners and/or your environment are a good fit. How do you "recognize" wrong fits? Review "when it doesn't work" and use it like a planning checklist. Ask your planning members to assess the presence of "doesn't work" elements and use these as starting points to discuss possible wrong fits.

Lack of Clarity/Misunderstandings

Communication is critical throughout any process; however, collaborative communication is extremely critical in the earliest stages. Using third party, unbiased facilitators or group/process leaders, hammer out what expectations are and what all planning group members want. Any process should be accompanied with written documents that explore missions, values, pert charts, decision trees, goals, outcomes, budgets, and assessment and evaluation tools. Every process should have a glossary or set of definitions for each organization, a pre-agreement, process documents, maintenance agreement, as well as maintenance of effort and then a divorce document with "custody" discussions. Write everything down! Detailing every partner's set of responsibilities or job description as well as establish user profiles before and after the agreements. The less discussion, the more verbal agreement, the greater the chance for lack of understandings.

Turf Concerns/Loss of Identity

Many collaborators are overly protective of their turf and the turf of their users, customers, or patrons. For whatever reason they are concerned, including loss of patron base, loss of finances, loss of status, and loss of their identity, etc. Therefore, all "turf" must be defined and discussed early in the process. Explorations must include collaborations that value and protect turf if turf is a major issue. Turf is often the reason why groups choose to pilot a project rather than planning for greater collaborations. In addition, turf may drive a group to choose to work side by side rather than join entities or organizational elements.

Dislike Change

Although disliking change is hardly the reason to ignore or cease discussions for partnerships, it *is* a real issue is many organizations and with many governing groups, administration, managers, and staff. Although solutions should include discussing change in and of itself, groups can and should also work to phase changes in, minimize changes at the beginning of the process, and plan closely for largely disruptive changes.

Time Is Money

Any discussions for partnerships and collaborations take time and time is money. Organizations must carefully plot who does what and how much time is spent for the entire process to avoid uneven commitments of time, which contribute to the lack of clarity and misunderstandings.

Money/Costs

Although most elements of failure discussions include budgeting and finance, the issues are important enough to identify more specific needs. These needs, where money is concerned, include establishment of financial calendars along with decision making calendars; early discussions on costs should include all cost elements such as in-kind, out of pocket, existing, and future needs. Costs should be discussed at each major meeting to ensure people are moving appropriately and groups should have independent financial consultants or overseers, specifically in the beginning of the project. In addition, future, ongoing support must be articulated, if only in the most general sense, early in the process. All aspects of money should be discussed including loss and gain of monies should partnership occur; variances in costs from funders; restrictions on how funds might be spent (resources or patrons); and, any salary and operating funding issues.

WHAT ARE CRITICAL RESOURCES, SERVICES, AND/OR ACTIVITIES TO USE AS CENTERPIECES FOR SUCCESSFUL COLLABORATIONS? (EX., INFORMATION LITERACY, ACCESS TO RESOURCES, BASIC LIBRARY SERVICES)

Most organizations join together to make things better for their patrons. Although this idea is simplistic in and of itself, often the simpler approach is the better one. Groups wanting to partner often do best by partnering with their strengths, attempting to join together in a project mode, letting staff explore working relationships for projects first rather than administrators leading organizations or even forcing organizations. Many of the most successful collaborations have been successful because of their focus on a specific element of their mission or their service. For example:

- Focus on a customer . . . both organizations serve some aspect of this person's life and together the groups can better serve (specific groups) . . . the one-stop service for the patron for reference, the single catalog of resources, the single interface for customers to use e-resources, the single adult program series.
- Focus on a unique service or resource of value to many . . . an information literate community is the better community so the two main libraries in a community can work together to offer seamless delivery of information literacy training, web environments are combined to provide standardized training for patrons across organizations, and access to a unique or special collection is made available to many, such as the business resources of an academic library being opened to the small business and community public library patrons.
- Focus on a strength . . . one organization is technologically astute or has resources superior to other groups; therefore it will partner to lead the others into updated, technological services . . . computer centers are opened to other patrons during certain hours, staff of one organization train staff and patrons of another . . . one organization provides access to wireless technology.

Focusing on a specific element of a partnership allows for easier evaluation, a preliminary look at greater partnerships based on success, a focus on customers or patrons more often than not (although two groups may form a staff development or training partnership which works to serve staff but ultimately serves the patron).

WHAT ARE CRITICAL PROCESS ELEMENTS TO USE IN PLANNING COLLABORATIONS?

Identifying, approaching, educating, maintaining, and appreciating collaborators and partners is everything. Even if a few original or even lofty goals are not met in the end, the process of bringing people together to discuss the critical issues can be the single most important element of the process. It is also critical that these steps be possible with non-existent, limited or only in-kind revenue to insure that all sizes of communities can realize a measure of success.

Identifying Possible Partners

- Environmental scanning for stakeholders and data on stakeholder environments
- Group brainstorming of organizational leaders and staff from a variety of levels of the organization
- Assessment and comparison of community marketing/commercial data and community group information:
  - Missions
  - Goals
  - Marketing plans/advertising
  - Strategic initiatives
  - Annual reports

Approaching Partners Identified

- Invitational letters for participants with invitations to discuss rather than partner initially
- Considering having some partners invited by designated community or organizational leadership
- Pre- and during meeting/event education of invitees to organizational missions, etc. (using documents gathered in the identification steps).

Maintaining Partnership Discussion

- Communication plan established for process with "e" (including lists and blogs), print, and in-person guidelines and resources
- Creating one timeline for discussions out of all timeline considerations by possible partners
- Creating decision trees and PERT charts for doing business within a specific plan of action
- Provide the widest possible samples of good and bad partnerships with written information and speakers AND consider field trips
- Discuss scenarios of budget options that include a variety of funding options:
  - Budget 1–no money
  - Budget 2–in-kind contributions and some money

- Budget 3–healthy resources (funding at a good level for one or more years)
- Budget 4–significant resources (funding is easily sustainable for many years)
- Establish an entity for the partnership with mission, vision, and goals for the partnership or collaboration no matter how big or small the initiative is
- Establish a "personality" for the initiative, that is, name it, have a logo, celebrate it, create a website
- Adopt a problem-solving model
- Adopt a conflict resolution process
- Discuss group dynamics information
- Provide ongoing team or group training with group member job descriptions
- Use outside facilitators throughout the process.

Appreciating Possible Partners

- Assessing needs of participants for appreciation for participation . . . asking what do they need to continue
- Appreciation plan of action including post press releases, letters to employers, supervisors, participants, and idea list for private/public recognition.

EXAMPLES OF COLLABORATIONS A-Z
(MINIMAL TO MAXIMUM INVOLVEMENT)

Academic Libraries

The constant 21st century changes in higher education environments are forcing librarians to rethink their vision and mission and institutional role, restructure their image or "re-brand" themselves, reposition themselves within the higher education environment, and redistribute some expertise and energy into the broader community. *Academic libraries* are playing a major role in this new higher educational environment by extending their reach and "designing new reaches" through strategic partnerships, collaborative relationships, and mutually beneficial alliances and creative ventures. These activities update/change their image, share their expertise, and promote their services. Many libraries, in order to successfully partner, are assessing older mission and goals statements and designing broader vision, mission, and goals to match the changing institutional vision and to play a leadership role in partnerships. Higher education libraries are:

- Expanding their roles of support for students, faculty and staff
- Expanding their role and the marketing of their role in providing critical general education and specialized instruction
- Articulating and marketing their expertise as librarians-as-discipline/department liaisons
- Becoming increasingly involved in campus wide interdisciplinary programming and cross-departmental partnerships such as college orientation, career counseling
- Increasing their marketing for their service and expertise in research support
- Creating a role of assistance in institutional enterprise activities, and
- Moving out beyond campus walls to provide and partner with a wide variety of groups and individuals.

Public Libraries

The constant 21st century changes in the public arena are forcing *public library* librarians to rethink their vision and mission and institutional role, restructure their image or "re-brand" themselves, reposition themselves within city and county government and community life. Public libraries, longtime supporters of the "whole" community, are now finding they must partner with others in order to offer complete up-to-date services. Public libraries are:

- Creating new public librarian teaching roles critical to working with the new info-laden public
- Expanding their role and the marketing of their role in support small businesses and community enterprise
- Articulating and marketing their expertise as information specialists
- Becoming increasingly involved in community workforce departmental partnerships such as job fairs, career information, and
- Realizing they must create a formal educational support role for distance learning.

School Libraries

The constant 21st century changes in K-12 education environments are forcing *school librarians* to rethink their vision and mission and school/educational role, reinforcing their teaching role responsibility and image, reposition themselves within their schools' and districts' technology arena, and educate themselves and their patrons on relevant and available resources in the broader community.

School libraries are playing a role in this new collaborative environment by thinking outside their box for strategic partnerships and becoming involved in discussions/collaborative relationships for themselves and their students/patrons. School libraries are:

- Expanding their roles of instructional support for students, faculty and staff
- Articulating and marketing their expertise as librarians-as-discipline/department liaisons
- Becoming increasingly involved in school interdisciplinary programming and cross-departmental partnerships, and
- Moving out beyond campus walls to provide and partner with a wide variety of groups and individuals.

General Partnership Examples

- Joint projects and programs with other child- and family-serving agencies dealing with information sharing including use of books, database information, web-based information, and other library resources regarding nutrition, health, and other related issues
- Organize workshops/resource days when information professionals move among types of libraries to experience breadth and depth of resources for their clientele
- Plan/attend general education/training/development for all types of librarians
- Partner to explore information literacy partnerships for seamless delivery of information/user education throughout a community
- Organize workshops on parenting for particular groups such as teen mothers, grandmothers, foster parents using library resources/expertise
- Design web environments for special partners (university web pages for college bound, community children, etc., . . . public library web pages served to guide distance learners . . . school library pages for distance learners . . . all serving home schoolers
- Design access/resource delivery for area home schoolers . . . tours . . . home-school reference hours . . . reference pass/referral
- Offer specialist/experts' day . . . a day when hobbyists, special interest groups can visit, see unique resources, get unique tours, specialized reference . . . open collections usually not open

- Open resources/unique help to book groups/clubs/special groups/sponsor or co-sponsor author programs
- Plan library experiences with resources for caregivers and family day home providers
- Partner together to offer space for family literacy sessions for students/families of students
- Create a resource and special training center for childcare personnel, especially home visitors, social workers, daycare, and Head Start, with well-organized videos, articles, games and other materials
- Offer programs or resources or special web pages for grandparents and others on how to tell real-life stories based on their own experience or folk tales from former homelands or family history and genealogy
- For a special event . . . enlist and train staff to work with parents or other volunteers to read and tell stories to children in some of their native or "home" languages for which your library or other area library staff have no speakers
- Create special tour days for K-12 environments
- Hire a K-16 coordinator/pull a committee together to handle resource access/information literacy
- Involve your staff parents/caregivers in summer programming offered by the library with other organizations such as museums, park programs, zoos . . . have academic library or school libraries sponsor parts or programs of the area public library summer reading club
- Design intergenerational programs in which children and parents/caregivers learn to use and understand the importance of new information technology
- Develop local programs patterned after successful national models such as "Born to Read" and F.A.T.H.E.R.S.
- Sponsor job fairs for local workforce
- Participate in community "read" programs/hold your own community reads (Cleveland, Detroit, Austin)
- Sponsor a family night at the higher ed library . . . once a quarter . . . once a month . . . let kids see firsthand what parents do . . . receive expert help with homework . . . partner with local school and public librarians so all staff are represented
- Partner with area librarians to design community web interface/end user pages
- Initiate resource centers where parents/families can connect with help lines, health information, computer training, employment and housing information. Recruit young adolescents to promote these services at

home and in the neighborhood, perhaps providing some incentive for bringing adults in

- Provide technical assistance/training to youth and family workers health, personnel of community departments such as police, parks, and recreation to fill them in on how libraries can collaborate to support their efforts with 10-14 year olds. Share outcomes with parents/caregivers
- Hold a "get acquainted" program for officials/staffs of community-based organizations serving young adolescents and their families to make them aware of library resources for themselves and the kids they work with. Provide lists of suggested activities involving library programming and resources linked to the community-based organizations' goals
- Work with leaders from Chamber of Commerce, service clubs, criminal justice, business, and others to match academic library staff, public library and school library staff with young adolescents with mentors who will serve as positive role models for staying in school, getting good grades, and contributing to the community . . . create an "information" or web partner like a "big brother"/"big sister" program
- Set aside a special area for teens seeking relief from the noise and chaos of their homes and streets . . . once a month . . . twice a semester . . . have an annual teen or youth day
- Create volunteer and other opportunities such as a youth advisory board for young teens to get involved in planning and producing library programs for their peers . . . for academic freshmen . . . create your own library orientation group for teens thinking of coming to that school
- Sponsor workshops in collaboration with resource local businesses, social and other agencies on such subjects as healthy physical and mental lifestyles, self-reliance and self-care . . . and areas such as economic development/small business
- Encourage leaders of youth organizations both adults and youth to hold meetings in the library and make use of library materials
- Join with other agencies to sponsor temporary or permanent youth resource centers which combine library and community resources such as counseling and youth employment, with a leisure center, "a place to go" for socializing, enjoying music, games and snacks, cruising the Web, and other youth-produced programs for personal enhancement . . . in the public library . . . in the academic library . . . in the local Y or in the Boys and Girls club
- Sponsor classes for local area librarians . . . or younger patrons on web design . . . tech classes in general
- Partner to discuss resources and services for virtual or digital sharing

- Partner to apply for local, state for federal funding to initiate or expand partnerships
- Partner to discuss purchasing processes and plans that maximize cooperative purchasing of e-resources and broad community access to those resources
- Open computer rooms for training area professionals/special community groups
- Link all area websites together and/or design one user interface for all or part of area online resources accessible
- Establish an e-list for all area professionals for threaded discussions or host Web chats or bulletin boards for posting area concerns including exchange of information about area school assignments as they move from school to public . . . college to public . . . etc.
- Have one organization host a training website for links unique/designed for area professionals for virtual collaboration for training
- Design print information centers on all area library services for every area library
- Adopt neighborhood projects
- Library staff members use their expertise to guest lecture for community groups and often work with local service groups on a consulting basis.

SHOULD YOU PARTNER AND COLLABORATE?

You already are.

The trick to making things work is for organizations to establish control mechanisms to insure that all partners are being dealt with fairly and all partners realize the maximum benefits available to them.

REFERENCES

Farmer, Lesley. 1999. *Partnerships for Lifelong Learning.* Worthington, OH: Linworth Publishing.

Illinois State Library. 1995. *Library Partners.* Illinois: Illinois State Library.

Laughlin, Sara. 2000. *Library Networks in the New Millennium: Top Ten Trends.* Chicago: American Library Association.

Lynch, Sherry. 1999. *The Librarian's Guide to Partnerships.* Fort Atkinson, WI: Highsmith Press.

Merriam-Webster Inc., *Merriam-Webster Online Dictionary,* 15 April 2003, <http://www.m-w.com/netdict.htm> (2004).

Managing the Grey Literature of a Discipline Through Collaboration: AgEcon Search

Julia Kelly
Louise Letnes

SUMMARY. AgEcon Search, http://agecon.lib.umn.edu, is an important and ground-breaking example of an alternative method of delivering current research results to many potential users. AgEcon Search, through a distributed model, collects and disseminates the grey literature of the fields of agricultural and resource economics. The development of this widely-used Web resource was possible through the cooperation between academic institutions, academic libraries, professional associations, and government agencies. This article will provide examples of other collaborative efforts, outline the development of AgEcon Search and its proposed growth into AgEcon Search International, and discuss the prototype it provides for other disciplines. *[Article copies available for a fee from The Haworth Document Delivery Service: 1-800-HAWORTH. E-mail address: <docdelivery@haworthpress.com> Website: <http://www.HaworthPress.com> © 2005/2006 by The Haworth Press, Inc. All rights reserved.]*

Julia Kelly is Reference Librarian, Magrath Library, University of Minnesota, 1984 Buford Avenue, St. Paul, MN 55108 (E-mail: jkelly@umn.edu).

Louise Letnes is Librarian, Waite Library, Department of Applied Economics, University of Minnesota, 1994 Buford Avenue, St. Paul, MN 55108 (E-mail: lletnes@umn.edu).

[Haworth co-indexing entry note]: "Managing the Grey Literature of a Discipline Through Collaboration: AgEcon Search." Kelly, Julia, and Louise Letnes. Co-published simultaneously in *Resource Sharing & Information Networks* (The Haworth Information Press, an imprint of The Haworth Press, Inc.) Vol. 18, No. 1/2, 2005/2006, pp. 157-166; and: *Libraries Beyond Their Institutions: Partnerships That Work* (ed: William Miller, and Rita M. Pellen) The Haworth Information Press, an imprint of The Haworth Press, Inc., 2005/2006, pp. 157-166. Single or multiple copies of this article are available for a fee from The Haworth Document Delivery Service [1-800-HAWORTH, 9:00 a.m. - 5:00 p.m. (EST). E-mail address: docdelivery@haworthpress.com].

KEYWORDS. AgEcon Search, grey literature, digital repositories, agricultural economics, economics

INTRODUCTION

AgEcon Search, http://agecon.lib.umn.edu, is a subject repository of working papers and conference papers in agricultural and applied economics. Established in 1995, it has always relied on collaborative relationships among libraries, professional organizations, and other interested groups.

Agricultural economists have a long tradition of producing grey literature, mainly in the form of working papers, which are organized in series sponsored by academic departments and other agencies. This "preprint culture" existed for many decades before the advent of the Internet, but the World Wide Web provided the medium to enhance the availability and organization of this literature via scholarly respositories (Luzi 1998, 130-139). These repositories also introduced a new environment for collaboration.

Scholarly digital repositories have many positive aspects from the perspective of faculty or researchers, including greater visibility and impact of their work, the ease of use, and availability of current material for their students (Gutteridge and Harnad 6/5/2004; Johnson 2002, 6/5/2004). It has also been noted that faculty members prefer access to electronic versions of documents, and that free online availability increases the impact of a paper (Friedlander 2002; Lawrence 2001, 6/04; Harnad et al. 2004, 6/5/2004). Scholarly digital repositories, whether they are focused on the work of a single institution or a subject discipline, introduce opportunities for librarians in a number of areas:

- Collaboration–with individual faculty members, departments, professional organizations, and other librarians
- Bibliographic enhancement and control–making it much more likely that a document can be located
- Open access–providing documents free of charge
- Organization–gathering a critical mass of material on a topic, and providing searching and browsing capabilities
- Preservation–changing the ephemeral nature of the print grey literature

The importance of involving librarians in the development and maintenance of digital repositories is noted by Huwe in his article about the University of California's Social Sciences eScholarship Repository (Huwe 2002, 38-42).

This paper will focus on the collaborative opportunities for libraries that are involved in development and maintenance of various types of grey literature repositories, using AgEcon Search as an example.

INSTITUTIONAL REPOSITORIES

Institutional repositories are "digital collections capturing and preserving the intellectual output of a single or multi-university community" (Crow 2002). The materials contained in an institutional repository may be in a variety of media, and often go beyond scanned documents to include data sets, photographs, and other digital objects.

The forces that are driving this relatively new movement include an interest in changing the current system of publisher-controlled scholarly publishing, the hope of highlighting the intellectual output of the university, and an attempt to locate and preserve materials that have often been overlooked in the academic environment. In some cases, they are seen as "part of the digital infrastructure of the modern university" (Ware 2004, 6/5/2004).

Libraries often play a large role in the development of institutional repositories, and in some cases, they are the driving force behind them (Smith 2004, 6/5/2004). Opportunities for collaboration between libraries and other campus units may come in several forms. Library staff may be active in recruiting departments or individual faculty members to participate, and they may define the standards or procedures for submissions. They may work with technical staff, trouble shooting, developing protocols, and selecting the software, as well as assisting individual researchers.

SUBJECT-BASED REPOSITORIES

Subject repositories of grey literature provide libraries even wider opportunities for collaboration than institutional repositories. Partnering can take place with academic departments, other libraries, research institutes, government agencies, professional organizations, foundations, and individual faculty members. Following are a few examples of subject repositories that have been built with a library/librarian as either the project leader or as a partner in a support role. The most robust subject archives exist in areas where there was already an established "paper-based preprint culture"–economics, computer science and physics (Ware 2004, 6/5/2004).

- RePEc (Research Papers in Economics) (http://repec.org) is a freely accessible, decentralized database of working papers, conference papers and journal articles. RePEc was developed (and is still maintained) by volunteers including economists, librarians, and computer specialists from several institutions worldwide. The goal of RePEc is to promote scholarly communication in economics and related disciplines. Individual institutions maintain an archive of the electronic publications and RePEc provides information and links to this information through RePEc Services such as IDEAS (http://ideas.repec.org). Presently over 100,000 documents are available online with over 300 archives providing information to RePEc. In addition to links to the archives of academic institutions, government institutions (such as the Federal Reserve System), research institutes (such as the National Bureau of Economic Research), RePEc has collaborated with professional organizations such as the Econometric Society, the American Economic Association, and the Royal Economic Society to provide electronic access to annual conference proceedings (NetEc 2004).
- PhilSci-Archive (http://philsci-archive.pitt.edu) is a multi-institution repository housed at the University of Pittsburgh. The center was established through the efforts of faculty from the Department of Philosophy and the Department of History and Philosophy of Science at the University. The current collaborators for this archive are the Center for Philosophy of Science at the University of Pittsburgh, the Philosophy of Science Association, and the University of Pittsburgh's University Library System. PhilSci contains over 600 documents including conference papers and reprints and is offered as a free service to the entire philosophy of science community. The goal of the service is to provide rapid dissemination of new work (University of Pittsburgh 2004).
- Digital Library of the Commons (http://dlc.dlib.indiana.edu) includes a working paper archives for the international literature of the commons, common pool resources and common property. Collaborators on this project include the Indiana University Digital Library Program and the Workshop in Political Theory and Policy Analysis, a research center at Indiana University drawing faculty from economics, political science, psychology, business, and public/environmental affairs. The goal of this global depository is to provide free access to scholarly research about human management of the commons to the developed and developing world. Scholars involved in this project are also collaborating with Makerere University in Uganda to test the creation of digital libraries of the commons for other research sites (Indiana University 2004; Indiana University-Bloomington Libraries 2003).

- DLIST (Digital Library of Information Science and Technology) (http:// dlist.sir.arizona.edu) is a project of the Arizona Health Sciences Library and the School of Information Resources and Library Sciences at the University of Arizona. This electronic subject repository contains published and unpublished papers, reports, and data sets in the fields of library and information sciences and information technology. Areas of emphasis include information literacy and infometrics. The service is freely available to the public (University of Arizona 2004).
- SPIRES HEP (Stanford Public Information Retrieval System) (http:// www.slac.stanford.edu/spires/hep) contains bibliographic information on preprints, e-prints, conference papers, journal papers and other reports in the field of high-energy physics. The system is managed and maintained by Stanford University's Stanford Linear Accelerator Center Library. SPIRES HEP collaborated with a central repository of full-text physics papers developed at Los Alamos National Lab (LANL) to link their bibliographic information to the electronic records provided at LANL (O'Connell 2002, 6/5/2004). "Through these linkages . . . each forum is made more useful than it would be without the other" (Kling, McKim, and Kling 2003, 47-67). Other collaborators include Deutsches Elektronen-Synchrotron and Fermi National Accelerator Laboratory, providing a broad base of resources of interest to the high-energy physics community. Currently, the database includes over 400,000 records with about half linked to full-text documents (Stanford University 2004).

LITERATURE OF AGRICULTURAL/APPLIED ECONOMICS

The agricultural economics profession has followed the path of the economics profession in the distribution of its literature via working paper series. Working papers, sometimes called discussion papers or staff papers, are first releases of research/policy findings and are distributed to peers as a form of informal review. Many of these papers were copies of presentations made at meetings of professional associations. After informal review, the information in the working papers is usually refined, shortened, and submitted for publication in the more traditional outlets for research reporting–usually scholarly journals. This working paper exchange initially took place in paper format with copies mailed either to colleagues who requested them, or to highly regarded researchers, in hopes of a review. This print-based working paper world was difficult and expensive to manage and maintain–both for libraries that attempted to collect this literature and for institutions that prepared and disseminated the papers. Many of the working paper series were never included in the major indexes for academic literature (CAB Abstracts, EconLit, AGRICOLA), making it among the most difficult of grey literature to locate and obtain. Huwe states that "working papers themselves retain historical and substantive value. Indeed, working papers are a record of intellectual inquiry that may gain value with time, instead of losing it" (Huwe 2002, 38-42). The fact that this working paper culture already existed has eased the development of electronic subject repositories to manage this literature. This elusive literature was a natural for dissemination via the Web.

AgEcon SEARCH BACKGROUND

AgEcon Search was launched in 1995. Its main focus has been to collect electronic working papers, conference papers, and other types of grey literature in applied economics (principally agricultural and resource economics) and to make that material available on the Web through a single search engine. The intent was to facilitate knowledge exchange of "work in progress" research and to archive this grey literature.

AgEcon Search is currently housed at the University of Minnesota, jointly sponsored by the Department of Applied Economics and the University Libraries. Over 80 academic institutions, associations, and government agencies contribute documents. The database currently holds over 14,000 items with over 600,000 paper downloads in the past 3 years.

STRUCTURE OF AgEcon SEARCH

AgEcon Search was organized to make the process for submitting, receiving, indexing, and mounting incoming papers as cost-effective as possible. The majority of the workload is placed on those submitting materials. Submitters follow an online submission process that elicits all the information necessary to mount a paper into the database. At most institutions a designated person serves as the AgEcon Search contact. This person gathers papers, verifies that the format is correct and submits the papers. This means that on the receiving end the paper needs little attention–just an approval of the submission form and the paper is available to the public. For projects that require more work (creating PDF files, scanning papers, etc.), the institution is asked to make a contribution toward the cost of staff time. Projects that have chosen this route are from organizations where individual members are submitting their own papers, or from organizations that want their journal articles scanned and archived on AgEcon Search.

GROWTH OF AgEcon SEARCH THROUGH COLLABORATION

AgEcon Search has been a collaborative venture since its beginning in 1995. Initially the collaboration involved the University of Minnesota Libraries and the University of Minnesota's Department of Applied Economics. Both provide a percentage of a librarian's time, and several hours of student help per week. Technical support comes from the University Libraries.

In 1995, the goal of the project was to disseminate electronically the working paper series prepared by many university agricultural economics departments in WordPerfect format via a Gopher server. Initially agricultural economics papers from the University of Minnesota and the University of Wisconsin were posted. Luckily, the World Wide Web and Adobe Acrobat PDF software became widely available at this time and made the database much easier to maintain.

At this point, the project took on many more collaborators. A library organization, AERO (Agricultural Economics Reference Organization) was approached for endorsement and participation. The members provided both–many new institutions papers were added at the encouragement of each institution's AERO member. The AERO group also provided a sounding board for new ideas, literature to include, and funding sources.

Next to join the effort was the American Agricultural Economics Association (AAEA)–the main professional organization for agricultural economists in the U.S. The executive board of the organization was impressed with the potential usefulness of such a service and decided to encourage members to deposit their institutional working papers in AgEcon Search. In addition, the AAEA provided funds for the coordinators of AgEcon Search to attend their annual meeting and host a booth in their exhibit hall–as well as funds to gather and post the selected papers from their annual conference on AgEcon Search. This funding has continued throughout the years with the AAEA becoming a true collaborator in the electronic dissemination of the grey literature of agricultural economics.

Other early collaborators included the Farm Foundation and the U.S. Department of Agriculture, Economic Research Service both of whom provided start-up funding for the project, viewing the service as a rich resource for their various audiences.

The database has grown from its initial collection of working papers and conference papers to also include journal articles and other digital collections.

This expansion was made possible by another set of collaborators–the regional agricultural economics associations, which publish the journals, and the AAEA Foundation, which financially supported the regional associations in their efforts to digitize their journals.

The following journals have been digitized and posted to AgEcon Search:

- Agricultural and Resource Economics Review
- Journal of Food Distribution
- Journal of Agricultural and Applied Economics
- Journal of Agricultural and Resource Economics

The full run of the journals minus their current year or two is available. The University of Minnesota Applied Economics Department has digitized its entire Staff Paper series (1969-present) for inclusion on the database. Michigan State University, Department of Agricultural Economics has digitized and posted all of the Plan B Master's Degree research papers done in its department since 1963. The database has also grown internationally to include papers from many countries other than the United States.

Another important collaborator continues to be the Farm Foundation. It provided funds to have AgEcon Search digitize and post its annual Increasing Understanding of Public Problems and Policies Conference Proceedings (1951-present), as well as several of its other annual conference proceedings. It also gave the coordinators a grant to attend an international meeting of agricultural economists as the first step toward AgEcon Search International.

AgEcon SEARCH INTERNATIONAL

Although the initial focus of AgEcon Search was the digitization of working papers from universities in the U.S., we are now moving beyond those borders to include papers from around the globe, and to encourage the use of the resource by students, researchers, and policy makers in every region. To move toward that new goal, we looked to current partners, and sought out new ones.

The International Association of Agricultural Economists was the perfect partner in the professional association category. At its meeting in 2003 in South Africa, it invited AgEcon Search to have an exhibit, publicized the service in the daily newsletter, and provided space to hold an interest group meeting. It also gave funds to mount the contributed papers from the meeting on AgEcon Search. Other associations have publicized AgEcon Search in their newsletters and on their Web sites.

A growing number of academic institutions from Europe, Asia, and Africa are submitting their working papers, and we are working with a few of them in hopes that they will become AgEcon Search "affiliate centers" for their regions, gathering documents and publicizing the service.

Library colleagues are proving to be important links in our effort to have a more global reach. Individual librarians have helped submit papers from their institutions, advised us about cultural practices in their countries, and assisted in promotion. Formal and informal associations of librarians are spreading the word about AgEcon Search, and suggesting additional institutions that might want to participate.

Non-government organizations are a new group of partners. They carry out much of the agricultural research and policy development in parts of the world. In addition to contributing their working papers to AgEcon Search, they are also publicizing the resource and encouraging other groups in their countries to do the same.

CONCLUSIONS

From our work in AgEcon Search, it is clear that a range of collaborators can strengthen a project and help it grow well beyond any initial expectations. The input from groups outside your home institution is valuable, particularly the professional associations in the field. The profession's feeling of ownership of the project is critical, since it is their literature, and can vary so much from discipline to discipline. Members of the association have contacts with colleagues that are invaluable, and they have a perspective that can help the resource grow in the most productive way possible.

REFERENCES

Crow, Raym. The case for institutional repositories: A SPARC position paper. Scholarly Publishing and Academic Resources Coalition. Washington DC, 2002 [cited 6/5 2004]. Available from http://www.arl.org/sparc/IR/ir.html.

Friedlander, Amy. Dimensions and use of the scholarly information environment. 2002 [cited 6/5 2004]. Available from http://www.clir.org/pubs/reports/pub110/contents.html.

Gutteridge, Christopher, and Steven Harnad. *Applications, potential problems and a suggested policy for institutional e-print archives.* Available from http://eprints.ecs.soton.ac.uk/archive/00006768/.

Harnad, Stevan et al. 2004. *Nature Web Focus: The green and the gold roads to Open Access.* Available from http://www.nature.com/nature/focus/accessdebate/21.html.

Huwe, Terence K. 2002. Social sciences E-prints come of age: The California Digital Library's working paper repository. *Online* 26, no. 5:38-42.

Indiana University. Digital Library of the Commons. 2004 [cited 6/5 2004]. Available from http://dlc.dlib.indiana.edu.

Indiana University-Bloomington Libraries. Digital Library of the Commons Earns Mellon Support. In Indiana University-Bloomington Libraries. 2003 [cited 6/5 2004]. Available from http://www.libraries.iub.edu/index.php?pageId=280&checkNewsId=49&year=2003.

Johnson, Richard K. 2002. Institutional repositories: Partnering with faculty to enhance scholarly communication *D-Lib* 8. http://www.dlib.org/dlib/november02/johnson/11johnson.html.

Kling, Robert, Geoffrey McKim, and Adam Kling. 2003. A Bit More To It: Scholarly Communication Forums as Socio-Technical Interaction Networks. *Journal of the American Society for Information Science and Technology* 54, no. 1:47-67.

Lawrence, Steve. 2001. Nature Web Debates: Free online availability substantially increases a paper's impact. *Nature* 411. Available from http://www.nature.com/nature/debates/e-access/Articles/lawrence.html.

Luzi, Daniela. 1998. E-print archives: A new communication pattern for grey literature. *Interlending and Document Supply* 26, no. 3:130-139.

NetEc. RePEc: Research Papers in Economics. 2004 [cited 6/5 2004]. Available from http://repec.org.

O'Connell, Heath B. 2002. *Physicists Thriving with Paperless Publishing*. Available from http://library.cern.ch/HEPLW/6/papers/3/ed.

Smith, MacKenzie. 2004. *DSpace for E-print archives*. Available from http://library.cern.ch/HEPLW/9/papers/3/ed.

Stanford University. SPIRES HEP (Stanford Public Information Retrieval System). 2004 [cited 6/5 2004]. Available from http://www.slac.stanford.edu/spires/hep.

University of Arizona. Digital Library of Information Science and Technology. 2004 [cited 6/5 2004]. Available from http://dlist.sir.arizona.edu.

University of Pittsburgh. Phil Sci Archive. 2004 [cited 6/5 2004]. Available from http://philsci-archive.pitt.edu.

Ware, Mark. 2004. Nature Web Focus: Universities' own electronic repositories yet to impact Open Access. *Nature*. Available from http://www.nature.com/nature/focus/accessdebate/4.html.

Collaborative Training in Statistical and Data Library Services: Lessons from the Canadian Data Liberation Initiative

Charles Humphrey

SUMMARY. New technology and knowledge push organizations to upgrade and improve the skills of their staff. Paying for professional develop programming is a common way of providing continuing education. This article describes a collaborative training program introduced to develop baseline competencies in Canadian academic libraries to support data services. In conjunction with an initiative between Statistics Canada and sixty-six Canadian universities, a data literacy program has delivered thirty workshops over a seven-year period training librarians how to provide services for statistics and data. A cost-sharing arrangement keeps these training expenses to a minimum for individual universities. *[Article copies available for a fee from The Haworth Document Delivery Service: 1-800-HAWORTH. E-mail address: <docdelivery@haworthpress.com> Website: <http://www.HaworthPress.com> © 2005/2006 by The Haworth Press, Inc. All rights reserved.]*

Charles Humphrey is Head, Data Library and Academic Director, Research Data Centre, Humanities and Social Sciences Library, 1-01 Rutherford South, University of Alberta, Edmonton, Alberta T6G 2J4 Canada (E-mail: humphrey@datalib.library. ualberta.ca).

[Haworth co-indexing entry note]: "Collaborative Training in Statistical and Data Library Services: Lessons from the Canadian Data Liberation Initiative." Humphrey, Charles. Co-published simultaneously in *Resource Sharing & Information Networks* (The Haworth Information Press, an imprint of The Haworth Press, Inc.) Vol. 18, No. 1/2, 2005/2006, pp. 167-181; and: *Libraries Beyond Their Institutions: Partnerships That Work* (ed: William Miller, and Rita M. Pellen) The Haworth Information Press, an imprint of The Haworth Press, Inc., 2005/2006, pp. 167-181. Single or multiple copies of this article are available for a fee from The Haworth Document Delivery Service [1-800-HAWORTH, 9:00 a.m. - 5:00 p.m. (EST). E-mail address: docdelivery@haworthpress.com].

http://www.haworthpress.com/web/RSIN
© 2005/2006 by The Haworth Press, Inc. All rights reserved.
Digital Object Identifier: 10.1300/J121v18n01_13

KEYWORDS. Professional development, data services, competency training, data literacy training, Data Liberation Initiative, Canada, collaborative training

The Canadian National Site License Project (CNSLP), launched in 2000 by sixty-four Canadian academic libraries, has been a widely publicized and successful collaborative venture.[1] Through this initiative, over 2,000 scholarly journals in the sciences, engineering, and medicine have been licensed for desktop delivery to staff and students at participating institutions. Portrayed as a digital library project, the substance of the CNSLP consists of a bundle of online full-text and bibliographic databases. If one has heard of a Canadian national academic library collaborative project, it likely has been the CNSLP.

However, a few years before the CNSLP, another national collaborative initiative had successfully established affordable access to Statistics Canada data for teaching and research purposes. Known as the Data Liberation Initiative (DLI),[2] this program enrolled sixty-six institutions in a subscription service providing access to statistical databases, public use microdata,[3] and geography files.[4] Hundreds of items exist under these product groupings (known as standard data products), which Statistics Canada sells publicly on an item-by-item basis. As a package, the total cost of this collection is in the hundreds of thousands of dollars. The DLI was established so that academic libraries could access these data through a flat fee that all member institutions could afford. Prior to the DLI, no single institution had acquired the complete collection and only a few of the better-endowed institutions had meaningful portions of the collection. Organized collectively, this resource became accessible to all participating libraries regardless of the size of their institution or their collections budget.

Many of the stories regarding library consortia are associated with resource sharing, such as the CNSLP mentioned above. Indeed, the formation of the DLI also consists of a story about building a service to share resources. A tremendous amount of energy was invested over a forty-month period from 1992 to 1995, mobilizing the political will to establish a mechanism to provide access to Statistics Canada's standard data products. Representatives from the academic community and government agencies worked together to influence the appropriate powers within government to establish a five-year pilot period for the DLI. Following a successful evaluation of this pilot, the program was established as a permanent service in 2001. The experience of building a relationship between a government agency and the academic library community is an integral part of this resource-sharing story.[5]

This article, however, focuses on a data literacy initiative implemented in conjunction with the DLI to provide professional development to staff at member institutions who were assigned the responsibility of providing local support for DLI resources. This particular story has been chosen for two main reasons. First, the data resources available through the DLI are not typical library materials. Traditionally, academic libraries collect, organize, and manage the outcomes of research, such as journal articles and books. The content of the CNLSP, for example, taps mostly materials disseminated from the outcomes phase of the research cycle. The resources available through the DLI, however, represent the evidence upon which research outcomes and new knowledge are based.

The digital resources in the DLI are the raw information that fuels much of Canadian social, economic, and population health research. Data were an unknown resource to many librarians when their institutions first subscribed to the DLI, causing library management challenges in both technical and reference services. While statistical information in print has long been part of the collections of academic research libraries, the organization of statistical information in digital format and the necessity of processing data before it is of use to others presented a new frontier for many libraries. By comparison, full-text databases generally do not require the user to compile and analyze the texts before the material can be accessed. Statistical databases and microdata do, however, require this kind of manipulation.

Confronted with the challenge of a non-traditional resource in their collections, library management faced the question: "What do we need to do to support DLI resources?" Unlike a full-text or bibliographic database that can be incorporated into an existing collection of online databases, statistical databases and microdata require additional skills by those providing reference and technical support as well as computational skills by patrons working with these resources. Library management needed new options to answer their question.

Second, the managers of the DLI program faced a similar conundrum. To be successful, the DLI needed to attract and retain enough academic libraries in the program to keep subscription costs at an affordable level. Furthermore, the resources available through the program needed to be easily accessible to member libraries and readily useable by their patrons. The DLI management found itself asking: "What do we need to do to help libraries support DLI resources?" The success of the DLI was contingent on the program's data resources being of value to libraries and being used by the staff and students at member universities.

A collaborative literacy program was developed after the first year of the DLI operation addressing key aspects of the two questions posed by management in libraries and the DLI. However, before a training program could be planned and implemented, pressure arose over an issue of equitable access to the DLI collection by all member libraries. This issue had a direct relationship to staff development and training.

THE DLI CONTACT AND THE ISSUE OF EQUITABLE ACCESS

As a subscription service, the rules by which all members in the DLI must abide are laid out in a license. This document stipulates the conditions under which DLI data may be used and who is authorized to access these data. To comply with the license, Statistics Canada requires each member institution to designate a DLI Contact who serves as the person not only responsible for administering the license locally, but also for downloading resources from a central data server. Requiring each member institution to have a DLI Contact and controlling who has access to the central data server establishes this as a mediated service. While some universities employ authenticated web services to disseminate DLI resources locally or with partner universities, the DLI Contact remains an essential requirement of membership. Consequently, the DLI Contact is instrumental in the provision of local services and in the long term, the local success of the DLI program.

Near the end of the first year of operation, download-count statistics from the central data server revealed an uneven usage pattern among member institutions. Furthermore, correspondence on an e-mail discussion list established for DLI Contacts suggested varying levels of difficulty with the service among this group. These two indicators raised concern that access was uneven due to unequal skill levels among DLI Contacts. Furthermore, DLI management worried that these uneven skill levels were a risk to the program because of the focal role that DLI Contacts play in the operation of the program.

It should be noted that about twenty-five of the sixty-six subscribing institutions had some experience with data in their libraries prior to the DLI program. Data had been introduced as a library resource earlier through two Canadian federations in the Inter-university Consortium for Political and Social Research (ICPSR)[6] and a collective purchase of data from the 1986 and 1991 Canadian Censuses organized by the Canadian Association of Research Libraries (CARL).[7] Within this group of libraries, eight institutions had well established data services prior to these collective memberships.

The uneven usage of DLI resources at the end of the first year of operation was partially due to the fact that approximately a third of the members in DLI had some prior experience with data in their libraries and could make use of the DLI resources more quickly. This was borne out in the statistics showing institutions with prior data experience downloading more data. Since one goal of the DLI was to create a level playing field for all member institutions, the need to establish a baseline of competency across the DLI Contacts was seen as a necessary step in making the program uniformly equitable.

Establishing a skill baseline for DLI Contacts and addressing the concerns of library and DLI management about what should be done to support data proved to be the motivation in organizing a data literacy program supported by the DLI.

ORGANIZATION HAS AN IMPACT ON COLLABORATION

The DLI was promoted early in its inception as a partnership between the academic community and Statistics Canada. This proved to be a novel relationship between a federal agency and the academic community. Both parties contribute revenue to the program's operation and a governance structure was established bringing together representatives from the agency and the academic stakeholders. Together, the members of this governing committee, known as the External Advisory Committee (EAC), set the program's budget and determine its policies and procedures. This Committee encouraged the creation of a data literacy program for DLI Contacts and made training a priority by providing funds through the DLI operating budget.

This overall governance structure proved to be an important factor in developing a literacy program for DLI Contacts. Once the case for training was presented, the decision was made quickly to plan and implement a literacy program. Because both parties have representation on the EAC and could allocate funds immediately to support this activity, the literacy initiative proceeded without administrative delay. This experience is an example of the importance of the organizational structure in initiating a collaborative project. Sharing representation on a governing board that has the authority to set priorities through a budget can accelerate the launch of a collaborative program. The planning for the initial training program began in December 1996 and the first instruction was delivered five months later.

BUILD ON THE SUCCESS
OF EARLIER COLLABORATIVE PROJECTS

As mentioned above, two groups of Canadian academic libraries joined the ICPSR as members of federations prior to the start of the DLI. The initial federation represented institutions affiliated with the Council of Prairie and Pacific University Libraries (COPPUL), which has a well-established history of cooperative library projects.[8] Under the auspices of COPPUL, thirteen university libraries applied for a federation membership in the ICPSR in 1993. As part of this group's COPPUL agreement, training was slated annually for those providing data services and member institutions–on a rotation basis–would take turns hosting the training event. Furthermore, library directors at these institutions agreed to fund travel expenses for their staff to attend these annual sessions. Because there was no training budget, institutions hosting the workshops provided computing labs and meeting rooms without charge. Peers did all of the instruction without compensation. The content of the training was determined by polling members and once this was determined an instructor was found from within the group to teach the material. An e-mail discussion list was created to facilitate communications between training sessions. It was a bare-bones operation but successful because of the sense of shared mission among those providing data services in the federation's thirteen academic libraries.

The first training session of the COPPUL data services group occurred in December 1992, six months before the ICPSR federation became official. This session focused on preparing staff to handle ICPSR data and on planning their local data service. The COPPUL data group met a total of five times before the first DLI workshop in 1997. It continues to meet annually now in conjunction with DLI training. The training experiences of the COPPUL data services group and the second Canadian ICPSR federation served as models for the DLI literacy program.

Following the go-ahead given by the EAC in late 1996 to begin a national DLI training program, useful ideas were gleaned from the training done by the two Canadian ICPSR federations. In particular, these programs had confirmed that training in this area had to come from within the data services community. No one else in Canada was offering professional development in library data services. None of the library schools in Canada offered permanent courses on this subject. Furthermore, none of the continuing education courses offered through professional associations provided this instruction. There was a reason that library management was puzzled over what to do with data in their libraries. Data as a library resource was not covered in the curriculum of library education. To fill this void, the curriculum would have to come from the professionals working in the field.

BUILD ON SIMPLE AND WELL DIRECTED PRINCIPLES

A small committee of three members from the EAC was assigned the task of recommending a data literacy program. Drawing from the experiences of the two Canadian ICPSR federations and training done through the International Association of Social Science Information Service and Technology (IASSIST), this committee began by identifying seven simple, clearly stated training principles.[9]

- Training under this program is being conducted specifically for (1) DLI Contacts at participating universities, (2) the staff who will provide services for DLI data at these institutions, and (3) Statistics Canada staff directly involved in the support of DLI.

The group targeted for this training was very specific. No confusion exists about who is to be trained. Planning for the program has been very directed because the audience has been so clearly defined. In the years since this principle was established, other audiences have been identified who would benefit from instruction about statistical and data services, including colleagues in reference services, library management, Statistics Canada management, and patrons of data services. This is a much larger mandate than is supportable through the DLI literacy program. To reach other audiences, new partnerships will need to be built. The DLI might contribute to the training of these new groups, but to remain true to this original principle, its training focus will remain on those closest to providing DLI data services.

- Training will be provided to all of those eligible under the first principle through a variety of formats, including subsidized workshops that are delivered regionally.

This principle underlines a factor that is paramount to the Canadian context. Many nation-wide initiatives are organized regionally in Canada because of its bilingual heritage and vast geography. Within the DLI literacy program, four regions are recognized: Atlantic Canada, comprised of Newfoundland, Nova Scotia, Prince Edward Island, and New Brunswick; Quebec; Ontario; and the West, consisting of Manitoba, Saskatchewan, Alberta, and British Columbia. The territories of the Yukon, North West Territories, and Nunavut form a fifth region but are not part of the DLI program because no universities are located in this part of the country.

In addition to the linguistic, logistic, and historical reasons for grouping Canada into four regions, one data-relevant motivation also existed. The original distribution of data services prior to the DLI was not uniform across Canada. As mentioned above, there were only eight institutions with data services prior to 1990. This distribution was split between Ontario and the West, with none in Atlantic Canada or Quebec. Consequently, the regions without established data services did not have champions to serve as local mentors. By the time the DLI literacy program was initiated, the base of established data services had broadened across the country through the ICPSR federations and the CARL consortia. Nevertheless, the culture of data services in two of the four regions lagged behind the other two. Therefore, the training needs were more remedial in some parts of the country and expertise had to be built to establish regional mentors.

There are at least two other realities expressed in this principle. First, a variety of methods exist for delivering instruction. This principle recognizes the validity of a mixture of methods, but in-person workshops have been the preferred instructional method. To create a culture of data services, a sense of community must be built among the professionals who work in this area. The experiences of the two ICPSR federations demonstrated the effectiveness of in-person workshops in establishing community.

Second, holding in-person workshops entails costs, which can become a barrier to attendance if these expenses are passed on to the participants. This training principle endorses subsidized workshops to help defray the expenses incurred in training. Each region faces its own cost factors to host an in-person workshop. For example, travel costs are the largest factor in the West. In Atlantic Canada where the travel distances are shorter, these costs are less of a concern (except for those traveling from Newfoundland). To address these differences, block subsidies were created for the regions to allocate in a way that best encourages participants to attend workshops.

The development of subsidies in the DLI training program has usually been employed as a cost-sharing mechanism with individual institutions. For example, in the West, an economy airfare is offered to one person from each member institution to participate in a DLI-sponsored workshop. The expectation is that the university will provide the costs of accommodations and meals. This does not prevent an institution from sending more participants. The instruction is free; there are no registration fees. However, the subsidy is only for one person per institution.

- Training will address concerns appropriate both to small and large institutions.

Redressing the equity issue mentioned earlier about access and use of DLI resources became part of the DLI literacy mission. Not all institutions started from the same point and the size of the institution appeared to be an important factor in separating those who were leading from those who were following. Therefore, attention was given to the curriculum to ensure that the content was not biased in favor of large institutions.

Other reasons exist for potential inequities among member institutions. For example, a little over a third of the institutions are research universities offering graduate degrees. The others tend to be undergraduate institutions where four-year degrees are the priority. Instructional and research uses of DLI resources differ and consequently, the services supporting data vary depending on an institution's primary mandate. While data services are relevant both for teaching and research, the challenge of the data literacy program is to ensure that fair treatment is given in both contexts.

Initially, a benign bias existed toward research applications of DLI resources largely because individuals from the research universities were providing much of the instruction. Their context placed a stronger weight on research uses of data, which ended up being reflected in their teaching. Even their examples of instructional uses of data tended to be about research methods courses. As more of the DLI Contacts at smaller institutions received training, they began to swing the balance toward a middle ground between research and teaching. This was noticeable in Atlantic Canada where a majority of the universities are four-year degree institutions. The training in this region introduced a number of topics relevant to those supporting data in smaller institutions. In particular, they were showing the instructional relevance for data as well as its value to research.

- Whenever possible, trainers will be recruited from the existing Canadian data library community with the expectation that those who are trained may some day be called upon to train others. This perspective operates on the principle that as one learns, one will teach.

As mentioned previously, the only instructors for training in data services were the professionals in the field. Peer-to-peer training had proven to be successful in the cases of the Canadian ICPSR federations and was endorsed as a principle in the DLI literacy program. Instructors could have been recruited from related fields. For example, survey specialists from Statistic Canada would be likely candidates to teach. However, the perspective about the knowledge or information that is relevant differs between the person providing data services, such as a DLI Contact, and the person who is involved in the collection of the data for a major survey. DLI Contacts can undoubtedly learn important information from survey specialists, but the relevance of the information needs to be framed by the librarian. For example, the survey researcher may need to know how to calculate a coefficient of variation (CV) table but a DLI Contact only needs to know why a CV table is important to a patron. Pairing a survey specialist with a librarian who provides the relevance to data services has been used with success in some workshops.

The notion that "as one learns, one will teach" instills a sense of steward-ship in the development of the field of data services. This approach makes ev-eryone partially responsible for the future of the profession. It also strengthens the community by emphasizing the importance of peer relationships. There is no pretentious hierarchy of experts in the DLI community.

A pool of eight instructors was recruited in 1997 to serve as lead instructors. With two instructors from each region, a train-the-trainers workshop was held to plan the inaugural regional workshops and to prepare teaching materials. Some of these lead instructors were also observers at workshops taught by fel-low trainers prior to leading their regional workshops. In 2004, a new genera-tion of trainers was assembled to renew and strengthen the process.

- All training will be conducted from a "service" perspective, that is, from a point of view that focuses on the clientele of DLI data. The purpose of this training is to prepare data services staff to assist university clients with DLI data.

Peer-to-peer instruction is an effective approach when imparting informa-tion and knowledge about a field that is not part of the formal education sys-tem. However, to be relevant, the nature of the work needs to be kept in the forefront. In the case of the DLI Contact, the nature of the work is "service." As mentioned earlier, the very design of the DLI program makes it a mediated service with the DLI Contact as the person between the supplier of the statisti-cal information and the end user. This is a perspective that is quite different from that of a person responsible for producing and releasing data and a person looking for some data to answer a question.

Furthermore, the goal of the DLI literacy program is not to turn librarians into statisticians or social scientists. Rather, the goal is to provide librarians with knowledge about data and skills to work with data so that they can deliver better service.

- The first training priority is to establish a basic level of data service skills for all participating institutions. This training shall be considered the en-try level for supporting DLI data and more advanced training shall build upon this basic level. Priorities for the advanced levels will be deter-mined by the needs of those supporting DLI and by the evolution of DLI.

To establish equity of access to DLI data across institutions, an initial task of the DLI literacy program had to be the establishment of a baseline of com-petencies. This consisted of a mixture of knowledge about DLI resources and skills to locate, retrieve, and work with these products. Defining these competencies has changed over the years as the technology behind DLI products has changed. As a consequence, the minimum skills to be an effective DLI Contact need to be regularly monitored.

This principle also recognized levels of service that can be provided locally. Many DLI Contacts wear multiple hats on their job and are responsible for several services. This is particularly true at smaller institutions where there are fewer librarians to cover a wider range of responsibilities. The larger research libraries tend to have specialists who look after one specific area, such as data. Therefore, a specialist with the time as well as the resources can develop a wider range of services for DLI products. The expectation is that DLI Contacts receive the level of training that enables them to help their patrons at the level of service that their institution provides.

- A global curriculum plan will guide the course content that is offered through this program. The DLI External Advisory Committee will be responsible for maintaining this plan and for periodically reviewing its content and direction.

The responsibility for the DLI literacy program ultimately belongs to the professionals who are providing library data services. Operationally, however, financial support for this training is made available through the DLI program where the EAC has final accountability. In 2003, the EAC formalized the structure of its literacy program, which had existed on an ad hoc basis over the previous six years. An Education Committee was given formal terms of reference and the composition of its membership was defined. This Committee reports to the EAC and makes recommendations regarding changes to the DLI literacy curriculum. The membership of the Education Committee consists of at least one person from each region who currently sits on the EAC and one of the region's training coordinators. Each region has two training coordinators who are responsible for organizing an annual DLI workshop in their region. This includes preparing a budget for the block grant that the EAC must approve. The members of the EAC from a specific region along with their regional training coordinators serve as the selection committee to fill vacant training coordinator positions in their region. Altogether, these administrative changes institutionalize practices and procedures to stabilize the DLI literacy program.

The above seven principles provided the guidelines by which the DLI literacy program was implemented. They also served as a touchstone in dealing with a seemingly paradoxical situation: how to facilitate decentralized training activities while satisfying strong centralized training goals. As described above, differences already existed across regions that had to be addressed regardless. Letting the regions tackle their own issues within the framework of the training principles seemed prudent while also providing them with some financial assistance to achieve national training objectives. The goal of establishing a baseline of skills among DLI Contacts across regions remained a national objective that was pursued through an educational committee working closely with all regions.

THE OUTCOMES OF COLLABORATION

Over the seven years since the first regional DLI workshops were held in 1997, thirty training sessions have been conducted, including one national event in 2003.[10] Institutional participation rates at these events have been at eighty percent or higher, indicating that the training is valued at the local level. Furthermore, workshop evaluations show a high level of satisfaction by those attending the training. Over the years, usage statistics of DLI resources have steadily increased. An independent evaluation of the DLI in 1999 attributed continued growth of the DLI to ongoing training.[11] This study also discovered a strong endorsement for training by library directors and librarians.

Education Committee discussions were begun in 2003 regarding providing better assessment of the competency levels of those providing data services. Evidence through the positive feedback given by DLI Contacts does suggest that the training has been viewed as relevant and well-delivered. Also, anecdotal reports from DLI Contacts indicate that the training they have received is helping them do a better job. However, no systematic assessment has been done to determine the level of skills attained. The Committee is now reviewing options that may include awarding continuing education credits or conferring a certificate to those who have demonstrated a specific skill level.

COLLABORATIVE PROFESSIONAL DEVELOPMENT PROGRAMS ARE A VIABLE OPTION

Providing professional development opportunities for employees has become an important service in the operation of today's organizations, whether public or private. To keep up with new technology and knowledge, organizations expect employees to remain current by regularly upgrading their skills.

An organization that does not offer staff development or training benefits runs the risk of falling behind. As part of the economy's knowledge sector, libraries also face these demands to keep the skill levels of their employees current.

A survey conducted in 2001 by the American Library Association found that academic libraries in institutions offering four-year degrees invested 1.5 percent of their payroll on staff development and training. This figure is not far from the average reported for American businesses in 1999, which was 1.8 percent of payroll.[12] Academic libraries in the U.S. appear to invest in the development and training of their staff at a rate similar to American businesses. Using expenditure statistics from the 2002 survey of libraries by the Association and College Research Libraries (ACRL), a rough estimate of the amount spent on professional development and training is $2.6 million.[13] In the aggregate, this is a substantial investment in human capital through these types of programs.

The DLI literacy program is an example of offering specialized skill training employing a collaborative model. Libraries that have encouraged professional staff to participate in this program have incurred only a small fraction of the overall expense of this training. Through a collaborative model, training not provided elsewhere has been made available to institutions that could not replicate this experience for their staff on their own campuses.

Recently, the DLI Education Committee began asking if library schools should be doing more to prepare librarians to support statistical and data resources. Over the past seven years, the DLI literacy program filled this void in the professional development of librarians in Canada. Understandably, the DLI has contributed to an increased need for data services training in librarian education. A decade ago data services were a very specialized area, but the growth of statistical and data resources has given it greater prominence. While data may not have become mainstreamed in the library, the resources are certainly now on the Main Street of libraries. Increasingly, the patrons of academic libraries expect to find data resources in their library.

This raises the question: should library schools take responsibility for preparing the foundation skills and building the basic competencies in data services? Without the large professional associations' or the library schools' involvement in data literacy training, the DLI program is the stopgap solution in Canada. Until there is movement by the professional associations and library schools to change this situation, the collaborative training program offered through the DLI will continue to prepare professionals with the knowledge and skills that they require to support data services.

NOTES

1. More information about the CNSLP can be found on the website of the Canadian Research Knowledge Network <http://www.cnlsp.ca>.

2. A more complete account of the beginnings of the DLI can be read in the report of the project's evaluation conducted in 1999. Goss Gilroy Inc., *Evaluation of the Data Liberation Initiative* (Ottawa, 1999). <http://www.statcan.ca/english/Dli/eval.pdf>.

3. Public use microdata are computer files containing the coded responses from respondents in social surveys. These files have been modified from the original data to minimize the likelihood of disclosing any of the individuals in the survey. Through a process of anonymizing the data, the detail in information that would increase the risk of identifying someone is reduced. For example, the place of residence provides very specific information that could in combination with other information in the file lead to the disclosure of a respondent. Therefore, one method of anonymizing the data is to provide only information at a gross level of geography, such as the province in which the respondent lives.

4. National statistical agencies rely extensively on geographic boundaries in reporting statistical information. For example, Statistics Canada produces a large collection of spatial data files with a variety of geographic boundaries. These files are used widely with Geographic Information Systems (GIS) in conjunction with statistical summaries employing the same geo-spatial boundaries.

5. For an account of the work that went into establishing the DLI, see: Watkins, Wendy and Ernie Boyko, "Data Liberation and Academic Freedom," Government Information in Canada/Information gouvernementale au Canada 3, no. 2 (1996). <http://www.usask.ca/library/gic/v3n2/watkins2/watkins2.html>.

6. The ICPSR is a membership-based social science data archive housed at the University of Michigan. This organization has one of the largest collections of research data in the world and while the majority of the holdings are data collected in the United States, there are a substantial number of files from international sources also.

7. CARL negotiated a single fee for one copy of the 1986 Census of Canada that was shared by several universities. The University of Toronto received the master copy and then made copies on tape for each institution in the consortium. This consortium was repeated for the 1991 Census of Canada and several of the Canadian General Social Surveys. This model proved to be a precursor of the DLI model operating on an ad hoc basis through separate licenses for each product.

8. For further information about the cooperative projects of COPPUL, see this organization's website: <http://www.coppul.ca>.

9. The seven training principles are reported in an appendix to a paper presented at IFLA in 2003 by Ernie S. Boyko (Statistics Canada), Elizabeth Hamilton (University of New Brunswick), Charles Humphrey (University of Alberta), and Wendy Watkins (Carleton University) entitled, "Lifting Ourselves by our Bootstraps: Developing a National Peer-to-Peer Training Program for Data Librarians in Canada."

10. The national DLI training session was held in conjunction with an Ottawa-hosted IASSIST conference. As an international professional association for data archivists and librarians, IASSIST provided DLI Contacts an opportunity to meet with colleagues around the world who do similar work. Four regional DLI workshops were still held in 2003.

11. Goss Gilroy Inc., op. cit., p. 33.

12. Mary Jo Lynch, "Spending on Staff Development (2001)," ALA Office for Research and Statistics. <http://www.ala.org/ala/hrdr/libraryempresources/spendingstaff.htm>.

13. This is a crude estimate based on the 2001 average percent of the payroll expended on development and training from the ALA survey mentioned above and the total expenditure on salaries and wages of professional staff in 2002 from the ACRL survey. <http://www.ala.org/ala/acrlbucket/statisticssummaries/2002stats/ 2002statisticalsumm.htm>.

Patent and Trademark Depository Libraries and the United States Patent and Trademark Office: A Model for Information Dissemination

Claudine Arnold Jenda

SUMMARY. This paper describes the network of Patent and Trademark Depository Libraries (PTDLs), a collaborative partnership with the United States Patent and Trademark Office (USPTO) for disseminating patent and trademark information in every state plus the District of Columbia and Puerto Rico. Typical information sources and services provided at PTDLs are given, followed by suggestions of areas on which to focus in the future for PTDLs to continue to be vital links of information that spur economic growth, business competitiveness, and the continued discovery of new scientific and technological knowledge and applications. *[Article copies available for a fee from The Haworth Document Delivery Service: 1-800-HAWORTH. E-mail address: <docdelivery@haworthpress.com> Website: <http://www.HaworthPress.com> © 2005/2006 by The Haworth Press, Inc. All rights reserved.]*

Claudine Arnold Jenda is Science Librarian and Assistant Chair, Reference and Information Services, Auburn University Libraries, 231 Mell Street, Auburn, AL, 36849-5606 (E-mail: Jendaca@auburn.edu). She has served as a PTDL Representative at Auburn, PTDL Fellowship Librarian at the USPTO, and Patent and Trademark Depository Library Association President.

[Haworth co-indexing entry note]: "Patent and Trademark Depository Libraries and the United States Patent and Trademark Office: A Model for Information Dissemination." Jenda, Claudine Arnold. Co-published simultaneously in *Resource Sharing & Information Networks* (The Haworth Information Press, an imprint of The Haworth Press, Inc.) Vol. 18, No. 1/2, 2005/2006, pp. 183-201; and: *Libraries Beyond Their Institutions: Partnerships That Work* (ed: William Miller, and Rita M. Pellen) The Haworth Information Press, an imprint of The Haworth Press, Inc., 2005/2006, pp. 183-201. Single or multiple copies of this article are available for a fee from The Haworth Document Delivery Service [1-800-HAWORTH, 9:00 a.m. - 5:00 p.m. (EST). E-mail address: docdelivery@haworthpress.com].

http://www.haworthpress.com/web/RSIN
© 2005/2006 by The Haworth Press, Inc. All rights reserved.
Digital Object Identifier: 10.1300/J121v18n01_14

KEYWORDS. Patents, trademarks, intellectual property, inventions, inventors, cooperative partnerships, information networks, Patent and Trademark Depository Libraries, Patent and Trademark Depository Library Program, United States Patent and Trademark Office

INTRODUCTION

The nationwide network of Patent and Trademark Depository Libraries (PTDLs) traces its beginning to the year 1871 when the United States Patent and Trademark Office (USPTO), then known as The Patent Office, first started distributing copies of patents to a small number of libraries. Until then, patent documents were housed at only one location, at The Patent Office, in Washington, DC. When the publication of the *Official Gazette*, a weekly publication of the USPTO that lists patent abstracts and a representative drawing of the invention, started in 1872, this title was added to the list of documents that were distributed to libraries. As an agency that operates out of one main location in Washington, DC, initially and then Crystal City, VA, with no regional or state offices, it was great foresight and planning that led the USPTO to view libraries as an option for providing easy access to patent documents for research into the respective locations of inventors, businesses, educators, and any member of the public with an interest in this subject. It took an Act of Congress, 35 U.S.C. 13, to enable the Patent Office to start disseminating patent information to the public.

Distribution of patent documents to libraries was done on a voluntary basis (Sneed 1999). Libraries were given the option of serving as a patent depository, and eight libraries received patent documents in 1871: The New York State Library, Boston Public Library, The Public Library of Cincinnati and Hamilton County, Science and Engineering Library at Ohio State University, the Detroit Public Library, Los Angeles Public Library, New York Public Library, and The St. Louis Public Library. By 1977, the number of patent libraries had grown to twenty-two. Patent librarians from eighteen of these libraries attended the first annual patent training conference hosted by the Patent Office in 1977. This meeting laid the groundwork for a series of strategic planning sessions that have continued to shape the nature of information resources, patent and trademark reference and search tools, and quality of services that PTDLs offer to their users. Most importantly, this meeting had set the stage for the type of close collaboration, consultation, and working relationship that exists between Patent and Trademark Depository Libraries and the United States Patent and Trademark Office.

HOW TO BECOME
A PATENT AND TRADEMARK DEPOSITORY LIBRARY

From these modest beginnings, the PTDL network has grown four-fold from 22 libraries in 1977 to 86 libraries currently. Overseeing, coordinating, and administering the work and services offered by PTDLs is the Patent and Trademark Depository Library Program (PTDLP), an office at the United States Patent and Trademark Office, that is led by dedicated and knowledgeable USPTO staff who ensure that the key patent and trademark information that inventors, businesses, and patent researchers need is made available to them in the desired formats at a PTDL location that is closest to the patent/trademark user. To become a Patent and Trademark Depository Library, a library makes a number of commitments that include:

- acquiring a twenty-year back-file of U.S. patents;
- providing free public access to patent/trademark depository materials;
- protecting the integrity and availability of patent/trademark depository collections for use now and in the future;
- maintaining collections of patent and trademark reference and search retrieval tools to support user inquiries;
- assisting the public in the accurate and efficient use of patent and trademark information;
- and supporting the continued training of a designated Patent and Trademark Depository Library (PTDL) Representative at every annual PTDL Training Seminar (PTDLP 2002).

A library that demonstrates a readiness to adhere to these minimum service standards is formally designated a PTDL by the Commissioner (Director) of the U.S. Patent and Trademark Office who is also the Under-Secretary of Commerce for Intellectual Property. Through this unique partnership between the PTDLs and the USPTO, Americans are guaranteed easy access to patent and trademark information at their local PTDL with facilities and services that mirror those offered in the public search room at the USPTO. Researching patent and trademark information at a local PTDL removes the expense, time, and effort that each searcher would spend in driving to Washington, DC. In 1997, the PTDL Program at the USPTO met the goal of having one PTDL in each state, and has now set the goal of having a PTDL in highly populated metropolitan areas that also have high patenting activity (Sneed 1999). The Appendix shows a list of Patent and Trademark Depository Libraries with their designation dates and web addresses. For a current list of PTDLs by state, go to http://www.uspto.gov/web/offices/ac/ido/ptdl/ptdlib_1.html.

PTDL COLLECTIONS, SERVICES, AND SEARCH TOOLS

Each Patent and Trademark Depository Library agrees to offer to the public free access to over six million U.S. patents and about three million federal trademarks. Patent and trademark information is made available to the public in a variety of formats such as: paper, microfilm, CD-ROM, DVD-ROM, and via the Internet at www.uspto.gov. Some PTDLs also offer access to the online patent systems of the USPTO such as the Web-based Examiner Search Tool (WEST). Starting this year, the WEST system will be made available at all PTDLs. Three PTDLs have partnership status with the USPTO which enables them to offer enhanced PTDL services that include the ability to host videoconferencing sessions with patent examiners, providing local filing of disclosure documents, and offering in-depth training seminars and workshops on intellectual property topics, policies and procedures.

At selected PTDLs, the U.S. patent and trademark collections are supplemented by foreign patents from countries like the United Kingdom, France, Germany, Canada, and others. The *Directory of Patent and Trademark Depository Libraries* (2003) provides an accurate description of the collections and services of each PTDL.

It is in the area of U.S. patent and trademark collections and search retrieval tools that the benefits of the partnership between the PTDLs and the USPTO have created the greatest impact. Since the first meeting between the USPTO and PTDLs in 1977, there have been continued discussions and dialogue on the best systems that the USPTO should design for the delivery and searching of patent and trademark information. Such discussions have been instrumental in the timely migrations of patent and trademark collections and search systems from paper to microfilm, then CASSIS online and CD-ROM, and finally current combinations of paper, microfilm, CASSIS DVD-ROM, online, and web-based. At any given time, the USPTO's Information Dissemination Organization(s) can be counted upon to provide the latest information search retrieval and storage system that ensures the widest possible access to United States patent and trademark information. Indeed it is, in part, at the insistence of PTDLs that the USPTO made the unprecedented move to provide the database of U.S. patent and trademark information on the web. And now more intellectual property offices around the world are following that lead. For a more complete listing of the achievements and milestones of the PTDL network, the PTDL Program, and PTDLA, see Jenda (2002).

As a cost-recovery agency that is fully funded by fees from patent and trademark applications, the USPTO makes every effort to listen to and address the information needs of its users, including PTDLs. Librarians and information professionals by training are also customer-focused individuals who pride themselves in providing excellent user-centered information services. This compatibility and overlap in interests creates a synergistic working relationship between PTDLs and the USPTO that has resulted in the design, testing and implementation of various innovative patent and trademark search and retrieval systems in a variety of media and formats. PTDLs are often at the forefront with the USPTO in articulating, planning, and designing newer cutting-edge search systems that they know their users need. This is based upon the knowledge of information needs PTDLs gain firsthand as they work with inventors, businesses, and researchers, the primary users of patent and trademark information products.

Because information delivery and search systems are always changing, PTDLs house an array of collections, reference, and search tools in a variety of formats such as: paper, microfilm, CD-ROM, DVD-ROM, online, and full-text. Typical information found at PTDLs is shown in Tables 1 and 2.

USER SERVICES:
TRAINING WORKSHOPS AND SEMINARS

Since 1977 when the first training seminar was held, Patent and Trademark Depository Library Representatives attend a weeklong Annual PTDL Training Seminar on the United States Patent Office campus, now in Alexandria, VA. PTDL Representatives receive intensive training on intellectual property topics from various USPTO officials, patent examiners, trademark examining attorneys, patent classifiers, and other USPTO experts and specialists. Patent librarians have the opportunity of interacting with various other levels of USPTO staff to include policy makers at the USPTO and other related agencies, and through the PTDL Association (PTDLA), the interaction is extended to members of the Committee for Intellectual Property, inventor groups, and other professional associations such as the American Library Association (ALA) with which PTDLA is affiliated, Special Libraries Association (SLA), Patent Information User Group (PIUG), and PATLIB, a network of patent libraries similiar to PTDLs in the European Union. The Annual PTDL Training Seminars often include presentations by representatives of other Intellectual Property Offices abroad. Such attendees have in the past included speakers from Finland, United Kingdom, Canada, Mexico, China, and Japan, and representatives of the European Union and the World Intellectual Property Organization (WIPO).

Armed with such training, patent librarians are well equipped to provide patent and trademark search services at their local PTDLs to inventors, students, faculty, researchers, small businesses, and others with an interest in us-

TABLE 1. Patent Resources Available at PTDLs

Patent Documents and Search Tools	Date Coverage
U.S. Patent Specifications and Drawings	1790 to Present
U.S. Design Patents	1842 to Present
U.S. Plant Patents	1931 to Present
U.S. Official Gazette	1872 to Present
Index to the U.S. Patent Classification	Latest Edition
Manual of Classification	Latest Edition
Classification Definitions	Latest Revision
Annual Index of Patents and Annual Report of the Commissioner	1790 to Present
Manual of Patent Examining Procedure (MPEP)	Latest Edition
35 USC-Patents, Laws	Latest Edition
37 CFR-Patents, Trademarks and Copyrights	Latest Edition
Patent Attorneys and Agents Registered to Practice before the U.S. Patent and Trademark Office	Latest Edition
General Information Concerning Patents	Latest Edition

TABLE 2. Trademark Information Resources Available at PTDLs

Trademark Documents and Search Tools	Date Coverage
U.S. Federal Trademarks	All available Dates, active & lapsed
Annual Index of Trademarks	1927 to Present
Directory of U.S. Trademarks	Latest Edition
Trademark Manual of Examining Procedure (TMEP)	Latest Revision
15 USC-Trademarks	Latest Edition
37 CFR-Patents, Trademarks, Copyrights	Latest Edition
Rules of Practice in Trademark Cases	Latest Revision
Trademark Reporter	1911 to Present
Trademark Acceptable Identification of Goods and Services Manual	Latest Revision
Trademark Trial and Appeal Board Manual of Procedure	Latest Revision
Basic Facts About Registering a Trademark	Latest Edition
Design Code Manual for Trademarks	Latest Edition

ing the business, legal, scientific, technical, and other information that is contained in patent and trademark documents. Patent librarians develop a wealth of knowledge and understanding of information resources and search tools to use to address their clients' needs. While patent librarians do not conduct the patent and trademark searches for their users, and do not provide legal advice, they can guide users through their prior art searches and refer questions to local patent attorneys as needed, as well as draw upon the expertise of experts at the USPTO and colleagues in the PTDL network. PTDLs rely on outstanding reference help provided by PTDL Program staff with whom they are in close contact as their first line of support.

PTDLs also engage in direct user education of their patent and trademark users. In periodic surveys on training and outreach activities of PTDLs, a variety of training activities are mentioned such as:

1. Providing patent and trademark instruction to students in elementary schools that do science fair projects or competitions on creative thinking;
2. Giving presentations at state and national independent inventor workshops, and meetings of small business owners;
3. Giving instruction on the use of patent and trademark literature to college and university students of chemistry, engineering, design, history of science, and technical writing courses;
4. Giving presentations to librarians and information professionals at state and national meetings;
5. Presenting seminars on patents and trademarks to faculty and research staff at colleges and universities;
6. Giving talks on the uses of the patent literature for collectors and hobbyists;
7. Giving patent and trademark presentations at state business fairs.

It is quite common for PTDL librarians to team up with USPTO staff in providing local patent and trademark training workshop sessions at most of these state and national inventor, business, and professional meetings. For example, when the American Inventors Protection Act (AIPA) was enacted on November 29, 1999, as Public Law 106-113, the USPTO did a nationwide campaign and tour of various locations meeting with inventors, businesses, attorneys, and researchers to educate and train them on implications of this important legislation and its impact on patent examining policies and procedures. Several PTDLs served as the hosts for these training sessions, and co-presented on some topics covered during this publicity campaign.

PTDL FELLOWSHIP PROGRAM

Started in 1983, the PTDL Fellowship Program was created to provide PTDL librarians the opportunity of working for one to two years at the USPTO, in the Patent and Trademark Depository Library Program Office to bring their firsthand knowledge of the needs and operations of PTDLs to the USPTO, and while at the USPTO to learn about the functions and procedures of the USPTO and PTDL Program. A total of 19 librarians have participated in the Program to date. They have collectively made many lasting contributions to the workings of the Office and the PTDL Program such as: the implementation of the CASSIS CD-ROM search computer system that is used at all PTDLs; the introduction and phasing in of the Automated Patent System (APS), a precursor system to WEST, at selected PTDLs that served as APS pilot test sites; developing search tools and guides for patent and trademark searching; producing a *Directory of Patent and Trademark Depository Libraries*; and serving as liaisons between PTDLs, PTDLP, and the PTDL Association.

The Fellowship Program is another example of the partnerships and exchange of information and expertise that occurs between PTDLs and the USPTO. The USPTO gains valuable knowledge about the information needs of patent and trademark users while the PTDL Librarians back to their home institution with a better understanding of the inner workings of the USPTO and PTDL Program in particular. With this knowledge, PTDL librarians can come up with better strategies for accomplishing PTDL objectives, information services, and programs by working through the PTDL Program, PTDL Association, or other programs of the USPTO or related agencies.

USERS OF PTDL SERVICES

PTDLs make patent and trademark information freely available to anyone who needs it. There are a variety of user groups that are repeat customers of PTDLs such as: elementary school students and their teachers; independent inventors; small business owners; corporations; college and university students, faculty, and researchers; and federal government and state officials. These users interact with PTDL staff over the phone, in-person, via e-mail, and to a small extent lately via online chat reference systems.

Because of the ready availability of patent and trademark information over the Internet at www.uspto.gov, users have the mistaken impression that they can conduct patent and trademark searches without the support and services of PTDL staff. This is an unplanned outcome of having patent and trademark information on the Internet. Patents contain legal and technical language that is often used to describe the subjects of inventions. To perform an effective keyword search that will not miss any relevant patents, an inventor has to think of all the different ways that a product, process, or service may be described and use those keywords in the search. Martin (2002) has given examples of the common ways of describing inventions in everyday language and contrasted them with the legal and technical terminology that patents use to describe the same inventions.

In a study of the effectiveness of keyword searching compared to patent classification searching, Martin (2002) concluded that searching patents by keyword retrieves many irrelevant patent documents and misses several relevant patents, while patent classification searches have a higher precision and retrieve the highest number of relevant patents for a given subject. PTDL staff, when they train inventors, promote the use of the U.S. Patent Classification System (USPCS) as the most effective way of searching patents. PTDLs need to address this situation and figure out ways of reconnecting with patent and trademark searchers who need search assistance while on the Internet. In a recent focus group survey of PTDLs, it was observed that PTDLs, as is the case with most libraries, are experiencing a much-reduced number of people who visit the PTDLs in person to conduct patent and trademark searches. As a result, not many patent and trademark searchers are benefiting from the search experience and expertise of PTDL librarians when they conduct their prior art searches.

FUTURE CONSIDERATIONS ON THE PTDL-USPTO PARTNERSHIP

As the marketplace becomes more global, more inventors and businesses are seeing the need to protect their trademarks and patents in other countries as well. It is becoming more important for more U.S. nationals, especially independent inventors, to start protecting their ideas abroad also. PTDL librarians will need to lead in this effort by enhancing their knowledge of intellectual property to cover intellectual property systems of other countries in addition to that of the United States. The way users access their patent and trademark information has changed markedly in the last few years. The emergence and wide use of web-based patent and trademark information systems necessitates that web-based patent reference support from PTDLs be made available also. The following five recommendations will go a long way towards helping PTDLs and the PTDL Program respond to the global nature of the economic market place and intellectual property protection, and the evolving information technology systems for accessing patent and trademark information.

Enhance PTDL Librarian Education and Training

Patent Librarians should be encouraged to seek additional training through degree programs to encompass patent and trademark law. Among the pool of patent librarians, there should be a sizable number that are conversant in patent and trademark law as evidenced by professionally recognized certificates or degrees. At a minimum, all patent librarians should undergo training similar to that given to patent examiners and trademark examining attorneys. Presently, patent librarians receive a significant portion of this type of education and training through the Annual PTDL Training Seminars (Sneed 1999). However, the education and training is not formally assessed nor is it formally recognized beyond the PTDL network and Association.

The need for a more widely recognized education and training in intellectual property will become more critical as librarians get more involved in providing patent and trademark reference support over interactive online reference systems to users who are at remote sites. In such situations, it is easy to see that patent librarians are more likely to be drawn into questions that deal with legal advice. While most patent librarians who have gone through several Annual PTDL Training Seminars most likely have received, over time, the equivalent of what would be taught in patent law and programs of training given to patent examiners or trademark examining attorneys, a structured course and training program would guarantee that such education and training has been provided and is credentialed as such. Such training and education would give patent librarians the readiness to deal with patent questions, especially via online reference, without too many referrals unless answering a question in a given manner would constitute an unauthorized practice of the law.

National Online Patent Reference Service

Many libraries currently participate in collaborative efforts with other libraries around the country that aim to provide reference services 24 hours a day, 7 days a week over live online reference chat systems (McKiernan 2003). Chat services are widely accepted as a means of communicating. In library settings, chat services provide another way to connect with users who are doing research in a place that is remote from the library. In the case of users of patent and trademark information on the USPTO website, a way needs to be provided for patent and trademark searchers on www.uspto.gov to connect with patent librarians who can assist them with their searches. Because it is known that researching of the patent literature is not intuitive, the USPTO website should do more to increase the visibility of PTDLs on www.uspto.gov. Providing a link to a nationwide online chat service on this that connects the patent and trademark searcher live to each of the 86 PTDLs would do much to help reconnect patent librarians with their users most of whom are relying on web-based patent and trademark information systems. PTDLs should explore the possibility of partnering with patent librarians in Europe through the PATLIB network in providing a global patent reference network (Jenda 2002).

Dedicated PTDL Representatives

One requirement for becoming a PTDL involves identifying one librarian, the PTDL Representative, to serve as the liaison between the PTDL and the PTDLP at the USPTO. The PTDL Representative at each PTDL receives continued training on intellectual property and is responsible for training other people at the local PTDL whose work involves helping patent and trademark searchers with their research. Typically, most patent librarians perform their PTDL Representative duties in addition to many other duties and assignments that their local library requires. It would be ideal if PTDL Representatives performed PTDL-related duties in a dedicated manner. We would expect PTDL Representatives to be much more effective in the performance of their duties, and PTDLs to become much more vibrant centers of creative and entrepreneurial activities, if at least one PTDL staff member managed and performed PTDL-related duties in a more concerted manner with better continuity than is the case at present where various work assignments complete for the PTDL Librarian's time.

Increased PTDL Outreach Activities

To help reconnect PTDLs to their users, PTDLs need to engage in an aggressive three to five year campaign of promoting PTDLs to their inventor groups, small businesses, students, librarians and information professionals, faculty and researchers, and many other user categories. Through an increased level of outreach activities such as giving class, seminar, and workshop presentations on patents and trademarks, more patent and trademark searchers will be aware that they still need to make use of the expertise of patent librarians to use patent and trademark information accurately and efficiently. Conversely, patent and trademark users will be more aware of the cost in time, money, and patent and product quality of basing their decisions on poorly done, incomplete prior art patent searches.

Patent librarians are also a great source of local information on additional sources of assistance for an inventor or small business owner such as small business centers or incubator centers that help evaluate the economic, business viability of a creative idea. Patent librarians often know about or actively participate in local inventor group organizations that are likely to have some experienced inventors who are willing to share their expertise with new inventors or entrepreneurs (Hayes-Rines 2003). PTDLs should also increase their efforts at training and networking with other librarians and information professionals at non-PTDL libraries in their state, who will in turn provide more effective referrals to prospective patent and trademark searchers to the PTDL. In an informal survey of independent inventors, Hayes-Rines (2003) also concluded that increased outreach to PTDL customers is needed for PTDLs to continue to provide effective support services to inventors, small business owners, and other users of patent and trademark information.

Continued Need for PTDL Services

In the face of the popularity of web-based searching, some may be tempted to question if there is still any need for PTDL services as we have known them for several decades now. Patent librarians and those patent and trademark users who have used PTDL services are well aware that PTDLs provide services and resources that are not replaced by the mere availability of patent and trademark information on the web (Sneed 1999; Fischlschweiger 2004). Patent searching is a complex process that can not effectively be reduced to simple keyword searching. Without the search expertise of a qualified patent search librarian or expert, implications of the outcome of a search are most likely not carefully reviewed or followed through by the novice searcher.

PTDL librarians guide inventors and other patent and trademark researchers through the patent and trademark search process. They teach patent and trademark research techniques to classes of students, inventors, small business owners, and various other audiences such as those at professional meetings and one-on-one sessions. PTDL librarians host and actively participate in inventor workshops and conferences where they showcase USPTO information products and PTDL services. The lectures and presentations highlight the accurate and effective use of patent and trademark information in science, technology, business, research, and instruction (PTDLP 2002). They also maintain close working relationships with inventor groups, patent and trademark attorneys and agents, Small Business Development centers, incubator centers, corporate firms, technology transfer centers, science and engineering faculty and students, elementary school teachers, science fair organizers, federal laboratories and research institutions, local chambers of commerce, and all other groups or individuals who are likely to be involved in the process of protecting, and transforming a creative idea into a successful product or service on the market. PTDL librarians use these individuals as a knowledge base and resource to whom to connect inventors or patent/trademark researchers who seek to properly protect their idea and develop it into a product or service.

It is important that PTDLs figure out alternative ways of reconnecting and working with their users who do not physically come into the libraries, so that these users can also benefit from the knowledge and experience of PTDL staff and all those with whom PTDLs interact. It is a great improvement that patent and trademark searchers are able to access millions of U.S. patent and trademark documents conveniently from their office or home computers without having to physically visit a PTDL. However, PTDLs should continue to explore ways of making it just as easy for these patent and trademark users to get the patent and trademark search help they need when they are on the web. At present, more should be done to increase the visibility and availability of PTDLs to patent and trademark searchers on the www.uspto.gov website.

CONCLUSIONS

Following a brief description of the nationwide network of Patent and Trademark Depository Libraries, the paper provides examples of patent and trademark services and collections that are provided by PTDLs. Through a formal partnership that exists between each PTDL and the United States Patent and Trademark Office (USPTO), the USPTO provides patent and trademark collections to each PTDL in paper, CD-ROM, DVD-ROM, online, and web-based formats for use, without charge, by all members of the public throughout the United States, District of Columbia, and Puerto Rico. This special partnership is the driving force that has helped shape the design, implementation, and testing of patent and trademark storage, search, and retrieval information systems from 1977 to date provided by the Information Dissemination Organizations of the USPTO and available for public use at PTDLs.

REFERENCES

Directory of Patent and Trademark Depository Libraries. Washington, DC: United States Patent and Trademark Office, 2002.

Fischlschweiger, Eileen. "The Fort Lauderdale Patent and Trademark Depository Library at the Broward County Main Library: A Key Community Resource for 20 Years." *Inventors' Digest,* September/October 2004. Forthcoming.

Hayes-Rines, Joanne. "Independent Inventors: Who They Are and How They Use the PTDLs." *Intellectual Property (IP) Journal of the PTDLA,* Vol. 3 (1) June 2003. Retrieved August 13, 2004 from: <http://www.ptdla.org/>.

Jenda, Claudine. "History of the Patent and Trademark Depository Library Association (PTDLA)." In: Oliver, Jeanne (Editor). *Celebrating 25 Years of Librarians and USPTO Cooperation.* Washington, DC: Patent and Trademark Depository Library Program, Chief Information Officer, United States Patent and Trademark Office. 2002, pp. 97-120.

Jenda, Claudine. "Providing Virtual Reference Assistance to Patent Searchers Using InfoChat." *PATLIB 2002*, Giardini Naxos, Sicily: European Patent Office, May 22-24, 2002.

McKiernan, Gerry. *A Registry of Real-Time Digital Reference Services*. Ames, IA: Iowa State University Library, 2003. <http://www.public.iastate.edu/~CYBERSTACKS/LiveRef.htm>.

Martin, Jason. "Loving the Manual: Effective Patent Searching Using the Manual of Classification." *Intellectual Property (IP) Journal of the PTDLA*. Vol. 2 (1/2) June/December 2002. Forthcoming.

PTDLP. *Notes on Becoming a Patent and Trademark Depository Library*. Washington, D.C. Patent and Trademark Depository Library Program, United States Patent and Trademark Office, 2003. <http://www.uspto.gov/web/offices/ac/ido/ptdl/noteson4.htm>.

PTDLP. *Patents: The Collection for all Reasons*. Washington, D.C. Patent and Trademark Depository Library Program, United States Patent and Trademark Office, January 2002. <http://www.uspto.gov/web/offices/ac/ido/ptdl/patreaso.htm>.

Sneed, Martha Crockett. "Fully Disclosed Yet Merely Descriptive: Intricacies of Training the Patent and Trademark Information Professional." *Journal of Library Administration*. 29, No.1, 1999, 59-78.

APPENDIX. Designation Dates and Web Addresses of Patent and Trademark Depository Libraries

City, State	Name of Library	Designation Date	URL Web Address
Akron, Ohio	Akron-Summit County Public Library	09-18-1995	http://ascpl.lib.oh.us/pat-tm.html
Albany, New York	New York State Library Cultural Education Center	1870	http://www.nysl.nysed.gov/patents.htm
Albuquerque, New Mexico	Centennial Science and Engineering Library. The University of New Mexico	11-03-1983	http://elibrary2.unm.edu/csel/
Amherst, Massachusetts	Physical Sciences and Engineering Library. University of Massachusetts	11-14-1984	http://www.library.umass.edu/subject/patents/
Anchorage, Alaska	Z. J. Loussac Public Library. Anchorage Municipal Libraries	12-04-1984	http://www.muni.org/library1/index.cfm
Ann Arbor, Michigan	Media Union Library. The University of Michigan	11-04-1983	http://www.lib.umich.edu/aael/
Atlanta, Georgia	Library and Information Center. Georgia Institute of Technology	1946	http://www.library.gatech.edu/
Auburn, Alabama	Ralph Brown Draughon Library. Auburn University	10-13-1983	http://www.lib.auburn.edu
Austin, Texas	McKinney Engineering Library. The University of Texas at Austin	06-16-1983	http://www.lib.utexas.edu/engin/
Baton Rouge, Louisiana	Troy H. Middleton Library. Louisiana State University	06-24-1981	http://www.lib.lsu.edu/index.html
Bayamon, Puerto Rico	Learning Resources Center. University of Puerto Rico-Bayamon Campus	04-06-2000	http://wwwbib.upr.edu/
Big Rapids, Michigan	Abigail S. Timme Library. Ferris State Library	08-22-1991	http://www.ferris.edu/library/patent/homepage.html
Birmingham, Alabama	Birmingham Public Library	08-08-1977	http://www.bplonline.org/
Boston, Massachusetts	Boston Public Library	1870	http://www.bpl.org/research/govdocs/patent_trademark.htm
Buffalo, New York	Buffalo and Erie County Public Library	1871	http://www.buffalolib.org/
Burlington, Vermont	Bailey/Howe Library	11-18-1996	http://library.uvm.edu/reference/government/patent.html
Butte, Montana	Montana Tech Library of the University of Montana	03-01-1984	http://www.mtech.edu/library/resources/ip.htm

197

City, State	Name of Library	Designation Date	URL Web Address
Cheyenne, Wyoming	Wyoming State Library	01-16-2001	http://www-wsl.state.wy.us/sis/ptd/index.html
Chicago, Illinois	Chicago Public Library	1876	http://www.chipublib.org/008subject/009scitech/patents.html
Cincinnati, Ohio	The Public Library of Cincinnati and Hamilton County	1871	http://www.cincinnatilibrary.org/
Clemson, South Carolina	R. M. Cooper Library. Clemson University	06-03-1992	http://www.lib.clemson.edu/GovDocs/patents/newpat.htm
Cleveland, Ohio	Cleveland Public Library	1890	http://www.cpl.org/
College Park, Maryland	Engineering and Physical Sciences Library. University of Maryland	01-25-1984	http://www.lib.umd.edu/ENGIN/engin.html
College Station, Texas	Sterling C. Evans Library. Texas A&M University	12-22-1983	http://library.tamu.edu/vgn/portal/tamulib/content/renderer/0,2174,1724_2062,00.html
Columbus, Ohio	Science and Engineering Library. Ohio State University	1870	http://www.lib.ohio-state.edu/phyweb/
Concord, New Hampshire	New Hampshire State Library	02-21-1996	http://www.state.nh.us/nhsl/patents/index.html
Dallas, Texas	Dallas Public Library	11-30-1977	http://dallaslibrary.org/CGI/patents.htm
Dayton, Ohio	Paul Laurence Dunbar Library. Wright State University	07-05-2000	http://www.libraries.wright.edu/find/gov/patent/
Denver, Colorado	Denver Public Library	11-11-1977	http://www.denver.lib.co.us/index.html
Des Moines, Iowa	State Library of Iowa	12-09-1988	http://www.silo.lib.ia.us/
Detroit, Michigan	Great Lakes Patent and Trademark Center. Detroit Public Library	1871	http://www.detroit.lib.mi.us/glptc/glptc_index.htm
Fort Lauderdale, Florida	Broward County Main Library	11-01-1984	http://www.broward.org/library/
Grand Forks, North Dakota	Chester Fritz Library. University of North Dakota	01-26-1990	http://www.und.edu/dept/library/resources/patents/index.jsp
Hartford, Connecticut	Hartford Public Library	10-07-1997	http://www.hplct.org/
Honolulu, Hawaii	Hawaii State Library	12-18-1989	http://www.state.hi.us/libraries/fedocs/
Houston, Texas	Fondren Library. Rice University	10-28-1977	http://www.rice.edu/fondren/ptd/

Location	Library	Date	URL
Indianapolis, Indiana	Indianapolis-Marion County Public Library	09-07-1983	http://www.imcpl.lib.in.us/bst_patents.htm
Jackson, Mississippi	Mississippi Library Commission	06-19-1990	http://www.mlc.lib.ms.us/
Kansas City, Missouri	Linda Hall Library	1946	http://www.lindahall.org/
Las Vegas, Nevada	Las Vegas Clark County Library District	05-10-1999	http://www.lvccld.org/
Lincoln, Nebraska	Engineering Library. University of Nebraska, Lincoln	01-05-1978	http://www.unl.edu/libr/libs/engr/engr.html
Little Rock, Arkansas	Arkansas State Library	01-18-1985	http://www.asl.lib.ar.us/patents/index.html
Los Angeles, California	Los Angeles Public Library	1870	http://www.lapl.org/central/science.html
Louisville, Kentucky	Louisville Free Public Library	03-28-1988	http://lfpl.org/
Lubbock, Texas	Texas Tech University Library	10-31-1995	http://library.ttu.edu/ul/index.php
Madison, Wisconsin	Kurt F. Wendt Library. University of Wisconsin-Madison	04-26-1976	http://www.wisc.edu/wendt/patent/patent.html
Mayaguez, Puerto Rico	General Library. University of Puerto Rico-Mayaguez	03-10-1995	http://www.uprm.edu/library/patents/
Miami, Florida	Miami-Dade Public Library System	07-25-1984	http://www.mdpls.org/
Milwaukee, Wisconsin	Milwaukee Public Library	1949	http://www.mpl.org/
Minneapolis, Minnesota	Minneapolis Public Library	09-12-1980	http://www.mplib.org/
Morgantown, West Virginia	Evansdale Library. West Virginia University	12-02-1991	http://www.libraries.wvu.edu/patents/index.htm
Moscow, Idaho	University of Idaho Library	11-03-1983	http://www.lib.uidaho.edu/
Nashville, Tennessee	Stevenson Science and Engineering Library. Vanderbilt	07-26-1985	http://www.library.vanderbilt.edu/patents/
New Haven, Connecticut	New Haven Free Public Library	10-07-1997	http://www.cityofnewhaven.com/library/
New York, New York	New York Public Library	1870	http://www.nypl.org/research/sibl/index.html
Newark, Delaware	University of Delaware Library	11-26-1980	http://www.lib.udel.edu/
Newark, New Jersey	Newark Public Library	1880	http://www.npl.org/Pages/Collections/bst.html
Orlando, Florida	University of Central Florida Libraries	12-30-1988	http://library.ucf.edu/GovDocs/PAT_TRAD.htm
Orono, Maine	Raymond H. Fogler Library. University of Maine	12-23-1993	http://library.umaine.edu/patents/default.htm

APPENDIX (continued)

City, State	Name of Library	Designation Date	URL Web Address
Philadelphia, Pennsylvania	The Free Library of Philadelphia	05-05-1986	http://www.library.phila.gov/index.htm
Piscataway, New Jersey	Library of Science and Medicine. Rutgers University	05-09-1989	http://www.libraries.rutgers.edu/rul/
Pittsburgh, Pennsylvania	The Carnegie Library of Pittsburgh	1902	http://www.clpgh.org/locations/scitech/
Portland, Oregon	Paul L. Boley Law Library. Lewis & Clark Law School	07-27-1995	http://www.lclark.edu/~lawlib/
Providence, Rhode Island	Providence Public Library	1901	http://www.provlib.org/
Raleigh, North Carolina	D.H. Hill Library. North Carolina State University	09-26-1977	http://www.lib.ncsu.edu/ptdl/
Rapid City, South Dakota	Devereaux Library, South Dakota School of Mines and Technology	02-10-1994	http://www.sdsmt.edu/services/library/library.html
Reno, Nevada	University Library. University of Nevada-Reno	05-16-1983	http://www.library.unr.edu/depts/bgic/
Richmond, Virginia	James Branch Cabell Library. Virginia Commonwealth University	09-26-1985	http://www.library.vcu.edu/jbc/govdocs/govhome.html
Rochester, New York	Central Library of Rochester and Monroe County	05-10-1999	http://www.libraryweb.org/
Sacramento, California	California State Library	04-13-1979	http://www.library.ca.gov/html/gps.cfm
Salt Lake City, Utah	Marriott Library. University of Utah	04-06-1984	http://www.lib.utah.edu/govdoc/
San Antonio, Texas	San Antonio Public Library	03-02-2000	http://www.sanantonio.gov/library/?res=800&ver=true
San Diego, California	San Diego Public Library	01-26-1984	http://www.sandiego.gov/public-library/index.shtml
San Francisco, California	San Francisco Public Library	01-19-1994	http://sfpl4.sfpl.org/
Seattle, Washington	Engineering Library. University of Washington	08-08-1977	http://www.lib.washington.edu/Engineering/
Springfield, Illinois	Illinois State Library	01-17-1984	http://www.cyberdriveillinois.com/departments/library/home.html
St. Louis, Missouri	St. Louis Public Library	1870	http://www.slpl.lib.mo.us/library.htm

Location	Library	Date	URL
Stillwater, Oklahoma	Patent and Trademark Library. Oklahoma State University	1956	http://www.library.okstate.edu/patents/index.htm
Stony Brook, New York	Engineering Library. Melville Library SUNY at Stony Brook	08-12-1997	http://sunysb.edu/library/sci-eng/
Sunnyvale, California	Sunnyvale Center for Innovation, Invention & Ideas (SCI[I]3). Sunnyvale Public Library	1963	http://www.sci3.com/
Tampa, Florida	Patent Library. Tampa Campus Library. University of South Florida	03-20-1990	http://www.lib.usf.edu/ref/
Toledo, Ohio	Toledo/Lucas County Public Library	1934	http://www.toledolibrary.org/discover/maintwo.htm
University Park, Pennsylvania	Schreyer Business Library. Paterno Library. Pennsylvania State Library	04-23-1979	http://www.libraries.psu.edu/business/patents/
Washington, District of Columbia	Founders Library. Howard University	12-08-1986	http://www.howard.edu/library/
West Lafayette, Indiana	Siegesmund Engineering Library. Purdue University	08-09-1991	http://www.lib.purdue.edu/index.html
Wichita, Kansas	Ablah Library. Wichita State University	01-31-1991	http://library.wichita.edu/govdoc/patents.html

Vendor/Library Collaboration– An Opportunity for Sharing

Kenneth E. Marks

SUMMARY. This paper presents a case study about the process of cooperating with a commercial vendor on a new product for library inventory. *[Article copies available for a fee from The Haworth Document Delivery Service: 1-800-HAWORTH. E-mail address: <docdelivery@haworthpress.com> Website: <http://www.HaworthPress.com> © 2005/2006 by The Haworth Press, Inc. All rights reserved.]*

KEYWORDS. Cooperation, vendors, library-vendor cooperation

Library and vendor relationships have always been doubtful. Perhaps, this is due to the very different environments in which the parties must operate. Vendors are in a competitive environment where they must generate a profit for their stockholders and continually upgrade existing products or create new products. The competitive environment means that many of a vendor's activities must be cloaked in secrecy with information being as closely held as possible.

Librarians are by their very nature non-competitive and the concept of "profit" is simply not part of the world view. Collaboration for the good of the

---

Kenneth E. Marks, PhD, is the former Dean of University Libraries, University of Nevada, Las Vegas, 4505 Maryland Parkway, Box 457001, Las Vegas, NV 89154-7001 (E-mail: kmarks@ccmail.nevada.edu).

[Haworth co-indexing entry note]: "Vendor/Library Collaboration–An Opportunity for Sharing." Marks, Kenneth E. Co-published simultaneously in *Resource Sharing & Information Networks* (The Haworth Information Press, an imprint of The Haworth Press, Inc.) Vol. 18, No. 1/2, 2005/2006, pp. 203-214; and: *Libraries Beyond Their Institutions: Partnerships That Work* (ed: William Miller, and Rita M. Pellen) The Haworth Information Press, an imprint of The Haworth Press, Inc., 2005/2006, pp. 203-214. Single or multiple copies of this article are available for a fee from The Haworth Document Delivery Service [1-800-HAWORTH, 9:00 a.m. - 5:00 p.m. (EST). E-mail address: docdelivery@haworthpress.com].

Digital Object Identifier: 10.1300/J121v18n01_15

community served is the impetus for librarians. The concept that secrets would be kept and advantages and progress not shared with others is anathema to librarians.

The result is a clash of cultures and philosophies with both parties viewing the other with a certain level of mistrust and reluctance to engage fully. Suspicions are confirmed and stereotypes are reinforced in both camps.

There are occasionally circumstances where these conditions have to be put aside if the self-interests of both vendor and librarians are to be served. These often arise when new products are being created, tested, and brought to market by vendors. They need to have "real-world" tests of their concepts and products. Librarians have a vested interest in this process because they should want products that will work effectively in libraries and that respond to clearly felt needs.

The UNLV Libraries found themselves presented with this opportunity in 1998. This is a first-person account of that experience–the good, the bad, the unwarranted assumptions, and the unexpected outcomes.

During Fall 1997, the 3M™ Library Security group sent letters to approximately thirty-six public and academic library directors inviting them to be members of the inaugural 3M™ Library Advisory Council. Individuals would serve two-year terms. Those directors agreeing to serve were asked to participate actively in a discussion group via the Internet. The first Council activity would involve participation in a discussion of a new product. Council members would also have to sign a confidential disclosure agreement. The Dean of UNLV Libraries, new to his job in October 1997, agreed to be a member of the 3M Library Advisory Council.

The first council meeting took place at ALA Midwinter 1998 with a half dozen individuals attending. A second meeting took place at ALA annual conference in 1998. Soon after the annual conference, 3M™ sent a letter to Council members asking if they would attend a meeting in St. Paul in late October 1998. There were two purposes for this Council meeting. One was to provide feedback on new product concepts which were going to be shown in the form of models and prototypes. The other was to attend a "Vision 2008" Conference.

The Library Advisory Council gathered in St. Paul on October 1998 for a day-long meeting with Library System personnel. During the meeting 3M™ personnel made a presentation about radio frequency identification technology (RFID) and the research work they had been doing about potential applications. The high point of the presentation was a demonstration of how the technology might work in a library setting focusing on check-out and check-in activities. It was immediately apparent to the advisory council members that the potential was fascinating. 3M™ staff made it very clear, however, that the research and development was ongoing and no final decision had been made about products for the library marketplace. They did indicate that if the development continued to be positive, it was likely that they would be looking for alpha and beta test sites for further testing of the product prototypes.

At the conclusion of the day's meeting, the UNLV Dean approached key 3M™ staff and indicated an interest in having one of the UNLV Libraries serve as a test site for future products. A brief verbal description of that library was shared. No commitments were made by anyone. Upon returning to Las Vegas, the Dean sent a letter to the head, 3M™ Library Systems Department officially expressing an interest in a more formal relationship.

> As I returned to Las Vegas and progress on our new building, I examined the plans and documents for 3M Library Systems products. While we will be installing the latest security gates and self-check systems, I wonder if we are taking advantage of all the possible products your division has to offer.
>
> I am interested in exploring whether there are other products that we should consider and whether there are new products you have in the pipeline that we could showcase as we open the new building in January 2000. We believe that our building will be an architectural showcase; but we want to make the operation a showcase, too. It is possible that 3M may have products that would help us achieve that goal.
>
> As you proceed with the development of the RFID product, we at UNLV would be very interested in deploying that system and helping test its functionality.[1]

UNLV had begun construction on what was to become Lied Library, a new 302,000 sq. ft. main library. All the architectural renderings made it very clear that the building would be distinctive. The goal was to have the opening of the new building coincide with the new millennium.

Midwinter ALA 1999 came and went with another Library Advisory Council meeting. While there was some discussion of the RFID development, there was no indication of a decision about whether to move forward with alpha/beta testing. The interest on the part of the UNLV Libraries in serving as a test site was repeated.

The Dean received an e-mail on February 19, 1999, requesting dates for a conference call with several 3M™ staff "*to gather some additional information about the library you believe would lend itself well to the field tests we would like to conduct and to answer other questions you may have at this point (so start your list!!)*."[2] The conference call was held on March 1, 1999. The UNLV branch library that was being proposed as the test site was the Curriculum Materials Library (CML) located in the College of Education building. The library had a collection of approximately 30,000 very heavily used materials, many of them very similar to those found in public libraries.

The current security system in the library was that of a competitor's of 3M™. The system had essentially been abandoned by CML staff as there was no vendor support. The conclusion of the phone call was that unless the UNLV Libraries were prepared to migrate to the 3M™ Tattle Tape Strips, using the library as a test site for RFID would not be practical. Since CML staff were ready for a security system that worked, this seemed like an opportunity to convert the collection so it would be compatible with the 3M™ security systems in the other libraries. It was agreed that this conversion would take place if CML was chosen as the test site. Dates for a possible site visit were identified for late March or early April.

One of the things that became evident very quickly was the importance of communication to 3M™ staff. Early on, 3M™ made the following observation: *"Third, let's all make sure we keep the line of communication open and we do it often. I'd rather err on the side of 'too much too early' than letting something slip through the cracks that will cost us time and/or resources later."*[3] A regular stream of e-mails and phone calls was quickly established and continues to this day. It became evident that 3M™ was prepared to invest in communication, as they inquired about the availability of teleconferencing capabilities on campus. While the equipment was available, the cost was beyond the reach of the UNLV Libraries.

The most dramatic confirmation of the commitment to communication was 3M™'s identification of a coordinator at the end of March 1999 who would be responsible for planning and implementation of the test. He would be the person library staff would work most directly with. This person had expertise in the technology and had been involved in the development of the products; in fact, he was an engineer not a salesman. His first action was to develop a detailed project plan for review by the UNLV Library staff and their approval. This individual managed the alpha/beta phases of the project, the deployment in the main library, and continues to be involved in the relationship even today.

The initial site visit took place on March 24, 1999. Several 3M™ staff toured the CML and met with the library's staff to discuss their possibly being an alpha/beta test site. The conclusion was that CML would meet 3M™'s requirements and the CML staff were pleased with the prospect that an unworkable security system was going to be replaced and they would be the first "working" library to test the RFID products. The only question that remained to be decided was when the conversion of the collection would take place.

3M™ provided UNLV Libraries with a Test Plan for 3M™'s Digital Identification Systems in the Curriculum Materials Library. The plan was very specific about many things, but two items stood out.

> UNLV understands that these are early test systems that may experience periods of instability and need updating. UNLV is prepared to revert to current procedures (bar code technology) when the new systems are temporarily unavailable.

> UNLV will provide 3M with appropriate usage data and feedback on the test systems. This will enable 3M to assess how well the new systems are working. 3M and UNLV will work together to improve design features as needed. When possible, 3M will implement improved design changes for retesting.[4]

The plan contained general descriptions of the new digital equipment that would be tested. These descriptions were important as they gave CML staff their first clue about the equipment they would be testing and using.

UNLV conducts three summer sessions each year. The first of these occurs from mid-May to early June. This would have been the ideal time to do the conversion, but there simply wasn't time between the late March decision to go forward and mid-May. Since UNLV Libraries were going to buy the Tattle Tape™ security strips, all orders had to be processed before fiscal year closings, which caused some discomfort with the university purchasing office. Timely processing of purchase orders has continued to be a challenge to this day due to inadequate staffing in that campus unit. RFID tags were considered part of the test so there was no purchase required. The reality was that 3M™ could not ship the equipment capable of reading RFID tags until some time in May. There were physical adjustments in CML that had to be made which required the university facilities personnel, and scheduling them was a challenge. Eventually, the equipment arrived, new power and data lines were installed, and the security strips were received.

The conversion project began in late June 1999. It had been made very clear that this was going to be a learning experience for both CML staff and 3M™ personnel. There were a number of 3M™ staffers who spent nearly the entire conversion period working along side the library staff. This developed a camaraderie among both groups that continues to this day. Library staff did the conversion work while 3M™ staff monitored every aspect of how books were tagged, how the equipment worked, and the most efficient manner in which inserting security tags could be combined with placing the RFID tags. Software that 3M™ had developed was upgraded several times and the design of the conversion station was changed. The meticulous manner in which 3M™ staff collected data and evaluated products was an eye-opener to all library personnel. Almost immediately, it was evident that the information being collected was going to offer opportunities for modifying library work routines. Library staff provided 3M™ personnel with insight on product functionality. Throughout the three weeks it took to convert the CML collection, there was an ongoing discussion of additional uses that could be made of the RFID technology in a library setting. It was evident that 3M™ had not fully considered all of the potential uses. A quality that was most valued by library staff was the openness and readiness on 3M™'s part to listen to ideas and suggestions. Nothing was dismissed out of hand.

All too often, there is a perception that library vendors give only lip service to what they are receiving in terms of feedback. Suggestions may be welcomed, suggestions may be received, but they disappear into a deep black void with no response. Working with 3M™ it was evident daily that suggestions from library staff were being considered and when they could not be dealt with, a reason for not doing so was provided. The outcome was genuine respect among all parties.

Another strategic move that 3M™ staff made while CML conversion was going on was a meeting with UNLV's President and Provost. This gave the alpha/beta test a new level of legitimacy within the university and established a new respect for the library on the part of the university administration.

There had been a belief from the very beginning of the alpha test that RFID technology being tested in CML would have its greatest impact in the UNLV's main library. The experience in CML quickly confirmed that this belief was correct. The challenge was how to accomplish tagging the main library's circulating collection. As summer 1999 drew to a close, work began immediately on the planned conversion of the main library collection that was scheduled to be moved to the new Lied Library at the end of the year. We were fortunate to be able to make the tagging of the main library circulating collection and the purchase of the appropriate equipment part of the equipment budget for Lied Library. This relieved library staff from having to approach the tagging in a piece-meal fashion that would have delayed the full impact of the RFID technology on library operations.

This conversion project would be different than CML's since the collection already contained 3M™ security strips. 3M™'s first plan was received in August 1999. Three points were made in this proposal and continued in all subsequent revisions.

> 3M will provide the necessary training for the conversion of materials and for the operation of the Digital Identification products.

UNLV will assign a "site coordinator" who will serve as the primary communications conduit with 3M and oversee the implementation of the technology.

UNLV understands that 3M is in an early stage of development with this technology. While we are making efforts to ensure that a reconversion of materials will not be necessary, this is recognized as a possibility. Reconversion, in the worst case, could mean replacement of tags on some items. Lesser reconversion might consist simply of updating the contents of some tags, requiring only a reprogramming operation. 3M and UNLV both understand these possibilities and wish to move forward understanding the risks and benefits of beginning conversion at this time.[5]

The plan covered the period from August 1999 through November 1999 when all of the conversion equipment was to be delivered. The thoroughness of the proposed plan came as a shock to some library staff as traditionally much of the libraries' planning had been only outlined in the most general fashion leaving the detail to be completed on site as a project progressed. This was not going to be the case working with 3M™. A new focus was instilled in library staff to make certain all of the possible activities were considered.

The information 3M™ wanted from library staff included the following items.

1. The number of operators and conversion stations that would be required for the project.
2. The size of the collection to be converted and the type of items in the collections to be converted.
3. Which items would be converted prior to the move to Lied Library.
4. The availability of data ports to enable the conversion equipment to be connected to the libraries' network.
5. Identification of space for storage of RFID tags.
6. Placement of conversion equipment in the Circulation Department in order to ensure that materials being returned would be converted before being returned to the shelves.
7. The hours and days when conversion would be performed.
8. Procedures for record keeping of the progress being made throughout the collection.
9. The order in which the collection would have RFID tags inserted.
10. How materials being swept (collecting books used in house) throughout the building would be tagged before being returned to the shelves.

Fortunately, there were members of the circulation department who turned out to be "naturals" in planning the conversion of the main library collection.

As this planning was taking place, there was a commonly held belief that the conversion of the main library's circulating collection of about 650,000 volumes might take a year to complete. The prospect that this project would begin in the old library and then continue in the new library was not welcomed. Before the planning was completed, it became very evident that Lied Library was not going to be opening in early January 2000. In fact, it would be almost exactly a year, January 8, 2001, before Lied Library opened. There was a sense of relief on the part of both library and 3M™ personnel when it became apparent that the delay would give a cushion for completing the tagging of the main library circulating collection.

The experience gained from having tagged the CML collection apparently caused 3M™ staff to review and reevaluate the content and location of data in the tag itself. They were cautious about moving forward on the tagging of the main library collection before finalizing the tag data and memory mapping. Their concern was to minimize the possibility of having to do a reconversion of the collection at some later date. The result was that the tagging of the main collection was put off until early 2000. Another consequence of the changes in tag data and memory mapping was that the CML collection had to have the tags in its books reconverted. This had to be done to ensure compatibility between the CML and main library systems. Fortunately, this was not as onerous a task as we had feared. Essentially, each book in CML had to be passed over a surface on the conversion station. There was no retagging needed. 3M™ reimbursed UNLV Libraries for all staff time expended in the reconversion.

A revised conversion plan was received from 3M™ in early January 2000, which projected the conversion beginning on February 8, 2000. Project completion was projected for late spring or early summer before the move into Lied Library. The uncertainty surrounding the completion of Lied Library and when it would be ready for occupancy must have been frustrating for 3M™ because it was a nightmare for library staff as they tried to plan for moving into a new building with a minimum of disruption to campus functions.

Library staff continued to refine the approach that would be taken to convert the main library circulating collection. Using data from the integrated library system the two dozen most heavily used two-letter LC classes were identified. Those were targeted to be tagged first along with all materials being returned from circulation as well as all new books being added to the collection. At the same time, the individuals who would do most of the tagging were identified. Three temporary personnel who had just completed another project preparatory to the move became available as well as student employees who ıld serve a supervisory role. During the actual tagging project, these individuals were supplemented by regular circulation staff and other selected library staff.

The conversion stations that were employed in the tagging process were attached to the library's network and were accessible remotely by 3M™ staff in St. Paul. As tagging moved forward, they were able to monitor daily production and determine if there were problems in the functionality of the equipment. While some of the conversion stations had been used in CML, there were additional new beta conversion stations with a variety of upgrades so the continuous monitoring was important. Tagging went faster than anyone was willing to forecast. Library staff had thought that at least a year would be required, but the tagging was done in six months, long before the move into Lied Library.

Rather than let the RFID development languish with the self-check and staff workstation, 3M™ research personnel continued to investigate other possible tools that might be used in libraries. As the CML tagging was completed there were discussions about the functionality that might be included in a "digital library assistant" and a bookdrop/sorter. Library staff participated in wide ranging conversations about the most significant problems involved in stacks maintenance. It was evident to library staff from the beginning that the digital library assistant was a tool that would have an impact on library operations. Library staff made a significant contribution to the development of additional capabilities for what became the digital library assistant. They identified weeding and pull lists as realistic functions for the tool. Neither of these were on the original digital library assistant development agenda.

One of the questions that had to be answered was whether suitable information could be extracted from UNLV's Innovative Interfaces library system and moved to the new handheld device. Only a few library staff had ever made extensive use of the "create list" function in the Innovative system. It was apparent that a variety of useful data had to be extracted regularly from the ILS if the digital library assistant concept was to be useful. 3M™ staff wanted library staff to find a way in which to extract a list of all items in shelf order, with status, full barcode, title and/or call number. A member of the circulation department soon became an expert on list creation and the unique ways in which those lists could be used to either expedite previously manual processes or combine previously independent tasks.

Throughout this phase of the project 3M™ staff were ready participants responding to the ideas and questions that library staff raised. Very quickly library staff began to feel as if they were equal partners in the development process which only reinforced their desire to discover further possible uses. It was evident that 3M™ personnel were interested in the most minute details of how we reshelved books, and how in-house-use books were collected and reshelved. They were interested in the differences in these processes between CML and the main library. Observation was always unobtrusive but circulation staff enjoyed the attention and liked answering questions about the rationale for the steps in various processes.

Early prototypes of the Digital Library Assistant (DLA) appeared during Fall 1999. As soon as library staff could use the DLA in a part of the collection that had been tagged, the benefit of RFID technology became dramatically apparent. Shelf-reading, which had always been a problem in the main library, took on a new status among student employees as it was no longer drudgery. It was actually fun. The fun was reinforced by the attention paid by 3M™ specialists who did time and motion studies comparing the traditional shelf reading methods to new ones using the DLA and conducted focus group sessions with library staff and student employees.

The bookdrop/sorter was an episode of a totally different kind that might have soured the working relationship between 3M™ and the libraries. An early prototype of a bookdrop/sorter had been shown to the Dean who had a preliminary interest in the product. The device was actually being developed by a third party that 3M™ was working with. An effort was made to find a way in which to place the bookdrop/sorter in what would be the new circulation area but construction of the area had been completed and it was not practical to make physical changes at that point. More important, after careful analysis it was clear that the device was better suited to a public library environment rather than an academic library. Academic libraries simply do not circulate the same volume of materials. There was disappointment among the 3M™ staff and the third party company but there was simply no justification for continuing to explore the subject.

Throughout 1999 and 2000, there were two parallel activities that brought 3M™ and library staff together. One was the alpha/beta testing of RFID and its deployment in Lied Library. The other was making certain that as construction of Lied Library was completed the latest models of various 3M™ equipment were going to be installed and that the contractors and suppliers were brought into the loop. Making certain that the correct equipment was installed was far more frustrating than any aspect of the alpha or beta testing. 3M™'s leverage on the supplier and contractor were indispensable in assuring that equipment was in place before Lied Library opened to the public.

The move into the new Lied Library took place between December 15, 2000 and January 8, 2001. The handheld device, now named "Digital Library Assistant" (DLA) and its Data Manager software were critical in making the relocation of the collection successful. The entire circulating collection had been shelf read before the move began and then as the collection was placed on the shelves in Lied Library by the movers, library staff followed with the DLA making certain the books were placed in order. The result was there was no subsequent shifting of any part of the collection. The stacks manager then claimed that our collection was the most "accurate" in the world. His claim was based on his having just completed an inventory of the circulating collection and the identification of hundreds of processing and cataloging errors that had caused books to be considered lost even though they were physically present in the collection.

It is always difficult to determine whether a collaborative relationship is viewed as successful to the parties involved. Our relationship with 3M™ was no different. It was apparent from the library dean's perspective that there was a clear and evident benefit. The RFID products were working and already having a dramatic impact on stack maintenance by keeping the collection in order, identifying cataloging and processing errors for correction, and inventorying the collection every ninety days. The library had no way of knowing what 3M™'s real assessment of the collaboration was until October 2, 2000, when a letter was received from the RFID product manager. The letter stated that 3M™ felt "this project has been a huge success." The letter continued by presenting an updated proposal "to continue with the pioneering partnership that we began over eighteen months ago." This relationship continues today.

An unexpected aspect of serving as the alpha/beta test site was the interest shown by other libraries, both international and domestic. As soon as the 3M™ public relations effort began to appear in the form of newspaper reports, trade publications, and materials distributed through the library press we began to receive calls. These calls fell into two categories. One was inquiry on the basis we used for selecting the 3M™ product; the other was a request to come and visit the UNLV Libraries. Our location in Las Vegas makes it very easy for individuals to get low cost plane fares, and who wouldn't want a legitimate reason to visit the city while doing business-related work? Many of the calls and inquiries came from 3M™ sales personnel in the U.S. and internationally. These have been extraordinary opportunities for library personnel to establish acquaintances and gain new perspectives on librarianship. Through international visitors, we have gained a broader appreciation for the exceptional developments in librarianship that are taking place in other countries. A number of library faculty and staff have had opportunities to write articles and make presentations on the RFID implementation and give programs on cutting-edge technology.

There are many factors that have contributed to the success of the collaboration between the UNLV Libraries and 3M™ Library Systems, but several factors deserve special mention. First, there was stability within 3M™ Library Systems group meaning there was no turnover in staff directly involved in the project. Too many library vendors have a revolving door approach to their staff who have direct contact with the customer. The outcome is a sales force that is always new to the territory having to learn who the customers are. The result of 3M™ staff stability was a continuity in effort that was important. No one had to be brought "up to speed." Second, there was a commitment to regular, extensive communication between 3M™ personnel and library staff involving email, phone calls, and face to face meetings. Calls to 3M™ personnel were returned in a timely manner and if a question could not be immediately answered, an answer was provided quickly. Third, if a specific commitment could not be made, there was an explanation. Similarly, if delays were anticipated, they were explained. Fourth, 3M™ personnel worked with library staff as peers and colleagues, which resulted in a far stronger relationship.

Hindsight can be a marvelous filter in assessing a relationship. Reviewing the collaboration between 3M™ Library Systems and the UNLV Libraries, it is unlikely that we would change any part of the experience if we were to do it over again. It has established a much higher expectation for our dealings with other vendors.

REFERENCES

1. Letter dated November 13, 1998 to Department Manager, 3M Library Systems from UNLV Dean of Libraries.
2. E-mail dated February 19, 1999 from John Yorkovich to Ken Marks.
3. E-mail dated March 30, 1999 from John Yorkovich to Ken Marks.
4. Faxed document April 21, 1999 from Paul Sevcik to Ken Marks
5. Faxed document August 20, 1999 from Paul Sevcik to Ken Marks.

Index

Page numbers followed by f indicate figures; those followed by t indicate tables.

BOOK ORDER FORM!

Order a copy of this book with this form or online at:
http://www.HaworthPress.com/store/product.asp?sku=5586

Libraries Beyond Their Institutions
Partnerships That Work

____ in softbound at $39.95 ISBN-13: 978-0-7890-2909-6 / ISBN-10: 0-7890-2909-X.
____ in hardbound at $59.95 ISBN-13: 978-0-7890-2908-9 / ISBN-10: 0-7890-2908-1.

COST OF BOOKS _____

POSTAGE & HANDLING _____
US: $4.00 for first book & $1.50
for each additional book
Outside US: $5.00 for first book
& $2.00 for each additional book.

SUBTOTAL _____
In Canada: add 7% GST. _____

STATE TAX _____
CA, IL, IN, MN, NJ, NY, OH, PA & SD residents
please add appropriate local sales tax.

FINAL TOTAL _____
If paying in Canadian funds, convert
using the current exchange rate,
UNESCO coupons welcome.

❑ BILL ME LATER:
Bill-me option is good on US/Canada/
Mexico orders only; not good to jobbers,
wholesalers, or subscription agencies.

❑ **Signature** _____

❑ **Payment Enclosed: $** _____

❑ **PLEASE CHARGE TO MY CREDIT CARD:**
❑ Visa ❑ MasterCard ❑ AmEx ❑ Discover
❑ Diner's Club ❑ Eurocard ❑ JCB

Account # _____

Exp Date _____

Signature _____
(Prices in US dollars and subject to change without notice.)

PLEASE PRINT ALL INFORMATION OR ATTACH YOUR BUSINESS CARD

Name

Address

City   State/Province   Zip/Postal Code

Country

Tel   Fax

E-Mail

May we use your e-mail address for confirmations and other types of information? ❑ Yes ❑ No We appreciate receiving
your e-mail address. Haworth would like to e-mail special discount offers to you, as a preferred customer.
We will never share, rent, or exchange your e-mail address. We regard such actions as an invasion of your privacy.

Order from your **local bookstore** or directly from
The Haworth Press, Inc. 10 Alice Street, Binghamton, New York 13904-1580 • USA
Call our toll-free number (1-800-429-6784) / Outside US/Canada: (607) 722-5857
Fax: 1-800-895-0582 / Outside US/Canada: (607) 771-0012
E-mail your order to us: orders@HaworthPress.com

For orders outside US and Canada, you may wish to order through your local
sales representative, distributor, or bookseller.
For information, see http://HaworthPress.com/distributors

(Discounts are available for individual orders in US and Canada only, not booksellers/distributors.)

Please photocopy this form for your personal use.
www.HaworthPress.com

BOF05